Seeds of Promise

World Consultation on Frontier Missions,
Edinburgh '80

PHOTO CREDITS: Pg. 126, E. Mooneyham, World Vision;
    Pg. 143, Zwemer Institute; Pg. 151, Dan Stearns,
    World Vision; Pg. 161, Cheri Goodman, World Vision.
    Others, Edinburgh '80.
COVER DESIGN: Gene Keller

Seeds of Promise

World Consultation on Frontier Missions,
Edinburgh '80

Allan Starling, Editor

William Carey Library

P.O. BOX 128-C • PASADENA, CALIFORNIA 91104

ISBN 0-87808-186-0
Library of Congress Card No. 81-69488

Published by
William Carey Library
P.O. Box 128-C
Pasadena, California   91104
Telephone (213) 798-0819

In accord with some of the most recent thinking in the academic press, the William Carey Library is pleased to present
this book which has been prepared from an author-edited and
author-prepared camera ready copy.

PRINTED IN THE UNITED STATES OF AMERICA

CONTENTS

CONTENTS

INTRODUCTION

THE PURPOSE OF THIS VOLUME

Another Consultation - another book? I hope not! This is not
intended merely to be a record of what happened in Edinburgh.
Certainly we want it to be that. But our prayer is that it will be
much more—hence the title "SEEDS OF PROMISE." In his welcome
letter Dr. Rigby said: "We are gathering to MAKE history," not
merely to review it. Likewise, our prayer for this volume is that it
will not only give the facts, but also transfer the vision which
prompted the consultation in the first place - to reach the Hidden
Peoples of the world with the saving Gospel of Christ.

SEEDS OF PROMISE

Chapter 13 gives us a glimpse of some of these seeds of promise.
Two groups, one comprised of European missionaries and the other of
Theological students "sprouted" at Edinburgh. Both were inspired to
start concentrating on Hidden Peoples. We hear many reports of others
just poking their heads through the soil. May they continue to grow, to
His glory and to the salvation of Hidden Peoples.

"STUDY AND IMPLEMENT"

For those who are serious about the task of finding Hidden
Peoples, this book contains much in the areas of both information and
inspiration. In his report of the conference, Dr. Ben Jennings of
International Missionary Advance said: "These addresses represented a
lot of creative thinking. They need to be studied and their ideas
implemented wherever possible." With this in mind, we have prepared a
fairly extensive index to enable you to correlate and study those
subjects of particular interest to you.

INTRODUCTION

Recent strategic missionary thinking and research has produced a number of new catchwords, technical terms, and descriptions, with which all our readers might not be familiar. For example, the term "Hidden Peoples" is not intended to imply that the people are hiding or are in any way invisible! A quick study of the Glossary before reading the book should help you understand the intended meaning of these terms.

A WORD ON THE VARIOUS ARTICLES

The majority of the text is taken from talks and speaches given at the Consultation. In transcribing and editing these presentations, we realized in a new way the difference between the spoken and the written word! Something that came across as a real inspiration in Edinburgh can look very disjointed and flat when quoted verbatim on paper. Also in the interests of space we have done a considerable amount of editing, always seeking to keep the tone and spirit of the original message. Where possible, this has been done in conjunction with the authors, so we are reasonably confident that nobody has been misquoted.

THE PRODUCTION TEAM

As with any such volume, a lot of people contributed their various skills in order to bring it to finalization. Special thanks to Mrs. Anna Perkins who did the lioness' share of typing and proofreading. Mrs. Roberta Winter did an excellent job of editing her husband's talks. The staff of the U. S. Center for World Mission also helped in many ways, and their Computing Center speeded production.

Allan Starling
Gospel Recordings, Los Angeles

THE PLEDGE

"A CHURCH FOR EVERY PEOPLE BY THE YEAR 2000"

By the grace of God and for His glory,
I commit my entire life
to obeying His commission of Mt. 28:18-20
wherever and however He leads me,
giving priority to the peoples
currently beyond the reach of the Gospel (Rom. 15:20-21).
I will also endeavor to impart this vision to others.

Developed by the sister conference-
International Student Consultation for Frontier Missions

EDINBURGH '80

Theme Chorus

A Church for Every People

Ben Jennings

Ben and Mary Jean Jennings

Go to ev-ery na-tion with the church of Christ; Let the world their only Savior see. A church for ev-ery people by the year two thou-sand; Lord of harvest, here am I, send me!

GLOSSARY

AMA	Asia Missions Association
BMS	Baptist Missionary Society
CCC	Campus Crusade for Christ
CMS	Church Missionary Society
Church	See Ch. 4 page 65 for definition
Closure Strategies	Strategies Designed to COMPLETE the Task
E Scale	see Ch. 4 page 64 for explanation
EFMA	EVANGELICAL FOREIGN MISSIONS ASSOCIATION (USA)
EMA	EVANGELICAL MISSIONS ALLIANCE (ENGLAND)
EMS OF ECWA	EVANGELICAL MISSIONARY SOCIETY OF EVANGELICAL CHURCHES OF WEST AFRICA
Edinburgh	1980 World Consultation on Frontier Missions, Edinburgh, Scotland
Evangelism	see Ch. 4 page 65 for explanation

GLOSSARY

FRONTIER MISSIONS	see page 114 for a definition
Haystack Meeting	Student meeting in 1897 which precipitated the founding of the first American Mission agencies.
Hidden Peoples	see Ch. 4 page 61 for definition
ICG	International Church Growth
IFMA	INTERDENOMINATIONAL FOREIGN MISSIONS ASSOCIATION (USA)
ISCFM	INTERNATIONAL STUDENT CONSULTATION ON FRONTIER MISSION 1980
IVCF	Inter-Varsity Christian Fellowship
LAUSANNE or LCWE	LAUSANNE CONSULTATION ON WORLD EVANGELIZATION
MEGASPHERE	see Ch. 4 page 62 for explanation
MELBOURNE	1980 Melbourne Conference on World Evangelism, Melbourne Australia
MISSION '83	1983 Missionary Conference in Europe for young people sponsered by TEMA
P Scale	see Ch. 4 page 63 for explanation
PATTAYA	1980 Consultation on World Evangelization, Pattaya, Thailand
Penetration of People group	see Ch. 4 page 64
People Group	see Ch. 4 page 64
SVM	Student Volunteer Movement
Third Era	see Ch. 4 page 50
TSFM	Theological Students for Frontier Missions
Unreached People	see Ch. 4 page 60 for definition
Viable Church	see Ch. 4 page 65

GLOSSARY

WCFM

World Consultation on Frontier Mission

WMF/MC

WORLD MISSIONARY FELLOWSHIP, MISSIONS COUNCIL

1
CONSULTATION OVERVIEW

WHAT HAPPENED AT EDINBURGH?

Rather than write a report ourselves, we have formed a composite of four reports which were published in journals of well known organizations. They are identified as follows: /1/ A report by Leslie Brierley in "THE WIDER LOOK"; /2/ A report by Ben Jennings in GLOBAL CHURCH GROWTH BULLETIN; /3/ A report by Gerald Swank for Evangelical Missions Information Service; /4/ A report in MISSION FRONTIERS.

HISTORIC DAYS

We have been living in historic days. "Melbourne 1980" discussing "Your Kingdom Come"; The Thailand "Consultation on World Evangelization" centering on How Shall They Hear?"; and finally "The World Consultation on Frontier Missions" or "Edinburgh 80", gathered round A CHURCH FOR EVERY PEOPLE BY THE YEAR 2000 – all in 1980! Seventy years after the first World Missionary Conference, when missionary leaders met together to study the effects the "Great Century" had had on the unreached peoples of the world! A comparison of the situation in 1910 with that in 1980 should give rise to echoing paeans of praise to God for such marvels.

Yet, as Dr. Rigby, Chairman of the Local Arrangements Committee said in his welcoming letter, we were gathering to MAKE history, not merely to review it! Did we? Only the future will give the full answer but we shall make a brief attempt. For the record we include a STATEMENT OF OBJECTIVES as circulated over a year ago:

1. To share the results of contemporary research and experience concerning the world's Hidden Peoples: those cultural and linguistic

sub-groups, urban or rural, for whom there is as yet no indigenous community of believing Christians able to evangelize their own people.

2. To stimulate Protestant evangelical missionary agencies to accept specific responsibility for reaching the 16,750 Hidden Peoples by the year 2000.

3. To facilitate the necessary strategy, planning and action to achieve this goal, recognizing that the majority of the Hidden Peoples are currently inaccessible to conventional missionary work.

4. To provide opportunity for leaders of non-Western and Western missionary agencies to help one another by fellowship in praying, thinking and planning together.

5. To stimulate spiritual enrichment, enlargement of missionary vision, and organized frontier missionary efforts by bringing together participants from as many parts of the world as possible.

6. To lay the groundwork for future conferences of a similar nature.

In the writer's view, we achieved all of these goals, not perhaps in the full sense some of us anticipated, but sufficiently to create and fan a flame of fellowship around, and focus more purposefully and meaningfully on the watchword given, we believe, by the Lord: "A Church for every people by the year 2000." /1/

FOCUS

The Thailand Conference brought together outstanding evangelical leadership, the opinion makers, including a wide spectrum of pastors, denominational officials, evangelists, and evangelism specialists, as well as a number of mission leaders. All of the non-Christians of the world, including nominal Christians, were the concern of that conference. At Edinburgh, the focus was narrower: concentrating exclusively on frontier missions—those populations where there is not yet any church at all. The meeting was composed of delegates sent by mission agencies./4/

ATTENDANCE

The earlier meeting in 1910 was larger in the number of people present, but was nowhere nearly as representative since not a single non-Western agency was represented (the only three known to exist at that time were left out by accident).

At Edinburgh 1980, three out of the four major plenary addresses in the morning sessions consisted of technical papers which were assigned to Third World mission leaders. The largest Third World agencies present—having about 100 or more missionaries—were the Evangelical Missionary Society of Nigeria, the Friends Missionary Prayer Band of India, the Indonesian Missionary Fellwoship and an Evangelical missionary group (A.M.E.N.) of Peru. (See APPENDIX II for a list of agencies and representatives)

In proportion to the size of the country represented, the largest delegation (40 people) was from the United Kingdom, while the U.S., with a population four times as large, had only 84. Sixty-nine came from Asia, 35 from Europe outside the United Kingdom, 24 from Africa, nine from Latin America, and three from Canada. /2/

Was this meeting necessary? Did it accomplish goals not accomplished by Pattaya? Should it have happened? These were questions asked by some U.S. agencies which were not represented. They hoped this Consultation was only preliminary so that a later one could be planned in which they could participate.

Perhaps it was that. The number of delegates could easily have been three times as many, though only two could officially represent an agency. And yet, under the providence of God, this meeting was as it should have been.

Why? 1) Non-Western agencies (they reject the term "Third World" as being a bit derogatory) were able to meet on a par with the older Western agencies in a way which would not have been possible had they been overwhelmingly outnumbered. 2) Of the major strategy addresses given in the morning working sessions, only one was given by a Westerner, in the absence of Dr. George Samuel of India, unable to attend at the last minute. These addresses represented a lot of creative thinking, and need to be studied by all mission executives, both East and West, and their ideas implemented wherever applicable. 3) For the first time, the newer agencies became known to each other and to the older agencies. /2/

THE INAUGURAL MEETING

The Deputy Lieutenant of the City of Edinburgh warmly welcomed the WCFM AND ISCFM (students) to the City. He reminded the audience of the long connection of the city with Missions. The Rev. David Lyon, General Secretary of the Overseas Council of the Church of Scotland, prayed that "Edinburgh-80" might be used of God as greatly as was the first World Conference held 70 years before in that city. Rev. Richard Fry, U.K. Home Director of Wycliffe Bible Translators Inc. (which played a large part in the practical aspects of the Consultation's task) brought greetings on behalf of the Evangelical Missionary Alliance in the absence of Mr. Ernest Oliver in Hong Kong. He reminded us that "the mustard seed is indeed becoming the greatest of all herbs ... " for, since the illustrious career of William Carey the Church had indeed grown and spread in a marvellous way.

Rev. Larry Allmon, Chairman of the Convening Committee declared the Consultation open. He recognized it as "a unique occasion paralleled only by the great gathering of 1910." He explained, "We have come together to face side by side the task that lies before us. That task which sees ourselves as the reality and the possibility of becoming Christ's instruments in reaching the remaining people-groups of the earth, planting in each one a viable, reproducing church by the end of this era—the year 2000—is that goal. This week we shall be praying in faith that all that we do will be aimed to realization of that goal under the moving of the Holy Spirit of God ... We must not forget Who it is that has brought us together ... It is not a committee but the Sovereign God ... "

At the chairman's bidding, we rose and acknowledged God to be "The Committee Chairman, the Patient Leader, the Shepherd, the Lord of Harvest ... " The preliminaries, inspiring and impressive, were over. The time had come for the "keynote message", by Dr. Michael Griffiths, Principal of the London Bible College, former General Director of the Overseas Missionary Fellowship.

He warned us he was "going to major largely on some of the difficulties and hindrances which stand in the way of the advance of the Gospel today." He then plunged into a listing and explanation of the deficiencies of the Church in its missionary outreach today. /1/ (See INAUGURAL ADDRESS, Chapter 3 - Ed.)

STUDENT CONFERENCE

A novel addition to the excitement of the conference was a sister consultation composed of 180 students from all over the world - the International Student Consultation on Frontier Missions - which overlapped the plenary sessions of the WCFM, but had a day and a half of additional sessions both before and after the main consultation as well as separate meetings every afternoon.

The young people adopted the same consultation goal, "A Church for every People by the Year 2000"; and demonstrated a zeal, a vision, and a competence which bodes well for world mission leadership and specifically for the goal defined for the year 2000./4/

On Saturday morning Brad Gill, from the Student Consultation, reported to us. He said that the genius of this entire event has been the convergence of the youth with the mission leaders. At times it had been awkward meeting in separate sessions, but it was remarkable and significant that on the final day, similar goals were in view in each of the sessions. He outlined their goals as: (1) The students would take initiative in seminars, universities and colleges throughout their countries to spread the news of our watchword. (2) The convergence with the mission world leaders was significant to the students. They had much opportunity to interact with them. (3) They are looking for 200,000 new missions recruits for church planting and pioneer missionary work in the next twenty years./3/

THE STRUCTURE OF THE CONSULTATION

Seven aspects of the Consultation formed the structure for our thinking, praying and action.

1. THE RESEARCH UNIT, under the leadership of Allan Starling of Gospel Recordings, was available to delegates throughout the Consultation. Information on Hidden Peoples, drawn from the combined

resources of Missions Advanced Research and Communications Center (M.A.R.C.), G.R., and Wycliffe Bible Translators (W.B.T.) was used as the basis for answering specific enquiries. /1/

This index, called "Peoples file," runs 2,700 pages, covering 168,000 items, mainly different languages and people names, many referring to the same populations. At the conference, delegates could obtain 12 celuloid microfiche cards containing the entire index for just $12. The project was rushed to completion in time for the meeting by Allan Starling using the computer facilities of World Vision and the U. S. Center for World Mission. /4/

2. THE PRAYER UNIT, led by Patrick Johnstone, author of "Operation World", functioned throughout the Consultation. Each morning Patrick led a prayer session on specific topics related to the subject of the day. /1/

3. FRONTIER MISSION STRATEGY was discussed each morning. . Dr. Ralph Winter first explained the vision God had given him of establishing a viable, witnessing, reproducing church in the midst of each distinct people-group, as a Pauline first step to the completion of the task Jesus entrusted to His Church. As the Rev. George Samuel could not be with us, on the second morning Dr. Winter continued his explanation. On Thursday Dr. Petrus Octavianus of the Indonesian Missionary Fellowship spoke on "Missionary Structures". From 20 years' experience of building an integrated structure, combining the resources of several mission-groups, both Western and non-Western, he was able to speak of INTEGRATION as a viable method, already tried and found to be effective. On Friday, Rev. Panya Baba of the Evangelical Missionary Society of Nigeria spoke on "Frontier Missionaries".

Each of these papers was followed by a response by chosen panellists, after which the subject was open to 'the floor'. Unfortunately, we didn't have the time to address ourselves adequately to the important questions raised. /1/

4. TASK FORCES AND GROUP STUDIES

After a slow start during which the groups got organized, the participants found the smaller group sessions very beneficial. The West Africa group, for example, began describing the people groups, sharing with each other what was being done and what yet remained to be done among certain ones, such as the Fulani and the Mandingo. This was followed through on the second day with development of other groups as well. Delegates also had opportunity to become familiar with the MARC research tool, the questionnaire for identifying people groups. Everyone was urged to make use of this tool to identify all the people groups possible in the areas where they came from. This will enable us to have a more complete file in the future. /3/

TASK FORCES RECOMMENDATIONS

Each Task Force Group submitted the following recommendations as "immediate steps toward establishing a church for every people."

1. DEVELOPMENT of Third World Agencies: The third world people on this task force felt that they themselves could do a more effective job of evangelizing the Third World than western missionaries. The group agreed, however, that western support of training programs would be helpful. An interchange between missionaries was also called for.

2. AVOIDING OVERLAP in Adoption and Penetration of Peoples: This group recommended that a) Each agency make an unofficial estimate of the number of hidden people groups they might be able to enter by 1985. b) That agencies compile data to be consolidated with other data available. c) That missionaries be informed of where to file the data and how to get the information they need. d) Sister Centers combine all their data for the use of everyone.

3. SHARING EXPERIENCE in Training Missionaries: This group felt that Western and Third World agencies could have complimentary roles in training. Western missions can supply the historical and theological training, while third world agencies can provide cultural, linguistic and "grass roots" training. The task force called for facilitation of exchange between agencies from a possible continuation committee.

4. DEVELOPMENT OF SISTER CENTERS of Mission: This should be done to research hidden peoples, develop and coordinate resources, raise missionary vision both in churches and students, and broaden cooperation in strategy and planning.

5. COOPERATION IN POOLING World Resources: Models of cooperation already in existence were considered. It was recommended that action be taken at this Consultation to facilitate the coordination at the regional level for sharing information, planning regional consultations, and to delegate regional representatives who could promote cooperation in outreach to frontier mission fields.

6. RELATIONS OF LOCAL CHURCHES and Agencies in Reaching Unreached Peoples: The vital role of the local church is missing from the Consultation. A problem clearly exists on both the level of the church and of the sending agencies. The group would like to convene again to make some recommendations to the full Consultation. /3/

5. THE SPECIAL-INTEREST MEETINGS

These were of various types to meet the diverse needs of delegates. I was able to attend only two such groups—that for Unreached Peoples Research led by Allan Starling of Gospel Recordings, and Mission Centres for World Evangelization, led by Ben Jennings, Exec. Vice-President of International Missions Advance, a group working from the U.S. Center for World Mission campus.

(a) UNREACHED PEOPLES RESEARCH. Here we were told of the exciting plan for M.A.R.C., W.B.T. and G.R. to combine their information on ethnic and linguistic groups, making it available on microfiche to those who can use such information. On the "ANIMIST" evening we were dramatically made aware of the need for such information. Who will ever forget George Cowan's 'audio-visual' as he flicked open a print-out of the linguistic data relevant to the 5,103 language groups listed in ETHNOLOGUE! Sheet after sheet, each bearing 66 names of ethnic groups and their need of Bible translation, fell in a cascade to the floor. Many of these names would be those of Hidden Peoples. Many more would be people-groups without a single word of the Scriptures. It was a convincing demonstration of the enormity of the remaining task.

(b) THE RESEARCH CENTRES: A Ring of RESEARCH for the Hidden Peoples: The concept of "sister-centres" had already been aired among us before the Consultation, so we were glad to meet others who had either begun such centres already, or who were eager to begin. There is a strong reluctance on the part of our American brethren to have such centres linked as subsidiaries of the U.S. Center for World Mission. However, they and we do see the advantage of forging strong links between us for the gathering of correct, well-documented information on Hidden Peoples from the 'grass roots'. Equally, such links would be useful for the dissemination—as pleaded for by Michael Griffiths—of better information" more adequately to churches across the world.

The Sister Centres would handle:

a) Research—on the Hidden Peoples, their location, description and groups available to reach them, etc.

b) Resources—the sharing of facilities, methods, approaches, etc. which other mission agencies could use effectively. The recruitment of personnel for the ongoing task would come within the purview of this aspect.

c) Strategy—agencies would plan together the penetration of given areas, groups, peoples etc. The Institutes of Tribal, Hindu, Muslim and Chinese Peoples already created within the USCWM would play a part here.

d) Training—better ways of utilising the facilities already available, coordination of efforts etc.

e) Prayer—an "Institute of Prayer" (as yet in embryo form)—building the prayer interest of the Church n Missions.

6. THE PUBLIC PRESENTATIONS

The splendid evening meetings were open to delegates of both Consultations and to the general Christian public. Each night was given over to the study of a different "world religion".

(a) THE ANIMIST WORLD, (b) THE MUSLIM WORLD, (c) THE HINDU WORLD, (d) THE BILLION-STRONG CHINESE WORLD /1/ (See Chapters 5 through 8 - ED.)

7. THE BIBLE MESSAGES

Dr. Mark Hanna had a hard time packing it all in as he presented the "Biblical Basis of Missions". Who is Dr. Hanna? He turned out to be a rare personality—a Phoenician Bible Teacher! Dr. Hanna thought we needed a REFORMISSION, not a Reformation!

THE TRANSMIGRATION OF PEOPLES. A major challenge of his daily teaching concerned the tremendous opportunity God was giving to this generation by what he termed the transmigration of Peoples. What is God saying to the Church through this phenomenon of our day? About one quarter of those who will be the leaders of the world's nations   are now studying in the West. In the 1990s some of these men will, by simply signing their name, be able to expel all of the ex-patriate missionaries within their country. We never know, he insisted, how the course of history can be changed by the way we treat those who may turn out to be key individuals, when they come within our orbit as they are now doing. He told the story of a church in Kansas City which had the foresight to designate a host-family to each foreign student studying in their city university—there are 250 such students. Last year, through this hospitable gesture, there were 70 converts from among them! Another aspect of this transmigration trend was the gap being built up between the increasingly-educated leadership of the developing countries and the leadership of the churches in those countries. "This will be one of the greatest threats", said Dr. Hanna, "to the Church in the next two decades."

After a round of teaching in Scottish universities, Dr. Hanna would be heading for Egypt where he would minister in this way. /1/

In the four Bible messages by Dr. Hanna, he emphasized THE TWO ASPECTS OF MISSIONARY WORK, THE CENTRIFUGAL AND THE CENTRIPETAL. There is the "Go" aspect as demonstrated by the obedience of Abraham as he left his country going whither he knew not at the express command of God. On the other hand, Israel was told to be friendly and hospitable to the strangers that came their way. It was in this way that these would come to know the true God. Hence, we have those who "come" and we are responsible to share Christ with them. The Queen of Sheba visited Solomon and was greatly impressed with the glory of the kingdom and the God whom he served. Later at the dedication of the temple, Solomon reminded the people of the need to reach the stranger within our land. We were reminded that in the USA there are 6,000,000 non-tourists, non-immigrant people from other lands who take up temporary residence in America. We have an obligation to share our faith with these people. In the University of Edinburgh, there are 1200 overseas students and the same is true of other universities in Nairobi, Cairo, Madras, Bombay and throughout the world.

The New Testament also provides examples of the centripetal mission of God. Perhaps the best known to us is that of the Ethiopian servant whom Philip led to the Lord and then he went back to his own country to spread the good news of Jesus Christ. Within the last thirty years, great changes have taken place in the distribution of people. Tens of thousands are moving out of the underdeveloped nations, looking for education. Many of these have come from otherwise closed lands where missionaries are unwelcome. The opportunities are before us wherever we are today to share Christ with them. Dr. Hanna felt that there needs to be a much greater emphasis on this aspect of reaching hidden people.

He suggested a possible model. We should begin to pray for twelve individuals. Six of these might be from priority people groups and the other six would be for the purpose of training reproducers. In three years time a veritable army would be raised up if many of us would adopt such a model for mission. /3/

SPECIAL EVENTS AND ITEMS OF SIGNIFICANCE

A theme song was composed by Mr. Ben Jennings and learned by the delegates. We believe this will be useful to help keep in view the spirit of the Consultation to plant a church in every people group by the year 2000. (The song is reproduced in the Introduction - ED.)

Eric Stadell of Mission SOS spoke to the assembled delegates in an impromptu speech, in which he urged us to give ourselves to the reaching of the goal expressed in the WCFM theme, "A Church for Every People by the Year 2000." He led us in a chant that rose in crescendo and aroused our great desire to see this goal accomplished./3/

CONCLUSIONS

Did we make history? The vision of "a Church for Every People by the Year 2000" has been defined, clarified and focussed—and enthusiastically taken up by a sizable number of the delegates and students. It is a specific vision within the total ministry of the Church—the "hidden bird" of the Hindu epic, which is the only thing many of us can see in the tree! Its progress will be measurable.

We did not accomplish all we had set out to do. There was no "sharing out of the Hidden Peoples among missionary agencies"; there was no monolithic structure formed to carry on the work of reaching Hidden Peoples; there was not even a concerted, coordinated Master Plan! BUT ... we did "share the results of contemporary research"; we did "facilitate the necessary strategy, planning and action to achieve our goal", at least in some measure. We certainly did "fellowship together in thinking, planning and praying together"; we "stimulated enrichment and enlargement of missionary vision" by the bringing together of participants from many parts of the world. And if the ongoing "catalyst committee" which did result from our deliberations feels it necessary and wise, the ground-work is laid for advance in both researching and evangelizing Hidden Peoples. Future conferences may be organized on a regional basis./1/

Were the two consultations worth it? The students gave a resounding yes, and insisted that they wished to be included at all future such consultations, both those of students and of the mission executives. The executives also voted yes. Some wished aloud that some churchmen had been invited as observers. But the general concensus was well stated by one mission executive from India when he said, "I hope it won't be another 70 years before we meet again." Following that lead, an International Catalyst Committee was set up and charged with exploring the time and place for another similar meeting and to act as a clearing house for the developing plans of the world's mission agencies to penetrate the last frontiers. /2/

As we now look back, we wish two weeks had been available instead of one. The afternoon working sessions by people groups were too short to move as far as was necessary in strategic thinking. More time was needed for discussion back and forth from the floor. It would have been nice if the students would have been able to finish their consultation in time to share with the executives what they had accomplished. This was a first for them, and the first in 70 years for the mission agencies. It was also a first for a joint international missions meeting of students and executives. Lessons were learned which now can be built upon in another such consultation.

When will that be? As one delegate put it, "We may not have 20 years to reach some of the frontiers. History is moving too fast." To take seriously the finishing of the Great Commission means moving ahead together by mission agencies from around the world, student organizations and those church leaders and organizations who met at Pattaya. The harvest is ripe now in more places than we know! /2/

At the close of the business session on Saturday morning, the chairman said, "Surely the Holy Spirit has moved us to unanimity." We have had a hard look at the hidden people and are convinced that this is our task for the next twenty years. He reminded us that we should also remember that there were many mission leaders who did not take part in this Consultation. The very fact that they were not here says a great deal. Again, there was still the problem of western domination. This was a recurring theme as the delegates spoke with one another. Nevertheless, there was real cooperation and a sense of unity throughout. Finally, it is important for us to remember the relationship of church and mission. We must have a closer cooperation between these two God appointed agents as we move ahead in our future task./3/

Did Edinburgh begin a new Student Volunteer movement? It may be too early to tell. The delegates did not feel that a large organizational structure was to be formed at this consultation.

Rather, God seemed to be encouraging a global movement composed of individuals within and outside of existing organizations who share a common commitment to reaching Hidden Peoples and to spreading that vision.

The clarion call has been sounded: "A church for every people by the year 2000!" Knit together by a week of rich, ear-opening experiences, the student delegates parted ways. Each took home this challenge for other people to share a lifetime commitment to the cause of frontier missions, whether at home or abroad.

This anecdote was given to us in the closing session. One of the missionaries in India, an Indian national, was giving a gospel message to a group of people. An aged Indian said, "I have a question. When did this person Jesus Christ come?" The answer was, "1900 years ago." And he responded, "Where have you been hiding all this time?" May God's people come out of hiding and reach out to those people who have been hidden from our view because of our lack of concern and unwillingness to sacrifice to give them the knowledge of Jesus Christ and a share in His blessings. /3/

RESOLUTION OF DELEGATES

We, the participants of this consultation, in order to maintain the vision of Edinburgh '80 agree:

1) That there should be a small international catalyst committee to carry on after Edinburgh '80 with the following tasks:

a. Maintain correspondence with regional and national efforts to promote "Hidden People" consultation.

b. Encourage development and support of materials to be used in provoking a vision for Hidden People.

c. Relate with the major evangelical bodies, e.g. WEF/MC, LCWE, AMA, EMA, EFMA, IMA, IFMA, and various other regional and denominational organizations, in order to continue to place the vision of the Hidden People before these bodies and their spheres of influence, and in order to continue to discuss further efforts to meet the needs of Hidden People before these bodies and their spheres of influence, and in order to continue to discuss further efforts to meet the needs of Hidden People both in outreach and consultation.

d. Look toward projection of another world conference of mission agencies and societies.

2) That the theological basis of the catalyst committee continue to be the theological criteria of Edinburgh '80, i.e., the statements of faith of the LCWE, WEF, IFMA, AMA, EMA, IMA, and other similar evangelical bases.

3) That the international catalyst committee include one mission agency or society representative from the following areas:

(a) Africa south of the Sahara.
(b) Middle East and North Africa.
(c) Europe.
(d) East Asia.
(e) South Asia.
(f) Latin America.
(g) North America.
(h) Oceania.

Note:
This catalyst committee be empowered to enlarge its membership for adequate area representation and to work out arrangements for its own continued functioning.

4) That the appointment of the personnel of the international catalyst committee should be detemined by the consultation, e.g., the asembly might request the ad hoc evaluation committee to serve as an appointing committee.

5) That the new catalyst committee select a chairman and that the chairman meet with the chairman of the ad hoc convening committtee for the transmission of information and to determine the transition process.

6) That the new catalyst committee establish a coordinating desk to facilitate accomplishment of its tasks.

RESOLUTION:

We the delegates of the Edinburgh '80 World Consultation on Frontier Missions express our heartfelt thanks, gratitude, and appreciation for the countless hours of work and labor of love the individuals of the convening committee have invested in making this gathering such a great success.

May the Lord richly bless and reward each of you.

Jim Downing

HOW LEADERS SAW EDINBURGH

Many of those who attened the Consultation were kind enough to send us their impressions. Some were negative, and these have been noted in the event of a further conference. We have chosen a few to reproduce as typical examples of how lives and ministries were effected.

From 2 to 20 People Groups:

"E-80 was a real eye-opener in my life. We were concentrating mostly on two people groups, but after Edinburgh we are moving into a little over 20 people groups in this hill country ... finished two surveys of the Lodakh region and will be opening his new station there in May, among half a dozen new tribes." - P.M. Thomas, Kashmir Evangelical Fellowship, India

Seeking Hidden People Among Seamen:

"We have established the relationship of mutual cooperation among seamen's mission organizations in Europe and America. Also we are expected not to miss any hidden people of seamen visiting Korean ports." - Korea Harbor Evangelism

50 Full Time Missionaries:

"As a direct result of E-80 we plan on having 50 full time missionaries on the field within two years ... this summer we anticipate sending 150-175 student-missionaries to work with over 20 non-North American mission agencies throughout the world." - National Encounter with Christ, USA

A Responsibility:

" ... we have a responsibility to spread the vision of frontier missions in Finland ... the involvement of students in E-80 encouraged me to challenge Finnish students to engage more in world evangelization ... our aim is also to do research work for finding unreached (or hidden) peoples in our exciting fields in Asia, Africa, and Europe." - Seppo Vaisanen, Finnish Lutheran Mission

Keep Priorities Straight:

"The consultation forced me to think through some strategy issues and precipitated actions and recommendations to my mission ... will help keep our priorities straight and give further impetus to pioneer evangelism among hidden peoples within our sphere of work in East Asia." - Dan Bacon, Overseas Missionary Fellowship, USA

Cross-Cultural Evangelism:

"Agreements with agencies such as Indonesian Missionary Fellowship, the Friends Missionary Prayer Band (India), and A.M.E.N. (Peru), whereby we can effectively channel people, funds, and resources into cross-cultural evangelism." - R. Larcombe, Regions Beyond Missionary Union, U.K.

E-3 Missions a Reality:

"WCFM told me that E-3 missions had become reality for the 3rd World churches." - Gerald Swank, Sudan Interior Mission, International

No Longer a Small Organization:

"By being there, HKEF was no longer a small missions organization way off in Hong Kong, we are now a member of an international movement, an integral part of an effort to fulfill the Great

Commission." - Edwin Keh, Hong Kong Evangelical Fellowship

Organizational Development:

"Contacts with similar groups at E-80 has helped tremendously in organizational development." - Willard Walls, Outreach International, USA

Reminded of a Responsibility:

"... identifying ourselves with like-minded Christians all over the world for the early evangelization of the hidden peoples among the Hindus, Buddhists, and Animists in the regions of the Indo-Burma and Indo-China... reminding us of our responsibility to this important region to which no Western missionary is allowed. As a result of E-80 we are going to plant churches among the Meitei people in Manipur Valley, the Nepalis in Manipur Hills." -T. Lunkim, Gospel Mission Society of the Kuki Christian Church, India

Adjust our Strategy:

"The WCFM goal challenged us to adjust our strategy... to make our plans in order to help reach the goal of the conference... share our own renewed vision with other organizations here." - Panya Baba, Evangelical Missionary Society of Evangelical Churches of West Africa

Plan Evangelism Among Hidden Peoples:

"My organization is now planning to arrange a meeting of all independent and voluntary evangelistic organizations in Andhra Pradesh to plan a strategy for the next two years for evangelism among Hidden Peoples." - P.D. Prasada Rao, Christian Dynamics, India

Share This Vision:

"I want to share this vision with my Home Board, churches, groups, and prayer supporters all over my country and also with our missionaries on the field... consultation was an important stepping stone for the road ahead." - A. Voreland, Den Norske Tibetmisjon, Norway

Slogan Heartily Endorsed:

"We in W.E.C. heartily endorse this vision for 'A Church for every People by the year 2000" - a more modern expression of the objectives of W.E.C. We earnestly desire to implement this vision within our mission, and to pass on information about Hidden Peoples and the vision to reach them to as many as possible." - Patrick Johnstone, Worldwide Evangelisation Crusade, Britain

Impressed by non-Western Representation:

"I was impressed with the number of non-Western mission agencies who were represented, and especially those who have no connection with any Western agency." - Don Hamilton, Association of Church Mission Committees, U.S.A.

CONSULTATION OVERVIEW

A Much Needed Conference:

"This is a very serious and much needed consultation." - George Verwer, Operation Mobilization

A Turning Point:

"Edinburgh '80 - a great turning point - to take away our false satisfaction - to open our eyes to see the Hidden People." - Thomas Wang, Chinese Coordination Center for World Evangelism

A New Beginning:

"Theological Students for Frontier Missions traces its origin back to Edinburgh '80." - Ward W. Shope, Theological Students for Frontier Missions

2
BEGINNINGS

EARLY STEPS TO EDINBURGH

Why was Edinburgh 80 necessary? How did it come about? In 1976 Dr. Ralph Winter, then professor at Fuller School of World Mission, wrote the following article for MISSIOLOGY (Vo. IV, No. 2, April 1976) This documents the circumstances which gave rise to the need for such a consultation as well as the events surrounding the Call. The foreword was written by Arthur Glasser, editor of the magazine - Ed.

1980 AND THAT CERTAIN ELITE - Ralph D. Winter

It was within the circle of American Society of Missiology (ASM) members who remained for a gathering of professors of mission in June, 1972, that a proposal was made of far-reaching significance touching the future of the Christian mission. Indeed, because Nairobi 1975 revealed the WCC's preoccupation with a long and valid agenda of churchly concerns, the strategic importance of this proposal has been immeasurably heightened. Our ASM Secretary-Treasurer Ralph D. Winter here provides a history and update of the proposal. It is reminiscent of the insights of Taylor, Warren, Beaver and a host of other advocates of "the voluntary sector" of the Church as the spearhead of her mission to the nations. - Arthur Glasser, Editor, MISSIOLOGY: An International Review, Vol. IV, No. 2, April, 1970

For a certain elite group in the world today the phrase "Nineteen Eighty" has crucial significance. Due to a strategic Call drafted in 1974, 1980 will hopefully be the year of the largest, most representative gathering of mission leaders in human history. The elite group to whom this phrase is significant consists of people for whom the fulfillment of the Great Commission is the primary commitment of their lives. Such people, very often career missionaries, have been meeting together "on the field" for well over a hundred years in "inter-mission meetings" of all sorts in virtually every country of the world. But once and only once in history, in 1910, was a conference held on the world level to which all Protestant mission societies sent representatives as the sole official participants. Hopefully the same kind of elite gathering can take place once more, now that the immense additional spectrum of the non-Western world has blossomed with its own hundreds of mission societies and thousands of missionaries.

In order briefly to evaluate this arresting possibility, we must 1) review the developments thus far, 2) exposit the central document of The Call, and 3) endeavor to envision the results.

The Concern of God for the recovery of all the world's peoples is plainly stated at least as early as the Abrahamic Covenant (Gen. 12:3). It is restated at the decisive moment of the reconstruction of the nation Israel in the Exodus (Ex. 19:5). It is reflected again and again in the Psalms. It is brilliantly restated at another critical national juncture in Isaiah 49:6. It is definitively clarified and detailed once for all by His Son, Jesus Christ, in the Great Commission.

The Emergence of an Elite Structure

In 1976 we look back on the brief intervening period of only nineteen centuries during which a certain elite—those who have tried consciously to fulfill that commission—have gone to virtually all corners of the earth. They penetrated the Roman Empire and then exceeded its furthest reaches both in the East and in the West. Such agents were echoed back from Ireland to win Southwestern Europe. They moved north to Russia and eventually to fierce Scandinavia. They were forerunners in the development of navigation skills and reached literally the ends of the earth once the means were developed.

In every age it has been primarily intentional efforts and mainly group efforts that have been able to cross cultural boundaries in this world-wide task. Such organized groups have been teams of Irish peregrini, groups of Franciscan Friars, transplanted industrial communites of Moravians, and self-supporting bands gathered around men like William Carey. They have been highly organized societies like the family of mission agencies that sprang up in England, Norway and Germany from Hudson Taylor's influence. These various organized teams have been closely and distantly related to the organizational structure of the various church traditions.

These groups are not to be confused with churchly entities, whether denominational, diocesan, district, parish or congregational structures. It is well known that where biologically perpetuating communities have become reconciled to God in Jesus Christ and the principal mechanism of perpetuation of the "faith" is through the process of socialization, a beneficial but eventually nominal Christianity results. The official churchly structures, representing as they do this mainly biological type of Christian structure, have in only rare and isolated instances initiated efforts effective in recovering distant peoples to a vital relationship to God. On the other hand, the organized team structure proposed by William Carey in his crucial ENQUIRY (indeed the meaning of the phrase in its long title, "The Obligation... to Use Means") was precisely not a church entity but a "society" structure, a structure which is characteristically an elite vanguard, a nonbiologically perpetuating structure—the kind of thing anthropologists call a sodality. (Latourette, 1970:18, also used this term. It is earlier a Roman Catholic term used in a slightly more restricted sense; Winter 1974). It is this kind of elite "vanguard" to which Max Warren refers, reflecting back upon a lifetime of distinctive service on a world level:

> A community becomes committed precisely in proportion as it has a spiritual vanguard that is committed. Indeed my own conviction is that to call an entire denomination a "missionary organization" actually obscures the real situation and prevents the average person ever making any progress at all towards becoming one of the vanguard. This is best achieved by voluntary organizations consisting of persons who have joined together on some agreed basis. - Warren, Max. CROWDED CANVAS; SOME EXPERIENCES OF A LIFETIME. London: Hodder & Stoughton, 1974:158.

The Development of a Unique Prototype: the 1910 Conference

The person most widely known for proposing a conference of members of such mission sodalities is, again, William Carey. His plan, actually quite feasible even in 1810, was scoffed at by church leaders, was dismissed back home as merely a "pleasing dream" not because it was physically impractical but because the people back home couldn't believe missionaries of widely different traditions would want to meet together (Rouse, Ruth. "William Carey's 'Pleasing Dream'". INTERNATIONAL REVIEW OF MISSION. 1949:181). One hundred years later that dream was fulfilled, at Edinburgh, now built upon more than a half-century of periodic field gatherings of missionaries of many backgrounds in various non-Western countries (Hogg, William Richey. ECUMENICAL FOUNDATIONS; A HISTORY OF THE INTERNATIONAL MISSIONARY COUNCIL AND ITS NINETEENTH-CENTURY BACKGROUND. New York: Harper & Brothers. 1952: 16-35).

But since the 1910 conference was a "first" in human history, it is not surprising that different people have seen it from different points of view. With the advent of the massive anticolonial revolt and birth of the new nations in the non-Western world following World War II, some have looked back on the 1910 meeting and regretted the small percentage of non-Western delegates, as though societies that did not yet exist in the non-Western world could have been invited. Certainly no African or Asian mission society was intentionally excluded.

Others have felt the 1910 meeting was itself at fault—and perhaps it was in part—because it failed somehow to prevent subsequent history from expanding the invitation to church leaders as well as mission leaders in a series of subsequent meetings. Thus the "fault" of the 1910 meeting was partly its attracted attention to the world-wide family of those reconciled in Christ. It inspired world-level conferences involving both missionary and church leaders of this family.

In 1910 only a _few non-missionaries_—church leaders like Henry Sloan Coffin from the USA and Bishop Azariah from India—attended. At Bangkok in 1972-73 only a _few missionary_ leaders attended. In 1910 church leaders came only as part of a delegation sent by a missionary society. At Bangkok virtually the only missionaries or mission executives there as voting members were part of delegations sent by councils of churches—just the reverse. In 1910 mission leaders outnumbered church leaders at least 10 to one. Bangkok reversed these quantities as well as the process of selection.

The Erosion of the Elite Pattern

Yet this profoundly significant change resulted from a gradual transition, fascinating and fatal. The 1910 meeting itself had been an abrupt and decisive transition in the opposite direction. Early thinking about the meeting had assumed that it would be another massive exposition of missionary interest like the 1900 Anglo-American conference had been, dominated as that conference was by supporters in the churches, and by church leaders and public citizens. In the new trend at the 1910 conference Mott's influence was probably decisive (Hogg, 1952:105). In 1907 it was finally determined that the meeting would be based upon appointed delegates of missionary societies. "Leading missionaries" were sought, "and if practicable, one or two [overseas church people]" (Hogg, 1952:109). But the basis was clearly the structure called sodality.

The centrality of the active agency of mission continued in the early thinking leading to the founding of the International Missionary Council, which was the organizational direct outcome of the 1910 conference. As the Continuation Committee met near The Hague in 1913, the conclusion was drawn that

> The only Bodies entitled to determine missionary policy are the Home Boards, the Missions and Churches concerned.
> -Hogg, 1952:161)

If the wording here is a bit fuzzy as it apparently mentions both missions and churches, the actual founding membership of the International Missionary Council, which consisted exclusively of mission societies, groups of mission societies, or councils of mission societies, clearly maintained a continuity with the nature of the 1910 meeting.

Yet the preamble to the Council's constitution reads:
> The only bodies entitled to determine missionary policy are the missionary societies and boards, or the churches which they represent, and the churches in the mission field.   - Ibid: 204

Here the mission society structure at least comes first with the home churches as an alternate (the "or"). A new entity—"the church on the field"—is not mentioned.

By the time of the Jerusalem conference in 1928 this new voice would be heard much more strongly, and its legitimacy was not questioned. But the trend from a conference of church leaders was now very clear as the roots (the mission agencies) and the fruits of missionary work (the churches overseas) became confused. This was no plot against the missionary societies. They still had a major voice in the various Christian councils in the non-Western world and were themselves eager for the precious fruits of their work to become known in the West.

However, the trend from missions to churches in the structural backbone of the IMC became even more pronounced as its constituent members—the National Christian Councils—began to enroll churches alongside of missions as their members and thus gradually became councils of churches rather than continuing to be councils or associations of mission agencies. Again, it is not as though the new national churches sought to shoulder the mission agencies out of the way. In most cases the earnest desire of the missions themselves was that the churches should increase and the missions decrease. This was a glorious trend, in some respects. There came a day when the largest of all National Christian Councils—that of India—voted to exclude mission agencies from the Council, thus making it virtually impossible for a mission society—even a national mission society—to have any direct voice either in the Council in India, or in any higher-level world gathering (Fey, Harold E., ed. THE ECUMENCIAL ADVANCE Volume 2 of A HISTORY OF THE ECUMENICAL MOVEMENT. Philadelphia: Westminster Press. 1970:98). By 1948 the Constitution of the International Missionary Council reflected the complete reversal. The phrase quoted above, which had put mission societies first now read:

> The only bodies entitled to determine missionary policy are the churches and the missionary societies and boards representing the churches.   - Hogg: 1952:373.

The remaining anachronism was that the associations of mission societies in most Western "sending" countries (but no longer the USA) still represented the missions—the elite structure. This input was lamely continued when the International Missionary Council merged with the World Council of Churches, becoming its new Commission on World Mission and Evangelism in 1961. Thus while the CWME theoretically continues the function and mandate of the 1910 meeting, for most of the world it has become structurally incapable of doing so.

BEGINNINGS

The Recovery of the Elite Pattern and a New Call

In light of all this, the Chicago Consultation in December, 1972 was a very curious phenomenon. Indeed, a stunning recrudescence of the long-lost meeting of missionary leaders was formed when an ad hoc committee under R. Pierce Beaver brought together a wide range of mission structures. At this date in history only the very oldest men present could remember the days when the Foreign Missions Conference of North America effectively gathered mission leaders from a wide variety of backgrounds. In the intervening years the Foreign Missions Conference had suffered by attrition in becoming merged with the National Council of Churches in the USA as those mission agencies representing church people who did not believe in church councils were lost in the transition. But at Chicago the unbelievable had happened again: the elite pattern reappeared. Since it was a conference not of churches but of mission leaders simply conferrring with each other, there was no more need for a creedal statement than in 1910, and the reasonable avoidance of theological issues about which there was known conscientious disagreement was well understood just as it had been in 1910. Thus highly conservative evangelical mission agencies along with mainline denominational mission board people as well as Roman Catholic missionary leaders were present, about one-third from each sphere, with a total of 97 different people registering. The sense of fellowship and great profit resulting from the theme of "The Gospel and Frontier Peoples" was impressive and unanimous. In the preliminary canvas of all American mission boards and societies (excepting those confined to work in Europe) there was a response of more than 90 percent, and only one board disclaimed any interest and concern.

But it was a minor tragedy of timing that the Chicago Consultation had not yet occurred when the idea of a full-blown successor to the 1910 conference was enunciated at the Association of Professors of Mission meeting in June of 1972, by Luther Copeland, the outgoing president. Even at the following meeting of the APM in 1973, when the writer seconded Copeland's proposal, there was at least one vigorous objection based on the assumption that the 1910 meeting had been merely a clique of Europeans. The structural significance of the Chicago Consultation had not yet fully soaked in. But by the following year, the idea had gained ground within the Association of Professors of Mission and the 1974 APM meeting was suspended at one point so that a discussion of the wording of a formal resolution could be discussed on a completely ad hoc basis. Luther Copeland lead the discussion. Twenty-four professors—almost everyone present—signed the resulting Call, which will be discussed below. The meeting was held at Wheaton College, and perhaps the majority of those who signed could be called conservative evangelicals, but there were Catholic and main-line denominational mission scholars as well.

Everyone agreed to discuss the Call in whatever circles they might find themselves. Inevitably, the meeting coming up a few days later at Lausanne, Switzerland—the International Congress on World Evangelization—gave opportunity for a slightly larger gathering to consider the Call. Due to the very nature of the Lausanne conference, the majority of those who indicated their support of the idea at this second meeting were evangelicals. But since there were Roman Catholic observers at Lausanne, some of them were also present.

(We asked Dr. Winter to document events subsequent to this article - Ed.)

The Realization of the Goal

The remainder of the above article discusses the essential elements of the Call and tries to anticipate the future steps necessary to carry the proposal into reality.

Now we know that the high hope expressed in the second sentence of the article quoted above were solidly realized. The year 1980 did in fact become "the year of the largest, most representative gathering of mission leaders in human history."

A second sentence in the article, beyond the portion quoted above, is also relevant. "In all ad hoc developments what has actually happened is often more important than what might have happened." That is why we have omitted the anticipation about what might have happened and will sketch here a few of the highlights of the next three years.

The Quickening Pace

The pace immediately quickened. Robert de Moss and Robert T. Coote of Partnership in Mission began to monitor developments. In their July 2, 1976 Newsletter they refer to the article above and to a number of other reverberations, nothing that "the possibility of a world missionary conference in 1980 is being widely discussed." Discussion at that time about what kind of a meeting should be held, and what it should cover, represented inevitably the full spectrum of existing opinion about the very contemporary phenomenon of missions.

Inevitably there were, on the one hand, those whose concerns were incubated in the context of mature mission fields, where the longstanding initiative-designed missionary structures, which were designed for Pioneer and Paternal stages, were now struggling for identity in the Partnership and Participation stages. Such observers naturally hoped for a meeting that would consider the various possible structural readjustments appropriate to the new mission/church relationships.

On the other hand, while some people felt honestly that the mission agency structure itself was an anachronism in the era of the younger churches, there were many others who just as honestly felt that such structures (whether non-Western or Western) were still very essential in new outreach to groups within which national churches had yet been planted. Observers of this kind seem to have had the greater influence in the framing of the wording of the Call. Some of them recognized that the 1910 meeting was made up wholly of mission societies and focused upon the frontiers in its day. Their expectations for the 1980 meeting were naturally significantly different.

Luther Copeland, himself a missionary in Japan, although he was the one at the blackboard when the Call was framed, tended to think in terms of a meeting of younger church leaders and Western church leaders as well as leaders from persisting mission societies, but he admitted the validity of the other concern (in personal correspondence) and generously welcomed it. The writer's own interpretation of the Call was very literal. The Call, in fact, made no reference to anyone but the representatives of mission structures. This, as mentioned, corresponded to the structure of the 1910 meeting. Furthermore, in keeping with the 1910 emphasis upon the penetration of non-Christian societies (In 1910 participation was limited to agencies sending missionaries among "non-Christian peoples."), the writer felt the Call's use of the words "missionary" and "cross-cultural" were intended to exclude any major emphasis on efforts for renewal within the church or local outreach within the same sphere of existing churches.

The Three Conferences

In any case, it is no exaggeration to say that the Call produced not one but three world-level conferences in 1980. Two major institutional traditions rose to the challenge. Emilio Castro of the World Council of Churches approached certain evangelical leaders about joining forces in the upcoming meeting of the WCC's Commission on World Mission and Evangelism. Although that did not work, the CWME meeting was pulled back from 1981 to 1980, and preliminary discussions began in November of 1977. In accord with the very structure of the CWME, it was clear in the beginning that their meeting would have to consist mainly of church leaders, not leaders of mission agency structures.

Also by the fall of 1977, the Lausanne Committee on World Evangelization began serious planning for its own next world meeting in 1980, eventually held in Pattaya, Thailand. It is not unreasonable that two well-developed insitutions would be better able to take initiative than a mere ad hoc group of serious mission thinkers. Beyond the article above, which was written in part in the normal course of his professorship in mission history, this writer's activities relating to the proposed conference were exceedingly minor. No one really carried the ball. Both the CWME and the LCWE were proceeding consciously in the direction of at least some of the aspirations of the 1974 Call, but both were aware of the waning probability of the original ad hoc initiatives to materialize.

The British Response

It is a matter of significant interest that the two leading mission statesmen who first responded to this proposal after 1974 were both

Englishmen—Max Warren, long the secretary of the Church Missionary Society, and Stephen Neil, even more widely known today. Then, as we shall see, as in the case of the earlier meeting at Edinburgh, it was a Scottish initiative that would make the timely offer to host the conference in Edinburgh, though earlier plans had talked of possibilities in Germany.

However, despite many enthusiastic responses to the 1976 article, during most of the year 1978 the idea of an ad hoc meeting, primarily of mission representatives focused on frontiers, continued on as little more than an idea. Indeed, in view of the other two meetings now in the planning stage, why continue to think about anything strictly comparable to the meeting way back in 1910?

However, in the fall of 1978, Roy Spraggett, traveling through from the Scottish Missions Centre of Glasgow, visited the writer at the U. S. Center for World Mission in Pasadena and expressed cautious interest in exploring the possibilities on return of forming a Scottish Committee of Arrangements. He then passed through Wheaton to talk with David Howard about the LCWE meeting then scheduled for January, 1980, and stopped over for a day in London to discuss the whole matter with both his own mission, Worldwide Evangelization Crusade, long noted for its special interest in frontiers, and with Ernest Oliver of the Evangelical Missionary Alliance. At this point in history it was suddenly difficult to defend a proposal still only an idea against two other conferences definitely in process of development. The very real differences between the three concepts were not always immediately apparent.

The Distinctions Between Three Consultations

The following two paragraphs represent an attempt by the writer to draw helpful distinctions. Here "M-80" refers to the CWME conference eventually located at Melbourne, Australia; "P-80" refers to the LCWE conference finally held at Pattaya, Thailand; and "E-80" refers to the originally proposed parallel to the 1910 World Missionary Conference, held in Edinburgh, Scotland.

"Will these three meetings conflict, duplicate, overlap? Or will it be like a three-ring circus where you can only try to keep your eyes on elephants, lions or tigers? M-80 is a meeting composed basically of official church representatives. P-80 is a meeting of invited, individual evangelical leaders. E-80 is a meeting of official agency representatives. In purpose at least, P-80 and E-80 are both going to deal with the issue of the Hidden Peoples, those unreached groups that cannot yet be won by evangelism from within. P-80 will deal seriously with Hidden Peoples; E-80 exclusively. However, in constituencies and potential results, these three meetings are very different. Due to its small size and diverse constituency, P-80 can invite only a small proportion of the world's mission leaders. For example, only 12 people from the United Kingdom can attend—most of them not even representing mission agencies. By contrast, all 100 mission societies of the United Kingdom that could probably qualify to attend E-80 (in terms of frontier commitment) are definitely invited to that meeting. Similarly in the United States, while not more than one-tenth of the 170 member organizations of the IFMA-EFMA can have individual, unofficial representatives at P-80, all frontier-concerned agencies may apply to participate at E-80.

"As far as potential results are concerned, the best way to see the differences between P-80 and E-80 is to see P-80 as assembling data, developing strategies, and alerting church leaders. Four months later E-80 will build on the P-80 documents as well as the preparatory studies of the participating missions. E-80 will allow the mission agencies to grapple with the question of what they are going to do about the specific opportunities defined by P-80. At P-80 we will see the conscience of evangelical leadership crying out on behalf of the world's Unreached and Hidden Peoples. At E-80 we will see the active agencies of mission sitting down to consider the concrete implementation of all that has been discussed at P-80 and anywhere else. P-80 is characterized by its question "How Shall They Hear." E-80 is the logical follow-through question: "Who Will Go For Us?" P-80 leaders can discover how the job can be done and reaffirm to their constituencies that it must be done. The E-80 representatives are then in a position to make it happen. Their agencies, in any case, are the major carrier vehicles, whether Western or non-Western."

Of course, none of these conferences achieved all of their potentialities, but this is what could be seen early in 1979.

The First, Bright, Concrete Events

If the Scottish initiative was the first, bright, concrete event to give hope for E-80, it was equally significant a few weeks later in March of 1979 that Leiton Chinn was seconded by International Students Incorporated to function as a full-time coordinator.

This introduced immediately a long series of very delicate steps, which Leiton Chinn carried out with sensitivity and skill. How do ad hoc meetings get started?

It was always assumed that the first few agencies that stepped forward to work together under the Call would inevitably bear the lion's share of responsibility and wield the lion's share of influence. Leiton established his office at the U. S. Center for World Mission in Pasadena, California, and as a result it is not surprising that the first few agencies actually to send official delegates to form a committee were mainly from the Southern California area. However, other major agencies based in the Eastern part of the United States often had Southern California representatives or responsible mission members who were able to participate—some officially, some not. While other organizations were present from time to time, the core of what came to be known as the Pasadena Convening Committee may be seen in the Appendix.

It may be added that even before this committee came into existence, the Scottish hosts had insisted that any participation by Roman Catholics in any capacity would have made their involvement impossible. Thus this condition was a "given" for all further planning. E-80 in fact became the only one of the three conferences where no Roman Catholics were present. On the other hand, none were turned away. In view of the pervasively "territorial" mentality of this church, which has long been patterned after the Roman Empire's civil "diocesan" structure, it is apparently true that contemporary mission leaders in the Roman Catholic sphere do not find it easy to think in terms of the non-geographical frontiers which this consultation emphasized—this despite some excellent Vatican II references to the contrary.

In view of the fact that the writer rarely attended the more than a dozen plenary meetings of the committee and was not a member of the Executive Committee, which met far more frequently, it is entirely proper that the final fruitful months of this story be carried forward by the capable, hard working chairman of the Executive Committee, Larry Allmon, of Gospel Recordings, Incorporated.

A final personal word may be appropriate. It may possibly be true across the years that the writer held on to this hope for E-80 more consciously than did anyone else. It is much more obvious that without the very real muscular response of more than a dozen agencies, specifically those which contributed Roy Spraggett, Leiton Chinn and Larry Allmon, this meeting would have endured only as a bit of spilled ink and wasted concern, and become no more than the same sort of "pleasing dream" which William Carey had for a similar meeting in 1810. In any case, by the close of the meeting which did indeed occur, with energy and flair, many others had invested far more time and effort than had this writer in this rare and wonderful gathering, whose impact and meaning has only begun to be felt.

FINAL COUNTDOWN TO EDINBURGH '80 - Larry Allmon

Following six informal gatherings in several locations in 1979 (Pasadena, Wheaton, Boston and Philadelphia), the first official gathering of an ad hoc committee actually to convene a World Consultation on Frontier Mission took place in Pasadena on August 30, 1979. Sixteen of the mission agency representatives present voted to constitute themselves as charter members of a convening committee and an Executive Committee was also selected. The meetings were charged with an air of expectancy as we wrestled with the basic concepts of the long contemplated worldwide meeting and necessary time frame within which we had to work. After much prayer it was with a true sense of urgency that we moved ahead with plans for an October 1980 Consultation in Edinburgh, Scotland.

At this first meeting of the committee, a coordinator (Leiton Chinn) was officially named, as well as myself as chairman of what

was then referred to as the "Pasadena Committee." You will find a
list of six qualitative goals of special interest. Basic Criteria for the
types of organizations to be invited to the consultation and for our
theological basis were also begun and sub-committees established for a
number of consultation matters. See Appendix III, page 247.

Before the first meeting, even, it had been decided to change the
original name suggested in the Call (World Missionary Conference) to
World Consultation on Frontier Mission at the request of Leighton Ford
of the LCWE, lest there be an unnecessary appearance of overlap with
the name they had chosen (Consultation on World Evangelization).

By the very next meeting, September 6, further drafts of the
theological criteria, criteria for participation and a definitive
statement of the goals and objectives were refined and adopted. The
program committee wrestled long and hard putting together a flexible,
non-pressure schedule that would allow for last minute input and
variables at the Consultation itself. Speakers were invited from around
the world, alternates sought, and various ideas for format were
weighed. All these things were discussed on various occasions where
executives were gathered, such as the EFMA meeting in the fall and
the Urbana meeting in December.

During the following months (September, 1979 to September, 1980)
the Executive Committee and sub-committees met almost weekly. I
travelled to Scotland on three occasions to coordinate our efforts in
Pasadena with those of the Scottish local management committee
coordinated by Roy Spraggett (Worldwide Evangelization
Crusade/Scottis Mission Centre).

"Progress Reports," invitational mailings and ads and articles in
various periodicals informed the mission world of progress towards the
Edinburgh event. Not all responses to the proposed Consultation were
positive, but a majority of those responding, especially from the newer,
non-European/North American agencies, were encouraging and supporting.

Long after plans had been almost irreversibly in process, some
American mission leaders continued to have misgivings about the
holding of the meeting in 1980. At one point, for a period of just five
days, there was actually an interlude during which the Executive
Committee voted to postpone the meeting until 1982. This action was
taken due to an honest misimpression that the IFMA-EFMA joint
committee would back such a meeting in 1982 if this postponement was
voted. However, it was soon clarified that no such action could be
guaranteed. Out of deference to the possibility of that backing for a
later meeting, the Executive agreed to consider the 1980 conference
"preliminary." Nevertheless, the rumor spread far and wide that the
meeting had been called off. This accounts for the fact that some
North American representation never materialized. Yet this may have
been a providential factor since it allowed the Third World
participants, untouched by the rumor, to constitute a husky, exhuberant
one-third of both agencies represented and delegates present.

The operating budget for all these preparations came from an initial prayer- commitment pledge of agencies (eventually 20) participating on the committee and others at a distance such as the Southern Baptist Board. Other gifts were received, and finally in the closing weeks prior to the Consultation, a substantial gift from the Aurora Foundation enabled us to meet our entire budget as well as assist in the travel for some additional third-world delegates.

By the final week of preparation in Edinburgh, the enthusiasm of the committee was at an all-time high, and the Lord's Hand was evident in retrospect as we reviewed how far we had come from those first ad hoc meetings well over a year before.

SISTER
CONFERENCE

INTERNATIONAL
STUDENT
CONSULTATION
ON
FRONTIER
MISSIONS
(See following
and page 219)

STUDENT CONFERENCE BEGINNINGS - Brad Gill

Towards the end of 1980, the year in which world-level gatherings would call Christian leadership together from across the globe more than any other time in history, there emerged yet one more international consultation. Its constituency was quite in contrast to those of the other high-level meetings in Melbourne, Pattaya, and Edinburgh./1/ The participants were younger, many quite inexperienced in actual missionary endeavor, and yet energized, potentially explosive, and carrying ideals which some observers would judge "triumphalistic." These were the delegates of the International Student Consultation on Frontier Missions(ISCFM) held concurrently with the World Consultation on Frontier Missions. They gathered from different parts of the globe to prayerfully consider how God might use them in this day to call forth a mighty army of young people which could realize the strategic objective of "A Church for Every People by the Year 2000."

BEGINNINGS

EARLY BEGINNINGS

The early beginnings which would ultimately lead to the formation of the Student Consultation can be traced to at least two occasions, each at the same location with very much the same participants.

MARCH 1979 The first gathering was recorded earlier by one of the participants, David Bliss, then a young seminary graduate on his way to Africa.

> Last evening I was with a small gathering of students and soon-to-be missionaries, staff-members of the U. S. Center for World Mission, at the home of Dr. and Mrs. Ralph Winter. Dr. and Mrs. Donald McGavran were the special guests on this occasion, and our dinner conversation excitedly ranged across the many miles, peoples, and years of Dr. McGavran's remarkable missionary life. After dinner we turned to questions of the future, matters of consuming and mutual concern to all present from the eldest to the youngest, from the most experienced to the least. "How will we play the most effective part possible in reaching the as yet unreached peoples for Christ?" and, "How will young people in particular best enter the stream of God's plan for the completion of the Great Commission, Christ's last command?"

> Dr. Winter produced a book containing John R. Mott's own description in 1892 of the first six years of the Student Volunteer Movement, that unprecedented and as yet unparalleled movement of the Holy Spirit among American students beginning in 1886 which so dramatically changed the world. Dr. Winter asked me to read, and I did so, stopping after practically every paragraph to allow for the brimming discussion, reflections of the heartfelt yearnings of everyone present.

> There we were, three generations of missions-minded people, Dr. and Mrs. McGavran, members of the old S.V.M., delegates to the 1920 quadrennial student missions conference before marrying and going out to service in India; Dr. and Mrs. Winter, one generation younger than the McGavrans, delegates to the first "Urbana" held in Toronto in 1946 before entering a life together of missionary commitment that has been so instrumental in focusing the attention of the Christian world today on the 2.5 billion "Hidden" people; and several other people who, like myself and my wife Debbie, are the "younger generation," with the majority of our missionary career years still before us. /2/

> Before the evening would end in a wonderful season of prayer, this small group would become convinced of the following:

> —that a new movement of student volunteers was essential if the Church of Jesus Christ was to cross the remaining 16,750 cultural thresholds which represented over 2.5 billion people;

—that "this movement must cooperate with any and all who would wish to raise up an international force of career, cross-cultural missionaries prepared to give their lives if necessary ... ; /3/

—that this movement must be based "solidly on the word of God, the enabling power of the Holy Spirit and the consuming passion for the lost ... ;"/4/

—that a simple watchword, challenging our faith with the strategic objective of reaching the Hidden Peoples, would be essential. After solid discussion, the group was to suggest the statement "A Church for Every People by the Year 2000."

JANUARY 1980 This same group had the unexpected opportunity to reconvene a few months later. The stimulus came from a group of 32 young South Africans who wanted to reconsider the convictions articulated the previous spring. They were in Pasadena during January of 1980 attending the Institute of International Studies. Sponsored by African Enterprise, their official name was the Unreached Peoples Pilot Project. They were convinced that the churches and student groups in Africa needed to take up the challenge of reaching these Hidden Peoples. The evening was spent in serious discussion on a number of related issues. Was there evidence that students were aware of these frontier regions? Were they volunteering for service? How best could this mandate be carried worldwide? How could organizational cooperation make this possible? The answers seemed few.

Later that week forty students, Africans and Americans, gathered to pray the entire night. Within a few short days an ad hoc group (comprised of three Americans and five Africans) came together to consider necessary action. It was felt unwise to simply start another organization. More perspective, insight, and participation was needed. If students and student mission leaders of like mind and heart were all over the world, how could they participate in the discussion? It was in this context, this critical period, that God introduced a special opportunity.

FEBRUARY 1980 Meeting on the very same campus was the Pasadena Convening Committee of the World Consultation on Frontier Missions (WCFM). It seemed wise to suggest the possibility of a "parallel" consultation. Its purpose would be complimentary to that being addressed by these mission agency delegates—i.e. the calling forth of needed volunteers for the ripening harvest fields of the world.

In the last hours before the South African members of this ad hoc committee returned home, the following proposal was drafted and submitted to the Pasadena Convening Committee:

MINDFUL OF THE NECESSITY to carry out the biblical mandate "to make disciples of all nations (ta ethne)," and BURDENED by the urgency of the remaining Hidden Peoples, and CHALLENGED by the remarkable and complimentary role which students played in Edinburgh 1910, we put forward the following proposal for the consideration of the Edinburgh '80 Pasadena Committee:

That the Committee take action to officially recognize the need for a simultaneous and complimentary consultation which would provide an international forum where students committed to frontier missions may consult with each other in the context of the World Consultation on Frontier Missions, concerning the principles, goals, resources, and implementation of a global movement which would call forth and develop student volunteers who would share the responsibility for the Hidden Peoples of the world.

At the February 7 meeting of the Committee, the proposal was accepted enthusiastically, given crucial advice and a unanimous vote of cooperation. As one committee member stated, "This could be one of the most important things that takes place at Edinburgh." Another observed that "this could be the passing of the baton." Two generations, experienced missionary personnel and young aspiring candidates, both sensed from the beginning the value of such a combined effort.

But to understand the specific intentions of the ISCFM one would need to study closely the proposal stated above and how God undertook and provided in ten short months. The major components are as follows.

"TO PROVIDE AN INTERNATIONAL FORUM." Already the South Africans and Americans had profited greatly from a month of interaction. This had to continue, expanding to include as many countries as possible. Because it was believed that a parity of Western and non-Western participants would be most profitable, a high priority was placed on international communications in the following months. "Seedbeds" of missionary outreach needed to be contacted in Asia, Europe, Latin America and Africa. It was hoped that 200 key individuals would be able to gather from these areas.

"WHERE STUDENTS COMMITTED TO FRONTIER MISSIONS MAY CONSULT WITH EACH OTHER." The application process was set in motion immediately. It was felt that participants would not need to be official representatives of any organization or country, but rather would sign the following Declaration of Purpose, thereby clarifying his or her commitment and direction:

I will make the Great Commission the commanding purpose of my life for the rest of my life, and I am willing, as God directs, to be a missionary to the peoples presently beyond the reach of the Gospel of Jesus Christ (II Corinthians 10:16)

It was also expected that some participants would be older than collegiate age, that all were "willing to consider formulating and eventually carrying out plans for a new international student effort," and that each would provide his or her own finances for the journey.

IN THE CONTEXT OF THE WORLD CONSULTATION ON FRONTIER MISSIONS." The value of the convergence of these two distinct consultations was recognized from the beginning. Penetrating new peoples would require that the logistics of missionary recruitment, training, and deployment be addressed. A delegate to one of the earlier consultations of 1980 was to articulate this very concern, stating that his "burden today is that we face the challenge of sending."/5/ And history had made it very clear that new frontier endeavors are accelerated, even initiated, by the participation of young people./6/

The Convening Committee established a student liasion office for purposes of continued participation and cooperation between both consultations. It was also determined that the student delegates would be welcomed into the plenary sessions of the WCFM for purposes of integrating frontier missions recruitment with the overall objectives of the mission agencies.

"CONCERNING THE PRINCIPLES, GOALS, RESOURCES AND IMPLEMENTATION OF A GLOBAL MOVEMENT." This was the major purpose and concern of the ISCFM. This delegation would set itself to determine the foundations needed to recruit laborers, which involved a studied consideration of the following:

Principles. The reappearance of any interdenominational, inter-organizational movement would require more carefully drafted principles than former movements. Biblical and historical insight would need to be applied to the spiritual character and strategic nature of this mobilization endeavor.

Goals. The mandate (A Church for Every People by the Year 2000) would require a quantum leap in the number of missionaries from all over the world. What would gauge the success of this movement? Was there to be "a strategy of closure" in the objectives? It was suggested at Pattaya that perhaps as many as 200,000 new laborers were needed./7/ Were numbers the actual measuring stick or would it be more critical to measure the penetration of each hidden people group? Participants would need to articulate their objectives.

Resources. Depending on which aspect or portion of student mobilization was considered (i.e. recruitment, training, deployment) certain resources, tools and understanding would need to be provided, especially to those involved in calling others into full time service.

Implementation. Finally, and most importantly, the question of proper organizational structure would need to be addressed. Was a new organization required? Is this the way God was leading? If so, how was it to relate to the present student organizations, churches, and mission agencies? Could it not simply reinforce present efforts? What new and vital distinctives were absolute and necessary? As planning for the event progressed, it became obvious that these would be critical questions—in fact, the watershed of the entire consultation. The progress and implementation of all activities demanded structure. The question was how it might be formed.

WHICH WOULD CALL FORTH AND DEVELOP STUDENT VOLUNTEERS: The focus was to be singular: recruitment. Students have the inherent ability to influence frontier missions. While they are not the best ones to design frontier mission strategies—which was the intention of the WCFM—they are instrumental in influencing the ratio of volunteers who will determine to reach the Hidden Peoples. The ad hoc committee felt that the identification and production of relevant "means" for calling forth and developing an army of volunteers might be determined by a grass roots student initiative alone.

During the months leading up to the consultation, God graciously intervened time and time again. Through a series of unlikely events, a local arrangements committee for the ISCFM was formed on sight in Edinburgh to supplement the administrative office (South Africa) and the liaison office (USA) already in motion.

Of all the actions taken by the ISCFM ad hoc committee, the most important action was the publication of 15 "prospective guidelines." They were understood to be a possible foundation for any student effort that was to emerge out of the ISCFM. They were drafted by one of the committee members, David Bliss, and two senior advisors: Dr. J. Christy Wilson, professor of missions at Gordon-Conwell Theological Seminary (USA), and Dr. Vivian Stacey, missionary to Pakistan and advisor to the International Fellowship of Evangelical Students.

They were to be discussed, amended, and/or adopted at the consultation itself. They were listed as follows:

Principles for Students completing Christ's Great Commission in this Generation

Knowing Jesus Christ as my Saviour and Lord, I vow to God the Father that, by the help of the Holy Spirit, I will devote my life to the fulfilling of the Great Commission. I promise to adopt the following disciplines:

1. Accepting the Bible as the fully inspired Word of God and recognizing it as authority in matters of faith and conduct, I determine to maintain a devotional life in the Word of God, reading at least one chapter of the Old Testament and one chapter of the New Testament every day (Luke 24:27; II Timothy 3:16; Joshua 1:8).

2. And as part of this daily personal devotion I agree to enter into prayer, for praise and worship and for intercession, and that this time (or times) of personal Bible study and prayer will command at least one hour in total throughout my day (Daniel

6:10; Mark 1:35).

3. A simple lifestyle, keeping possessions to a minimum, to tithe, and to make my surplus available for the completion of the Great Commission (Luke 3:11).

4. Recognizing that the servant is not greater than the Master, I expect to suffer for Christ. I am willing to die for Him (John 15:20 ; I Peter 4:1; Revelation 2:10).

5. I acknowledge my need of the fellowship of a local church and my responsibility in belonging to it, to support it with my presence and giving, and to report back to the church of the mighty works of God (Hebrews 10: 24 and 25; Acts 14:27).

6. To set aside one mealtime each week for fasting and prayer (Joel 2:12).

7. To devote one night each month to open-ended praise and prayer together with those of like mind (Luke 6:12).

8. To memorise at least three Bible verses each week (Psalm 119:11).

9. To pray that God will lead me to witness to key people in key places at key times to the end that others may be saved (Acts 8:29).

10. To believe that the Living God will perform mighty acts before our eyes, in our lives, and in the lives of those He seeks to save (Daniel 11:32; Ephesians 3:10).

11. To enter into the discipling of other believers (II Timothy 2:2).

12. To take practical steps to affiliate myself with a mission or a tentmaking agency (Acts 13:2-4).

13. To dedicate myself to help carry out Christ's ministry to the whole community in all its areas of need (Luke 4:18 and 19; Matthew 25:31-45).

14. To learn a language other than my own for the purpose of being a cross-cultural witness to a "Hidden Peoples" group.

15. To pray for additional labourers and to encourage others to commit themselves to these principles (Matthew 9:36-38, John 4:35 and 36).

Three other actions were crucial in helping the ISCFM to build a proper foundation and common vision. (1) A series of pre-consultation study materials were distributed for prior study by participants./7/ (2) An inquiry was begun into the strategic definitions and technicalities surrounding frontier missions in order to insure proper understanding by the student generation./8/ (3) The ISCFM schedule was extended forward two days in order to provide a series of "briefing sessions."

By the time discussion began at Edinburgh, ISCFM delegates would already have formed definite convictions regarding their roles in frontier missions.

NOTES

1. The 1980 Melbourne Conference on World Evangelism, Melbourne, Australia; the 1980 Consultation on World Evangelization, Pattaya, Thailand; the 1980 World Consultation on Frontier Missions, Edinburgh, Scotland.

2. David Bliss, in his preface to the reprint edition of Student Mission Power: report of the First International Convention of the Student Volunteer Movement for Foreign Missions ... 1891 (Pasadena, Calif.: William Carey Library, 1979).

3. Ibid., xi.

4. Ibid., xi.

5. J. Robertson McQuilkin, "Unless They Be Sent ... "; message to the 1980 Consultation on World Evangelization, Pattaya, Thailand.

6. David Howard, Student Power in World Missions (Downers Grove, Ill.: Inter Varsity Press, 1979); Ralph D. Winter, "Missions Today: the Long Look: the Dynamics of the Story" (Pasadena, Calif: U. S. Center for World Mission, 1980)

7. These materials included Timothy C. Wallstrom's The Creation of a Student Movement to Evangelize the World (Pasadena, Calif.: William Carey International University Press, 1980); Ralph D. Winter's "The New Macedonia" (1980), and other assorted articles dealing with the subject of frontier missions endeavor.

8. McQuilkin, ibid.

3
INAUGURAL ADDRESS

HINDRANCES TO THE GOSPEL
Dr. Michael Griffiths

"From Jerusalem all the way around to Illyricum, I have fully proclaimed the gospel of Christ. It has always been my ambition to preach the gospel where Christ was not known, so that I would not be building on someone else's foundation. Rather, as it is written: 'Those who were not told about Him will see, and those who have not heard will understand.' This is why I have often been hindered from coming to you. But now that there is no more place for me to work in these regions, and since I have been longing for many years to see you, I plan to do so when I go to Spain." Romans 15:19-24.

PAUL - THE TRAILBLAZING PIONEER

Paul sees Jerusalem as the spiritual metropolis and starting point for the gospel. It was from this center that Christ's empowered witnesses were to radiate outwards through all Judea and Samaria and to the ends of the earth. Now the limit of progress that Paul is able to speak of is as far as Illyricum. We have no record of Paul himself traveling that far, but in his Commentary Cranfield writes: "We understand his claim to have completed the gospel of Christ, to be a claim to have completed that trail blazing, pioneer preaching of it, which he believed it was his own special Apostolic mission to accomplish." And it is that trail blazing, pioneer preaching which makes this passage relevant to our discussion of frontier missions. Paul here expresses his ambition, his passionate desire. Not a small ambition to be given up, but a great ambition to be grasped, to press on to people who have never heard the gospel. And that is a desire and ambition which I trust motivates everyone of us who've come to this consultation.

PAUL - THE FOUNDATION LAYER

Men have differing gifts and perform different functions. The front line rugged pioneer missionary is essential to reaching the frontier peoples. He's often an extrovert and usually an individualist. Once churches have been planted and foundations laid, and national leaders appointed, that kind of person finds it hard to take a back seat. The church perfecting work takes a more introvert, tactful temperament who is able to work in a team. But Paul sees himself here as a foundation layer, not one who builds where others have already begun. He then quotes Isaiah 52:15 and this passage is significant because it also tells us that God's servant will be greatly exalted, and will sprinkle many nations, many peoples, one of the themes of our gathering. And these people include those who have no news of Him and who have not heard. Encouragingly that same passage gives us the assurance that Jesus Christ will see of the travail of his soul and be satisfied and will divide the booty with the strong. But until that consummation, we are called by God to preach Christ where He's not been named to those without good news of Him who have not so far heard.

How are we going to fulfill these great spiritual ambitions? What is the motivation that must lie behind a consultation such as this? Paul had preached the gospel and established new congregations throughout what's today called Turkey, and Greece. Now he was looking to Spain, at the western end of the Mediterranean. We may well ask how it is that when we had men with such ambitions, it has taken us so long to spread the gospel to the rest of the world. In verse 22, Paul speaks of hindrances to his plans and in thinking of the problems which confront this consultation, I am going to major largely on some of the hindrances which stand in the way of the advance of the gospel today.

OBSTACLES TO EVANGELISM.

Some hindrances have come from outside the church, but many are internal, self created problems rising from our faithlessness, or our lack of confidence in the whole gospel, or indeed a failure to preach the whole gospel at all. We are privileged to live at a time when the church is partially mobilized to reach those who have not heard. We also recognize that we have a long way to go.

LACK OF INFORMATION

The whole world has not been reached, and there have been some remarkable failures in recent history. Why, we may ask, was a country of 6 million people, like Kampuchea, ignored for so long. May I remind you that there are (or rather there were) more Kmers than there are Scots, or Swiss, yet there were never more than 30 church planting missionaries, at any one time, working there? Why is it that still today in the refugee camps there are many short term welfare and medical workers, but only a tiny handful of Christian workers who actually speak the Cambodian language? Why that failure to reach those people not hidden? What about the 3 million Moros of the southern Philippines or the 5 million Minangkabau in Central Sumatra, both of them now (they weren't always of course), almost entirely Muslim. Why were they neglected for so long? And why are they prayed for so little? Why are certain places neglected? It's all very ad hoc, hit and miss. There's a lack of rational criteria. We ought therefore surely to welcome genuine attempts to provide accurate information. We non-Americans should not sneer at this or dismiss it merely as an American obsession with applying success criteria, business methods to Christian work.

PLANNING AND GUIDANCE

In vs. 24 Paul says, "I PLAN to do so". Now there's nothing unspiritual or unbiblical about planning. There are other occasions where it is clear that the Apostle and those who worked with him planned to go to certain places and to do certain things. It is said that he visited the towns in Galatia in order. In other words, there was a certain plan behind what they were doing. There were occasions when there was direct divine intervention as in the call to Macedonia. But also we read many times that the Lord guided people when they got together and planned and sought His leading. So we ought to be grateful that some are endeavoring to collate information that will help us to identify neglected areas and to avoid unnecessary overlap.

I was in Mindanao in the southern Philippines recently and was appalled to find little villages of no more than 20 houses in one street, with a competing congregation at each end, and other small towns with four different church buildings on four adjacent lots. Everybody was trying to build new churches on other people's foundations, and yet nearby there are the animistic tribal people, until recently almost totally neglected, as well as the millions of Moros. In metropolitan Manila, there are still huge areas waiting for the gospel. We need better information, better disseminated, in all the churches. We need to know which people are unreached. Accurate information will stop us trying to start new organizations if there is already a group doing the job, and therefore we shall be able to find genuinely neglected areas and reach out to those.

FUND RAISING

Money always seems to cause problems. Instead of balanced objective information, there's a kind of public relations free-for-all. Information is selective according to who writes sensational books or pays for advertising. There are 3 or 4 big internationals who have an income close to, or in excess of, a million dollars a week. They have employed successful fund raising techniques, produced excellent magazines and are thus able to disseminate information widely about projects in which they personally are involved. This is the kind of structure which we have made for ourselves in Christendom today. It is doubtful to my mind whether all the work of these organizations is necessarily strategically the most important for the spreading of the gospel, or more important than that of smaller and less well known organizations.

Christian people are being unwittingly manipulated by the clever use of modern media so that certain Christian para church "brand names" are kept constantly before them. They are answerable to no one but themselves. I'm sure that as Christians these groups are seeking to be as responsible as they can, but one questions whether the set-up allows the churches to think objectively about the relative significance of Christian work as a whole. In other words, the Christian church is not being given a fully objective picture because of this advertising rat race. We need more thought on how information is presented and disseminated among Christians. Competitive advertising is not a spiritual method. Can this consultation find a valid and more objective alternative to our present, chaotic advertising, competitive approach?

ANCILLARY WORKERS.

My wife owes her missionary call to the Edinburgh Medical and Missionary Association, and I myself have been closely associated for many years with the medical work of the Overseas Missionary Fellowship. So don't misunderstand me, but for some reason, it's always much easier to raise money for medical and agricultural work, for development aid programs, as though those were the most significant. It's much harder to get money for evangelism or for theological training, for example, and this seems to me a very short-sighted policy. We are seeing that as countries develop, it is almost a slight on their own ability to produce doctors, nurses and agricultural experts, that these have to be provided from overseas. And missionary work, based upon that kind of specialization, is bound historically to diminish more and more, and such missionaries returned with thanks. But the need for church planting and church perfecting continues in some parts of the world undiminished, if not increased.

The missionary body is cluttered with self-styled experts in ad evangelism, film evangelism, etc. There are too many missionaries pottering around campsites and doing chores around white elephant buildings. The basic task is pioneer church planting and patient church perfecting, concerned with a quality of church growth. It's always easier to opt out of those difficult basic tasks, of going to a place where there is no church.

There are still cities of 40 or 50 thousand people where there is not yet a single congregation of Christians. It's not easy to go into places like that, and start from scratch. It's still harder to go to a church that has become institutionalized and to try to change it by the grace of God. It's difficult. It's always much easier to become an expert with an office, bogged down in masses of paper clips and carbon copies. We are being side tracked from the basic task of what McGavran calls, "saving souls, baptizing bodies and planting churches".

SHORT TERM WORKERS.

I was in Nepal in January, speaking to the group of missionaries there, and I discovered that half the missionaries had less than 3 years experience in the country, not yet capable of expressing the gospel in the national language. In a year it is unlikely to have changed much, because the majority are short termers! We have failed to press the need for long term missionaries. Again, don't misunderstand me, I have no problem with tentmakers where that's the only legitimate means of entry. What is worrying me, is Christians opting for short term when long term is possible. I understand that Bangladesh is probably worse, full of short term "missionaries" who spend their spare time in expatriate clubs outside of what they call working hours and who never bother to learn any language well enough to communicate the gospel. There are always glorious exceptions, but they are far too few. And all of that in a country of 80 million people, the seventh largest country in the world.

Our missionary statistics may be totally misleading. The number of "Missionaries" tells us nothing. How many of them make it their main business to plant and perfect churches? How many of them can communicate the gospel effectively in the indigenous language? Missionary superintendents in Thailand were asked what sort of missionaries they needed, and they said they wanted old fashioned missionaries under 25! What they meant was, people who would get on with the essential task of preaching the gospel, and who learned a language really well, and stayed long enough to earn the respect and affection of national Christian leaders.

There was a time when most missionaries were short termers. Many never lived to learn the language well enough to preach Christ. They never went home again. But today in most places, when people can live safely, in good health, to a ripe old age, so many refuse to do so, and return to their home lands. In those days missionaries worked to deadlines, literal ones. Like Henry Martyn who translated the New Testament into three languages before he died at the age of 31, one of them Persian, the language of Iran. Today Iran has a population of 35 millions or more, but only about 5,000 Protestant Christians. What have Christians been doing since Martyn died in 1813? Why did so few see the need to follow up the work which he'd sought to begin?

MISLEADING REPORTING

Another of our problems is the lack of a clear conscience. At A.L.C.O.E., a consultation of Asian leaders, we were told of groups all too ready to build on others' foundations—in one case, offering money to churches if they would add one word to their names, so that somebody might claim them for their own work. So often we only know what our own group is doing. I remember being asked at a college in Canada whether I knew the missionaries in Japan. I asked who they meant and they named three couples who I happened to have met. I replied that I knew several hundred of the 2,500 missionaries working in that country, but they behaved as though their own six from their denomination were all there were.

I know of only a few missionary magazines which regularly make a point of mentioning sister societies working in the same area, even when they actually cooperate on the field. This is part of the problem of a success-orientated public relations, which puffs up successes and makes big news items of them with singular lack of objectivity about actual achievement. When will crusade-organizing groups report honestly on surveys carried out five years after a series of meetings. I remember a crusade lasting six nights with a hundred professions every night but our rejoicing over six hundred new Christians was short lived. Two weeks later we had only twenty actually showing evidence of conversion. But our reports tend to reflect the glow of the final night rather than the realism after the first month of follow-up.

Are our church growth figures honest? Let's face the fact that many have come into the churches in Indonesia because they like roast pork, and as Muslims, they can't eat it. Or again take the matter of Third World missions. I am as delighted as anyone, indeed I think more so, about the mobilizing of the whole church. I know your hearts thrill with me when we read of tribal people from Mindoro in the Philippines, a g-string culture, themselves only having had the gospel some 20 years, sending out missionaries to reach the Negritos in Luzon. But here also we must be honest.

The statistics of Third World missions are absurdly inflated by Chinese going to Chinese, Koreans to Korea, Japanese to Nisei, and so on. I'm not saying they shouldn't go. Of course they should! They have a responsibility to win their fellow countrymen, but we need to recognize that whatever else it is, it is not E-3 evangelism. A Chinese friend of mine, speaking recently in a Chinese Congress, was urging that the word missionary should be restricted to cross cultural E-3 missions, and the response was that this was impossible, because it would reduce the marvelous statistics of men and money down to a mere 5% of the present figures. We need more honesty and less promotion in P.R. It is not honoring to God to encourage Christians with inflated statistics that talk triumphantly and lack objectivity and honesty.

DOCTRINAL CONVICTION

We know that we must evangelize but not all believe that it matters whether people are evangelized or not. There is a creeping universalism in the churches which is not convinced of the lostness of men without Christ. We have to ask whether our enthusiasm for hidden peoples is motivated by a kind of spiritual numbers game or by the conviction that men are lost and perishing without Christ. Many of us here are missionary professionals who are concerned about how many missionaries we have and how much effective work they are doing. And in the business of being organization men, we can lose our spiritual edge. Do we still have a passionate concern for men lost and perishing, or are we like the promotion people in Joe Bailey's Gospel Blimp, so obsessed with impersonal gospel ad balloons and committees that we no longer take the gospel personally to real individual people? If there is a lack of doctrinal conviction, then no wonder motivation is lacking for people to come forward as missionaries. Good theology produces good missions.

FAITH AND PRAYER

All of our statistics and surveys, important and necessary as they are, will be wasted unless they provide fuel for believing prayer. So many of our meetings do little more than pay lip service to the necessity of prayer. So I hope that in this consultation, the daily place for prayer and for the ministry of the Word will not be seen as an opportunity for chatting outside in the lobbies but for getting together before God on our knees. Frankly so much of our organization of committees and conferences could carry on without the Holy Spirit at all, without any spiritual input except lip service to an accepted norm of spirituality. So let's not kid ourselves that a list of so-called hidden peoples or a conference about them will in itself achieve anything. Discussing things or making covenants or devising statements can be useful preliminaries to define what needs to be done but they are not a substitute for action. And there is only one way I know of to bridge that gap, that is by genuine dependence upon God. We need to confess depending on our organizations instead of on God. We need to pray that God will work among us. There are no hidden peoples as far as He is concerned. But again and again, talking to God is dropped in favor of talking to men.

PEOPLE.

The poster read, "How to identify Hidden Peoples", and somebody had drawn a pair of eyes on it! Who are they hidden from? Not from God. Usually not from the thoughtful missionary or national Christian on the spot. They are hidden from the legions of the willfully ignorant in the churches who don't want to know and who are not motivated to find out. What hides them? Sometimes as we have seen, it is our lack of honesty, our failure to give objective information and frequently our deceptive and selfish public relations exercises that only speak about our own work.

Let's reach PEOPLE. I shudder when I read in literature about people being targets for something. Scripture uses the military metaphor in many ways, but it seems that speaking of people as targets is quite unbiblical. It's a de-personalization and we need to recognize and stress that word "People". It is not merely groups of unreached peoples but individual people, millions and millions of them, who need to be reached with the gospel.

FIVE POSITIVE STEPS.

I have concentrated on problems and hindrances, but my fear is that if we do not break ourselves free of the assumptions of our religious worldliness and talking as though the solutions are primarily to be found in better organization, more statistics, more jargon, more frequent conferences, if we do not pray, then we shall not get anywhere. Let me try and state all this positively.

HONESTY: Let's tell it the way it is, and not the way we would like it to be. Let's not puff up what we are doing out of proportion to the work of others, and let's stop trying to form new structures and new organizations when we ought to be trying to make the existing ones work.

THEOLOGY: Let's be sure that men are lost, without Christ, and because it is also theological, let's have a doctrine that helps us relate church with church, that helps in our little denominational groups not merely to ignore the issue but to decide what these other people alongside us are. Are they Christians or not? Are they preaching the whole gospel, are they preaching Christ or not?

COOPERATION: Let's stop wasting Christian resources on money-raising activities and competing between ourselves for the attention of the Christian public.

FAITH AND PRAYER: Put your faith in God, and not in men and methods. We need more prayer and dependence on God.

COMMITMENT: We need a greater challenge to costly cross-cultural identification on a long term basis and determination not to be side-tracked into alleged specialization in becoming expert on something. Paul's ambition was to keep planting and laying new foundations for new congregations, not for his own satisfaction, nor to feel that he built up some organization which would carry on his name, but building the church for Christ. The pioneer spirit is well described in Flecker's words, "We are the pilgrims, Master. We shall go, always a little further. It may be beyond that last blue montain barred with snow, across that angry or that glimmering sea." And if we are to reach these unreached sub-cultures, there are still plenty of cultural frontiers to be crossed. That's why we are gathered here. If this group is ready to pray, then I think we shall see progress towards taking the gospel to the world in this generation.

4
FRONTIER
MISSION
PERSPECTIVES

FRONTIER MISSION VISION - Ralph D. Winter

I want to quote from Billy Graham's final talk at the Lausanne meeting in 1974.

> While some people can be evangelized by their neighbors, others and greater multitudes are cut off from their Christian neighbors by deep linguistic and political chasms. They will never be reached by near-neighbor evanglism, that is to say, normal evangelism. To build our evangelistic policies on near-neighbor evangelism alone is thus to shut out at least a billion people from any possibility of knowing the Savior. Many sincere Christians around the world are concerned for evangelism. They are diligent at evangelizing in their own communities and even in their own countries, but they may not yet see God's big picture of world needs. This is ... the global responsibility that God has put upon the church in His word. The Christians of Nigeria, for example, are not just to evangelize Nigeria, nor the Christians of Peru just the people of Peru. God's heartbeat is for the world. World evangelization needs continued and increased sendings of missionaries and evangelists from every church in every land to the unreached billions.

I know of no other quotation that could more precisely sum up the burden and the vision of this conference.

The topic "Frontier Mission Vision," encompasses a broad spectrum. Certainly it should include the inspiration which is all important for frontier missions, as well as technical details, definitions, etc. I have handed out separately a few sheets of definitions (See FRONTIER

MISSION TERMINOLOGY-Ed.)

Let's begin with some of the non-technical aspects of the word "vision." Dr. Mark Hanna has already given us an excellent foundation of missions in the Old Testament, and in the next few days he will continue to pursue this into the New Testament period. Since this Biblical background is so essential to anything I might say about frontier vision, I hope you will not mind if I take a moment to sum it up in my own way.

THE ROOTS OF FRONTIER MISSION VISION

What could be the ultimate roots of frontier mission vision? Vision for the frontiers obviously was not an idea which originated with William Carey or Hudson Taylor. Nor was it first enunciated by Jesus Christ, although when He came, He definitively restated the Abrahamic Commission of Genesis 12:3, authoritatively putting it back into action again. I have been impressed by the continuity of mission vision throughout the entire Bible. I grew up in a dispensational church, with the Scofield Bible as my study Bible, and I still consider myself part of that tradition. Perhaps because of this, it has come to me in recent years somewhat as a glorious surprise that God's plans for reaching all mankind, references to which I had long noted all through the Bible, were not first put into force with Christ and the early church. Like scales falling off my eyes, I came to see how much earlier God acted on His concern for all nations, such that this "mission vision" can be seen throughout the entire Bible. Paul was so amazed when God led him into what must have been this same discovery that he realized he was now able to understand what to most others was still a "mystery." Yet he readily admitted that it never had been a mystery to God. All too often today we also have a veil before our eyes which prevents us from seeing the glory of His presence and the significance of His Great Commission first given to Abraham, renewed to Moses, known through the Psalms, etc., right down through Old Testament times to the present. Because of this veil and also due to our similar unwillingness to obey, things that are brilliantly clear in the Bible and should be well known in our churches today we find "hard" or "difficult to understand" or "puzzling" or "confusing"—all terms which could have been used to translate Paul's word "mystery."

In other words, vision to reach people we do not see is fragile and precarious, easily destroyed by disobedience and disinterest. It is not merely an intellectual achievement. It is not possible for me or anyone else simply to throw statistics on the screen and talk in terms of "unreached peoples" and expect "vision" to result in the hearer. Vision cannot be imparted simply by presenting cold, hard facts. Vision consists of an understanding given by the Holy Spirit. And it will die unless acted upon in obedience to the Lord.

A "Hard" Verse?

Let me illustrate. At a recent convention featuring displays from many evangelical organizations, the one representing the U. S. Center for World Mission was located directly across the aisle from one which emphasized the Rapture. One of our people walked across the aisle, looked at all the Bible verses across the back panel of the booth, then commented, "Well, you seem to have all the verses except one." "Which one do you mean?" asked the man behind the table. "The one in Matthew 24:14," our man answered. "What's that?" "You know, the one that says, 'his gospel must first be preached in the whole world as a witness to all peoples, and then shall the end come.' Why did you leave that one out?" "Well, you know, that's a hard verse! It's confusing ... really mysterious," was the answer.

An Old Commission Restated

But is it, really? This morning we reviewed the covenant to Abraham. He was to be blessed, and he was to be a blessing to all the families of the earth. Peter understood this commission to Abraham, and quoted it in Acts 3:35. Paul understood it, quoting it in Galatians 3:8. In other words, the Great Commission given by Jesus in Matthew 28:18-20 was essentially an authoritative restatement of what we find in Genesis and in Isaiah 49:6. The latter verse was quoted in the New Testament by the Apostle Paul in Acts 13:47 and Acts 26:23. Peter clearly understood and restated in 1 Peter 2:9,10 the missionary commission of the restored nation of Israel coming out of Egypt (Ex 19:5,6), which in turn is itself a restatement of the Abrahamic covenant.

Thus we see that the vision that moved Peter and Paul was one recognized—and intended to be recognized—long before, yet in their day it had been lost because of a decline in spiritual understanding and obedience.When Jesus definitively restated that same vision, He stated it to a people who, in effect, had already rejected it. Oh, He had hoped to help them fulfill it. He worked, prayed, and wept in His incessant efforts to show them what kind of obligations their God-given blessings brought to them. Due to their hardness of heart, Jesus could not talk all the time about their mission to the Gentiles, but He did demonstrate God's concern for the little people, the lame, the halt, the blind, the women and the Greeks, to see if there would be a flicker of interest. He did not find that kind of concern, even among the disciples.

Obedience to the Heavenly Vision

As a result, one might almost say that Jesus did not come to give the Great Commission, but to take it away—to take it from one nation and to make sure it got to others. Lamentably, those other nations—our own Gentile nations—have left no better a record in understanding and attempting to fulfill that vision in the last 2,000 years than did the Jewish people in the preceding 2,000 years.

Paul did understand! Look carefully at those verses in Acts 26 where Paul said to Agrippa, "I was not disobedient to the heavenly vision." You'll find that he is referring to a vision that clearly encompassed more of the peoples of the world than his own. That breadth was the bizarre, disturbing feature of the vision. Note that the very moment Paul mentioned the Gentiles, Agrippa (according to the New Testament "an expert on Jewish laws and customs") broke in and said, "You're mad! You're out of your mind!" We recall other times in the Bible when the word "Gentiles" triggered anger. In the synagogue at Nazareth, Jesus' reference to two Gentiles provoked fury—homicidal fury! With ominous similarity, when Paul referred to the Gentiles in his sermon at Antioch of Pisidia, the Jews sat down and worked out a plot to kill him. Jesus found that the chosen, Missionary Nation, after 2,000 years, registered no adequate response to its obligation to share its blessings. To this day Israel as a nation is characterized by guarding, not giving, its blessings. Very simply (and mysteriously) the Bible says that's not safe; that's not the way. But is our nation, is your nation, any better?

FRONTIER MISSION VISION SINCE NEW TESTAMENT TIMES

Ever since the time of Paul we can detect this same deadly dangerous, visionless pattern. In our day we evangelicals don't plot to kill people who mention missions; we just don't invite them back. Vision today is killed by other methods—by disuse, by disillusion, by spiritual declension, and in a thousand other ways. Indeed, a genuine concern for strange peoples has been shockingly rare among Christians across the centuries. Since the close of the Biblical period, it has been really only the Irish Christian scholars—the Scottish, as they were called back in the medieval period—who sent missionaries as part of any kind of a major national undertaking. We are amazed that there is no other example of a missionary nation in the entire first thousand-year period of Christian history. The Irish, Scottish, Celtic missionaries infiltrated not only the British Isles after the pagan Anglo-Saxons had invaded, but were the primary force in reconquering the continent of Europe for Christ. They were even called to teach Latin in the city of Rome itself. That Celtic outpouring was so important that Satan had to employ a whole series of his diabolic stratagems to knock it out. Those wandering Irish missionary saints— the Celtic Peregrini, as they are called—today seem very unusual and mysterious, and their vision was both rare at the time and is still difficult for modern, greedy, materialistic Christians to understand.

Protestants Took 200 Years!

Later on there were other groups who recovered the vision. The friars—the Franciscans and Dominicans—like a new breed of mobilized monks not confined to monasteries, traversed all of Europe and the known world preaching a vision which had long been lost. They were followed by the Clerks Regular, including such great missionary statesmen as Matteo Ricci, Roberto de Nobili and Alesandro Valignano. Centuries before the Protestants had awakened to the existence of the Great Commission in their treasured Bibles, these ordered groups were out across the world, at work preaching the gospel. By contrast, although they were furiously reading the Bible, Protestants failed to discover for almost two hundred years after the Reformation the mysterious vision of which Paul spoke—the mystery that other peoples, strange peoples, are to be included in God's kingdom, and are to be a major concern of all those nations that receive the Gospel and are blessed in the lineage of Abraham's faith.

The Moravians - A Trickle

Finally, however, born out of a profound spiritual awakening, there appeared in the Protestant world a trickle of missionaries of Moravian brand who pushed out across the world virtually alone. They were scoffed at and accused of being off on a tangent. They were considered fanatics simply because their vision, however central to the Bible, seemed peripheral to the Reformers, to the Reformation and to the Protestant movement as a whole. It is to our shame as Protestants that our ancestors took so long to rediscover the vision those others obeyed.

The First Era: William Carey and the Coastlands

One Protestant who did discover frontier vision in the Bible was William Carey, a young lay preacher–cobbler–teacher, still in his twenties, who lived not so far from this city of Edinburgh. His little book, An Enquiry into the Obligation of Christians to Use Means for the Conversion of the Heathens brought about a spectacular new understanding of God's age–old intent for all mankind. It also provided the principal literary basis for the deliberate creation of Protestant missionary orders. On the very first page of his book Carey started to repair the damage that had been done in the Protestant sphere to the Biblical text of the Great Commission. He maintained that it had applied all along to all Christians, not just to the disciples. He then added table after table of carefully worked statistics covering the unreached peoples of his day, who composed most of the world. He appealed to the Christians of England to obey Christ's command to go and disciple the nations. And, he went himself!

After a number of years, because of Carey's impetus, the coastlands of the world became well occupied by missionaries. But the interiors had been barely scratched.The vision for frontiers initiated by Carey had already been lost in a little over half a century. Then James Hudson Taylor, another young man also under thirty, moved into the breech and, like Carey, began talking like a fanatic. Taylor agreed with the mission leaders of his day that the work along the coasts must not be abandoned. The churches there were still young and needed missionary help. Yet, he insisted, God's concern did not stop at the coasts. Inland in every continent there were still vast unreached areas, with thousands and thousands of potential mission fields. Instead of being attracted by these new challenges, mission leaders in effect told Taylor, "Hudson, the one thing we don't need is another mission organization! Moreover, those areas are unreachable!"Seventy years before, Carey had also been reproved by the church leaders: "If God wants to save the heathen, He will do it without your help or ours!"

The Second Era: Hudson Taylor and the Interiors

At least ten years passed before anyone paid much attention to Carey. It was even longer with Hudson Taylor. Then gradually his vision began to gain momentum. Within twenty years there arose a major student movement for missions, much larger but reminiscent of the earlier "Haystack" student movement, which had sprung up ten years or so after Carey went to India. And, as before, this new student movement, this time called the Student Volunteer Movement, brought a new era of missions into full forcew. Sooner or later, partly because of student pressure, the older mission societies frantically retooled and plunged out into the new frontiers which Hudson Taylor years before had highlighted with that single terse word "inland." Meanwhile, the China Inland Mission, the Africa Inland Mission, the Heart of Africa Mission, the Sudan Interior Mission, the Regions Beyond Missionary Union, the Unevangelized Field Mission—all these agencies had already sprung up in response to that renewed frontier mission vision, the vision for people in groups where Christ had not yet been named.

THE (RECENT) RECOVERY OF FRONTIER VISION

As we now approach the year 2,000, we may look back on even greater accomplishment. We have already gone to the coastlands. We have already gone inland. There are Christians today within all politically defined entities of the world—what we call "countries." But if we look at the smaller entities the Bible calls "nations," we discover that here and there, both in cities and rural areas of every country of the world, there are still forgotten or bypassed peoples— "Hidden Peoples," as this conference calls them. Thus, by taking a Biblical magnifying glass to the social fabric of the societies of the world today, we discover that there are still thousands of such mission fields unreached with the gospel. These are the "nations," the ethnic or social groups where there is no internal, indigenous church to reach out in ordinary evangelism. As in the case of Paul's outreach to the Gentiles, there may in fact be some believers already within these Hidden People groups, but such believers are usually forced to worship outside their group, like the Gentile "God fearers." These "devout persons" were on the margins of the Jewish synagogues in the New Testament, at the point where there were not yet any Gentile synagogues. In such cases, because there is not yet a witnessing church within the group, there can be no indigenous, "full-time Christian worker." All evangelism must come from somewhere outside that culture.

The Third Era: McGavran, Townsend and the Hidden Peoples

The growing recognition and response to the existence of many still unpenetrated groups constitutes the third and final era of Protestant missions. The first era reached the coastlands; the second, the inland areas. Now frontier vision is automatically defined not as new geographical locations but as the Hidden, bypassed cultures of the world. Carey was the early prophet of the first era; Taylor, the early prophet of the second. Were there also symbolic pioneers in this third era of Protestant missions?

The observations of a third-generation missionary in India, working as a young man in the late 1920s, have become famous for taking note of and making strategic sense out of the mosaic of caste distinctions so profoundly embedded in the social structure of that vast subcontinent. Caste has long been known, ridiculed, and resisted by outsiders, eventually even by Indian leaders. It was early rejected by missionaries as un-Christian and was not therefore understood as something to take seriously nor as something we should deal with even on a practical level in initial communication.

Donald McGavran and the Homogeneous Unit Principle

Thus, Donald A. McGavran's insistence that both in India and in other countries Homogeneous Units be acknowledged and approached strategically was an idea that virtually by itself produced an entire school of missiological thought. "People group evangelism," winning a people group one at a time, has become by now probably the most pervasive perspective in mission circles around the world, although its full implications are still being widely explored.

From this basic insight it is only a small, logical step further to note the strikingly practical value of looking at all of mankind in two major categories: 1) the category of all those groups within which there is a viable church, and 2) the category of all those groups where that kind of missiological breakthrough has not yet taken place. The first of these two categories forces into view the existence of the Hidden People groups, and allows us to detect and then define this vast, remaining, non-geographical frontier that is otherwise easily overlooked and readily "hidden" from our eyes. Indeed, these groups continue to remain effectively hidden if we insist on laboring under the supposition that these often small units of mankind be expected immediately to "come over to," "join in with" and otherwise assimilate to those cultural traditions where the church has already become indigenized.

Standing squarely against such an "integrationist" supposition is the insight of Donald McGavran and a vast number of others who have with him detected and respected the right to a sort of theological self-determination by these smaller groups. But it was McGavran more than anyone else who first spoke up for this revolutionary perspective in the early 1930s, and whose classical work Bridges of God first enunciated the Homogeneous Unit principle.

Cameron Townsend and Tribal Peoples

However, at the very same time McGavran was first pondering the configurations in India, another young man, like McGavran a Student Volunteer from the later period of the SVM, and like McGavran, Taylor and Carey still under thirty, William Cameron Townsend was being dragged by circumstances into a similarly unwelcome complexity which he found, even in the very small country of Guatemala. Like Carey and Taylor before him, and like McGavran across the world of whose existence he knew nothing, Townsend reluctantly recognized a significant category of people groups that had been overlooked by the main evangelizing and missionary force of the Second Era. The Apostle Paul in his day had insisted that God could redeem Gentiles as Gentiles; they didn't have to become Jewish proselytes first. In Guatemala, Cameron Townsend realized that the main efforts of missionary endeavor were essentially insisting that the Mayan Indian population (which numbered two-thirds of the population) had to learn Spanish in order to truly follow the Lord. Many of the "Spanish" of Guatemala were, after all, only a small step away from the pure Indians. Why shouldn't the rest come over? Trying to sell a Spanish Bible to an Indian one day, he was startled by the question: "If your God is so smart, why can't He speak our language?"

Thus, with the tribal peoples of the world as his main focus, Townsend in 1934 founded what has become one of the largest mission agencies in modern history—the Wycliffe Bible Translators. McGavran wrote the vision in technical and general terms. Townsend founded a mission, and focused specifically on tribal peoples. McGavran began to be called as a consultant to other fields all over the world and has by now been the impetus behind serious missiological studies of more different people groups than any other person in history. Similarly, Townsend has been the impetus for more technical analyses of human tongues than any other person in history. McGavran's concept of the "social mosaic" of "homogeneous units" has sometimes been employed merely to allow Christians of one group to concentrate on their own people. But the most cogent meaning of his vision is that special efforts are necessary if we are to take seriously the unpenetrated groups that still remain.

The "People Group" Strategy

As in the beginning of the Second Era, it was a number of years before anyone paid much attention to either of these young men. They were, at first, too young. Neither attempted to start a new organization right away. Both spent immense efforts to move existing mission boards to the frontiers they had discovered. In regard to tribal societies, opponents of Townsend found it easy to say, "There are not very many tribal people in the world, relatively speaking. And who cares about them anyway? Let's win the people that are the major cultures of the various countries, and the tribal peoples will eventually follow suit." But if Townsend had not eventually started a new organization, it is doubtful if ninety different languages in the country of Mexico alone (hundreds elsewhere) would have been reduced to writing. Just as Hudson Taylor, in referring to the inland people of China had in effect pointed to the inland peoples in all the continents of the world, so Townsend and McGavran, in referring to the bypassed peoples of Guatemala and India, pointed out the general category of all groups of people everywhere that have yet to be reached by missionary and evangelistic effort. Although Townsend specialized on tribal peoples and McGavran caste groups, our definition for overlooked or Hidden Peoples as formulated by this conference covers both ethnic and social distinctions. It does not depend on geographical boundaries but rather on the presence or absence of an indigenous church. What matters is, do the people of a given group have a witnessing church which is able to reach out to them from within their society? Why is this necessary?

I remember Dr. McGavran asking a group, "How many of you have ever had a really good chance to become a communist?" There wasn't a person in the group who hadn't learned a great deal about communism. I know that when I was in college I couldn't avoid it. I was running into communist sympathizers all the time, and I read a lot of the things that Marx wrote. (I remember, for instance, reading his essay on India where he in effect said, "These people are so depraved that we have to send colonial powers to take control of them." If that quotation were highlighted around the world today, I wonder if the whole Marxist movement might not collapse!) The point is, everyone in that group knew about Marxism, just as millions upon millions of people know something about Jesus Christ. Yet all of us had to admit to Dr. McGavran that just as we had never been in a situation where we could sit down, sign a statement and join an acceptable group of people as a member of the communist party, so many people in the world today have no opportunity to become Christians, because they have no way to join an acceptable group of Christians in a face-to-face relationship.

Yet, realistically we know that unless nonbelievers have at least that good a chance to become Christians, we are kidding ourselves if we simply sprinkle the name of Jesus around the world. That isn't enough! It's those hard-core communist cells that make communism a force in today's world. Structurally it is the same with Christianity. The power of Christ today does not consist in the statistics of denominational offices. Fortunately, there are three times as many truly committed evangelicals in the world as there are communist party members, and evangelicals are scattered more widely. Yet Christians will still have to extend to non-Christians that same basic apparatus whereby people find fellowship and accountability in a local church. If we don't, we must confess it is a fallacy when we say people have already been evangelized. Oh, yes, they may have heard the gospel over the radio, or by some other casual encounter. Radio gospel messages are helpful, but the radio is just the air force. It still takes foot soldiers to complete the job. We still have to go where people are. We have to sit where they sit. We have to pay attention to the groups they belong to. We have to be content with nothing less than an indigenous, evangelizing church planted within a society before we can say that such a group is no longer a frontier population and is now able to be won by normal evangelism. This is what is required by the phrase "a church for every people by the year 2,000." This is Frontier Mission Vision. It is today what it has always been: people—group in focus, church-planting in method and indigenizing in orientation. However, in our era the frontiers are no longer "coastlands" or "inland" but the remaining bypassed people groups discovered for us by McGavran and Townsend.

THE HOPES AND HAZARDS OF FRONTIER MISSIONS TODAY

We have seen that the vision for evangelizing all mankind had its roots in the very beginning of the Bible. And we have traced that vision throughout the rest of the Bible and down through history. We have seen it recovered and redefined for our time. But what have been the fruits? Is this vision worth pursuing? What obstacles does it face?

Probably the chief hazard frontier vision faces today is the deep vacuum of knowledge about it. Yet the truth is that the fruits of the vision to take the gospel to all mankind have been so extensive, so worldwide in scope, that sometimes it is hard not to over-believe and assume that the job has already been finished. Some say that since there is now a church in every country, outsiders are no longer necessary. Much more often, however, people have no real grasp of the massive impact of the gospel, and they have lost all hope.

Such "hopeless" souls do not realize that it was the Christian missionary movement which brought 85% of the schools of Africa into being, founded 600 hospitals in the country of India, and started thousands of other major institutions all around the world. (For example, the largest technical university in Brazil, and in Asia, both the largest medical research institution and the most prestigious agricultural center, plus hundreds of other developmental projects, were all started by Christian missions.) The Christian missionary movement did all this long before the phrase "international development" was popular. Indeed, if the story were ever fully written, it would show that the missionary movement has been successful all out of proportion to the energy put into it, and that almost solely because of intentional mission efforts Christianity is by far the largest and most widespread religion in the world today. No matter how you examine it, the fruits of this vision of which we speak have been enormous.

Nevertheless, the Second Era frontier vision that produced all this has mainly gone into eclipse today. Why? For one thing, the McGavrans and Townsends are octogenarians, and their greatest influence has been relatively recent. But to a great extent it has been due to a growing mood of pessimism starting with the First World War, reinforced by the

Great Depression, the Second World War and more recently the Korean war, the Viet Nam war and numerous civil wars throughout the world. At the very moment Cameron Townsend was speaking up for a major thrust into tribal areas, many of the older, more successful mission agencies were beginning to speak of retrenchment. Many mission agencies have welcomed so enthusiastically the resulting national churches in every country that they have become too deeply involved with them to see what McGavran and Townsend saw so clearly—the bypassed and as yet unreached thousands of tribal, ethnic and social groups still without an internal, corporate witness. It has not always been clear that either McGavran or Townsend would ever be heard.

Recovery of Vision

In the last decade, however, numerous signs of a recovery of pioneer missionary vision have surfaced. A number of articles have been written. (1) A series of world-level conferences on world evangelization have been held—at Berlin, Lausanne, Pattaya in Thailand, and now Edinburgh. Most mission agencies are now talking seriously about the new frontiers. And (2) more and more we are thinking in terms of strategies of closure. In this sudden resurgence we can see some fascinating and illuminating parallels with the past. For example, from the beginning of the Second Era (which I feel was that day in 1865 when Hudson Taylor founded the China Inland Mission), it took 45 years before there was a world-level gathering of mission agencies probing the newly discovered frontiers consisting in that day of inland peoples beyond Christianized areas. Interestingly, from the time that Cameron Townsend founded the Wycliffe Bible Translators (and McGavran was producing his classical work <u>Bridges of God</u>) until this second world-level meeting of mission agencies in 1980, again in Edinburgh, it has been exactly 46 years!

In the now much larger and more diverse world of Christian initiatives today (than existed in 1910) it is more difficult for "everyone" to be present at a single meeting. But this meeting 70 years later has attracted delegates from a larger number (if not percentage) of mission agencies than have ever before participated together in a world-level meeting. Even more impressive, by contrast this time at least a third of the agencies represented are non-Western! Furthermore, this consultation is focused more precisely, or at least more publicly, on the frontiers. Seventy years ago the organizers of Edinburgh I focused on frontiers by deciding early on not to invite agencies working solely in geographically defined Christianized territories. Today, because of the very success of that Second Era, we face the complexity of focusing more precisely on the sociologically defined Hidden People groups of the world, wherever they are found, as the rallying cry of the Third Era. Finally, the 1910 meeting used younger people only to run errands. Here at this meeting 170 student leaders, the mission leaders of tomorrow, have come from all over the world for serious meetings of their own.

Getting There!

The rediscovery of vision in our time is in some ways as painfully difficult as it was then. Young leaders are still being put down. I'm sure George Verwer of Operation Mobilization and Loren Cunningham of Youth With a Mission have been told many times what the mission leaders told Hudson Taylor, "We don't need more mission agencies." These two agencies are not yet full-fledged missions. They're still young. They may not be quite sure where they're headed, but they're getting there! You add up the force of those two agencies, and you have the largest single bloc of overseas workers in the Protestant world today. They can learn, just like Hudson Taylor learned. He didn't know everything when he went out. Few today recall, for instance, that when he founded the China Inland Mission he was absolutely determined never to plant churches; he wanted his missionary staff to concentrate their attention totally on evangelism. But what happened? He simply learned that wasn't the best way to go, and eventually the China Inland Mission (now known as the Overseas Missionary Fellowship) became a mainline, church-planting mission in China, working with and serving 7,000 missionaries from many boards. Wasn't it refreshing to hear Michael Griffiths, one of Taylor's successors, bear down so hard and so unapologetically last night on the necessity of planting churches? Or, take Campus Crusade. What a young, vital force across the world! What amazing strides it has made in global terms in the past few years! Their hallmark is strategies of closure. They, surely, have the end in sight.

Who knows the future of these three youthful agencies at which some have scoffed across the years? They are getting older, and they are getting wiser. Some of their twenty-year men are among the keenest thinkers on the face of the earth today in terms of mission strategy. Soon they will no longer be waiting for the older missions to follow along behind them to do church planting. You just wait and see!

Obstacles!

Thus in our day and age, as we now sense the rapid build-up of the Third Era of missions, we see obstacles as well. As in the early stages of the Second Era, many of the older societies are very proud of the national churches that have grown up under their work. In many cases those national churches have so fully captured their attention that the younger churchmen have successfully insisted that all future missionary work done in their countries—even a thousand miles across the country with utterly different people groups—be screened through the office of the first church established in that country. Such a proposal may be perfectly logical and often reasonable, and courtesy demands every respect for the so-called national church, wherever it is found. However, I can only observe that it was a very fortunate thing for my own country that such a pattern was not followed in the early days of the United States. At the time it was born as a political entity, only 3 percent of the citizens were members of Christian churches. If in those days permission to evangelize or to plant new churches had always to be requested from those churches first founded—the Anglican and the Congregational—perhaps America today would still be largely unevangelized. The pluralism which is characteristic of American Christianity may not, after all, be of the devil, as some think! On the contrary, this very pluralism has penetrated many different strata and sub-societies of the U.S., something a single organization or two, clearing plans through a central office, could never have done. I believe the American experience might warn us to be careful before we assume that decentralized frontier outreach to the Hidden Peoples might somehow be opposed to the very legitimate unity movements which we also favor.

Another caution:

Toward the end of the First Era, when Hudson Taylor was trying to promote the Second, there was a puzzling period of transition which lasted at least twenty years.In the very same year the China Inland Mission was founded to go to the vast inland frontiers of China, all the missionaries were called home from the Sandwich Islands, then a separate country now known as the Hawaiian Islands. Why? Their work was done! The church was strong and well able to carry on by itself. Even at that early date, this national church was sending missionaries to other parts of the South Pacific.

But to assume that same degree of maturity was true everywhere in the world where missionaries had gone would have been a great mistake. Remember that the Hawaiian Islands are all "coastlands," with only volcanoes in the interior. By contrast, the inland territories of Africa, China, India and large sections of Asia contained large numbers of people, and were still largely untouched. Pioneer work there had hardly begun.

Two Voices

Thus a similar tension is observable during the transition between the Second and Third Eras.Because national churches are often strong where they exist, all too readily Christians in the homeland leap to the conclusion that the job is done. Yet often only a hundred miles away, or maybe even right next door in another culture, the crucial initial breakthrough into another tongue or people has yet to be made. Thus, while people in some circumstances are preaching, "Now is the time for the missionary to go home," others are saying, "Let's go to the vast unreached frontiers with the gospel." Both voices in this friendly disagreement are right if understood in the light of their particular reference. It is true that the missionary job is over in the case of many of the people groups of the world. At the same time the job has not yet begun within others. There are, in fact, at least 16,750 people groups today which are still mainly hidden from our sight.

But all such facts, and the strategies necessary to deal with them must be discussed elsewhere. Here, finally, there is room only to note that for a vision to be obeyed it must be precise and technical. It is absolutely essential for us to know the facts, to both know as much as possible about the various cultures yet to be penetrated, but also have at our fingertips detailed information about the resources available in order to do the necessary strategic planning. To wander into the task without faith and vision means only failure. But to wander also without planning means endless frustration. As Michael Griffiths said last night, "Planning is essential!"

Not Against Flesh and Blood

Then, too, we recall the technical detail of William Carey's epoch-making little book, and the fact that Hudson Taylor's precise "accusing maps" spurred him on in his frontier vision. These facts do not imply that only strategic planning is neccesary and that we don't need the guidance of the Holy Spirit. All human planning is of no avail unless He is very much a part of the entire process. As the Apostle Paul reminds us, "We struggle not against flesh and blood, but against principalities and powers in high places.." Only the constant presence of the Holy Spirit can enable us to gain and maintain frontier missions vision for the world's least reached peoples.

FRONTIER MISSION TERMINOLOGY – Ralph D. Winter
Concepts and Labels Applied to Them

(This paper was distributed to delegates at Edinburgh, but has since been revised and amplified – Ed.)

INTRODUCTION: A few thoughts on the use of labels.

1. The definition and usefulness of a concept or entity is more important than the label attached to it.

2. Even an ill-chosen label for a carefully defined concept can assist in understanding and using the concept while better labels are considered.

3. A commonly used word like mission or missionary, may have such widely different and firmly understood meanings that we might do well to use special adjectives to create a precisely definable phrase, e.g. frontier missions, frontier missionary.

4. Newly coined words or phrases (like Hidden Peoples) have no previous baggage to get rid of but may take longer to be accepted. Their very newness warns people to ask for the definition rather than to suggest their own. Of course, people do not have to use them.

I. HISTORICAL TERMS

Four Stages of Mission Work

At the meeting of the (U.K.) Evangelical Missionary Alliance in November of 1979 Geoffrey Dearsley of the S.U.M. Fellowship suggested very helpfully that (in effect within each era) we have been going through four stages:

Stage 1. A Pioneer stage - first contact with people group.
Stage 2. A Paternal stage - expatriates train national leadership.
Stage 3. A Partnership stage - National leaders work as equals with expatriates.
Stage 4. A Participation stage - expatriates are no longer equal partners each one of Three Eras.

Three Eras: First Era/Second Era/Third Era

Each of these eras is an apparent cycle, passing through the Four Stages mentioned. These are Protestant (not general) eras, and they overlap. Each begins at a symbolic point when a new mission agency was established with a pioneering emphasis.

	First Era	Second Era	Third Era
Start	1792	1865	1934
Focus	Coastlands	Inland	Bypassed Peoples
Dominance	English	American	3rd World
Early Prophet	Wm. Carey	Hudson Taylor	Cameron Townsend, WBT
	BMS	CMS	Donald McGavran, ICG
Student Mvt.	"Haystack" Soc.	SVM	IVCF/CCC/ISCFM/TSFM

(My designation of the William Carey Era or the First Era is not intended to slight the trickle of valiant efforts by Protestants or the massive organized efforts by Catholics which preceeded 1800. Quantitatively (not qualitatively) the build-up in what I have called the First Era eclipses all previous Protestant efforts, and for the first time introduces among Protestants on a widespread scale the concept of the missionary society. This "invention" or re-invention, written out in detail with Carey's discipline in the famous book An Enquiry, had an impact that was very significant. As a result, enough agencies became involved so that a First Era is discernable as the four stages we have described unfold all across the world more or less simultaneously.)

Two Transitions: First Transition/Second Transition

Historic world-level conferences of mission agency leaders were proposed in each era. William Carey proposed one for 1810, but it did not happen. There was one in the Second Era, in 1910, after a 45 year transition from the beginning of that era in 1865. The first such conference in the Third Era occurred in 1980, after a 46-year transition from 1934.

Predictably, each transition is characterized by a great deal of honest confusion resulting from the fact that the latter two stages of one era (Partnership and Participation) may very well coexist simultaneously with the earlier two stages (Pioneer and Paternal) of the next era. For example, missionaries in one field (in Stage Four) may be turning things over and even coming home, while other missionaries elsewhere (in Stage One, in the early period of the next Era) will be setting forth to begin work in people groups that have no church there yet at all.

II. "PEOPLE" TERMS

People group. This has been defined by the Lausanne Strategy Working Group as "a significantly large sociological grouping of individuals who perceive themselves to have a common affinity for one another." This concept has reference to what the Bible calls nations, a term we cannot easily use due to its recent use as a synonym for country. But in the Bible nation, people, tribe, tongue, family (as in Gen. 12:3) are all synonyms for people group. American anthropologists speak of subcultures, but in Latin America, at least, this is understood as derogatory. An older term which is synonymous is McGavran's Homogeneous Unit. No concept is more significant in current mission thinking. (See FRONTIER VISION IN GRAPHIC FORM – Ed.)

Unreached People Groups. Since we do not easily speak of a group as being born again, this term has been defined predictively by the Strategy Working Group of the Lausanne Committee for World Evangelization as "a group that is less than 20% practicing Christian." Furthermore, a group 0-1% is initially reached, 1-10% minimally reached, 10-20% possibly reached. I believe it would be fair to say that the intent here is that these Christians be "practicing" along indigenous lines, since their potential to win the rest of the group would otherwise be in question.

This now constitutes a whole family of predictive terms which take as their measure the number of reached individuals in proportion to the total number of individuals in a people group. However, while, this scale makes a predictive classification on the basis of the percentage of individuals who are practicing Christians, the practical intent of this family of definitions has to do with the question of whether or not the newly planted church in an unreached people group has yet gained the potential to evangelize its own people such that outside, cross-cultural efforts can be safely terminated. This potential may be roughly predicted by measuring the percentage of practicing Christians, as above. Thus, the 20% was established to be on the safe side, but is not crucial if in a given case you happen to know that a viable church has finally been achieved.

Hidden Peoples. The World Consultation on Frontier Missions has
defined Hidden Peoples as "those cultural and linguistic subgroups,
urban or rural, for whom there is as yet no indigenous community of
believing Christians able to evangelize their own people." Once there
is sufficient data, this term is ultimately the same as Unreached, since
it also refers to the presence or absence of a viable church. It could
possibly be called "definitely unreached," since it was not coined as a
"safe side" designation for groups where outside work was no longer
necessary, but where you would have to say the work had not yet
been safely begun. Thus, Reached implies definitely completed while
Hidden implies definitely not completed. In one sense all groups are
therefore either Reached or Hidden. But, in the absence of full
knowledge, many groups are neither definitely Hidden nor definitely
Reached, and we may fall back on the predictive scale of the
Unreached series of terms. Thus, this term asks not how much is
done, but how little. It asks whether for a given group outside
cross-cultural evangelistic efforts are still necessary in order to make
the minimum true missiological breakthrough. Thus a group is still a
Hidden People if there is not yet a viable church that is an internal
indigenous fellowship doing evangelism.

Thus a group is no longer in the hidden category once a viable
fellowship of believers can conceivably handle the remaining task, not
when it can safely handle the job. On the other hand, a Hidden People
is not necessarily one where there are zero Christians, but rather
where there is not yet a viable church. Neither is a Hidden People
one where there are no missionaries, nor even where there is no
church of any kind (in case the existing church is either
non-indigenous or non-evangelizing.)

Synonyms that have been used for Hidden Peoples are frontier
peoples, forgotten peoples, bypassed peoples, unpenetrated peoples.
Hidden People Group is a label which was originally an alternative to
Unreached People Group, but in view of the later definitions of the
latter, and references to the presence or absence of a viable church,
it might be possible to say that a Hidden People Group is simply a
"definitely Unreached" People Group. It is in any case primarily the
name of a group. We ought not properly to speak of individuals as
Hidden People (e.g., Hidden Persons) although such individuals would
presumably be people who are part of a Hidden People (group). It is
estimated for mid-1981 that there are about one million true Christians
and 2,479 million other individuals in 16,750 Hidden People groups.

We should note that by definition the members of Hidden People
groups cannot be reached by E1 evangelism. E1 evangelism properly
understood requires incorporation of the believer and therefore must
build out from existing congregations. But by definition a Hidden
People Group has no such congregation, even though there may in fact
be some individual believers who have no indigenous church home but
rather attend a congregation available to them which represents a
different society. Since such believers cannot easily get others to

follow them out of their culture, this is not an ideal way to win others. We do well to say that a group remains a Hidden People until there is within it a viable indigenous church, and that only then can E1 evangelism in the best sense be employed.

The origin and the metaphoric sense of the word Hidden may be derived by reflection upon Paul's ministry. The Gentile "devout persons" or "God fearers" in the Jewish synagogues of Asia were quite visible as persons, but their ethnic or cultural peoplehood was not taken seriously: the Jews could not readily conceive of a Gentile synagogue, just as today some Gentile believers recoil at the idea of a Messianic synagogue.

We may presume that there were many God-fearers/devout persons who were believers in Christ before the appearance of Gentile synagogues. Such "devout persons" could share their faith with other Gentiles, yet not without the grave handicap that the only organized fellowship available was culturally Jewish. The truly missiological breakthrough made by the Apostle Paul was thus the formation of indigenous congregations that were essentially Gentile synagogues. It is this kind of breakthrough that reclassifies a Hidden People Group, and this kind of activity that defines Frontier Missions.

Today all over the world there are Hidden Peoples who by definition have no indigenous church of their own, but who are on the margin of churches of quite different, often dominant cultures, and whose peoplehood is not seen as an evangelistically strategic factor. Such marginalized peoples are often mis-treated through ignorance or accident. Members of the majority culture, even church people, seem often as pleased for minority aliens to take on the dominant culture as they are reluctant to take seriously the minority language and culture. Almost everywhere people assume refugees have no rights to their own culture.

III. STRATEGY TERMS

Megasphere/Macrosphere/Minisphere/Microsphere. These terms have been chosen for purely practical reasons to try to deal with groups that are part of larger groups. As an example, see "Frontier Vision in Graphic Form, Figure 12, where five columns are entitled megaspheres.

A megasphere, theoretically is a group totally distinct from all others. But for evangelistic purposes, a megasphere is simply a group whose cultural kinship to any other megasphere is not sufficiently close to be of strategic significance. A megasphere is not necessarily a large group. It could be a small group, if it is in lonely isolation from all others. On the other hand, we have for practical purposes lumped all tribal people groups into one megasphere because, different though tribes may be linguistically and racially, they have become marginalized to the extent that they can identify with each other to some significant extent.

Whenever a megasphere has within it evangelistically significant sub-communities, we then need another term. I have chosen macrosphere for the immediate constituent groups, should there be any within a megasphere. In case a macrosphere has significant divisions, I have suggested minisphere. A microsphere is, in the same way, a breakdown of a minisphere, but in this latter case we shall agree that the microsphere differences are not sufficiently great enough to require a separate missiological breakthrough.

I feel that the most practical way to employ these terms is to assume a given people group is a minisphere unless proven otherwise. However, people group, after all, in terms of contemporary "people group strategy," usually means a group sufficiently small enough and/or homogeneous enough so as to be reachable by means of a single missiological breakthrough. Therefore, whenever we discover that a people group is internally too diverse for a single breakthrough to be sufficient, we must then employ the term macrosphere and pursue the details of the missiologically important minispheres which are within it.

The reality of human diversity is, of course, immeasurably more complex than these four levels imply. One can easily imagine cases where there are far more than four levels. But at least four levels seem to be handy, as will be seen in the next chapter, and in Figure 12 of that chapter.

P0, P.5, P1, P2, P2.5, P3 Groups. For several years the E0, E1, E2, E3 categories have been employed, the numbers referring to cultural (not geographic) distance. That is, for some time it has seemed helpful to differentiate the various cultural distances an evangelist must "traverse" in order to evangelize. Now, however, it would seem equally helpful to observe how far away (culturally) the individuals in a people group are from the culturally nearest, settled, congregational tradition. The same numerical scale, amplified at two points, can classify people and people groups from a missiologically strategic standpoint:

P0: These are nominal Christians, not yet real believers, who are nevertheless participating to some extent in a local church. Yet they face no problem of cultural distance in understanding the Gospel. They are at zero (0) distance from the local church.

P.5: These are nominal Christians who are decidedly on the fringe of the church. They are rarely exposed to the influence of the gospel message; nevertheless there is a church within their minisphere.

P1: These people consciously do not consider themselves Christians, but they are, nevertheless, part of the same minisphere within which an indigenous, evangelizing church is to be found, and can thus, on this score at least, be readily won into existing congregations.

P2: These people are part of a minisphere as yet unpenetrated but nevertheless similar culturally to a cultural minisphere possessing an indigenous church. They are in the same cultural macrosphere but are part of a sufficiently different minisphere so as not to be easily incorporated into an existing church.

P2.5: For these people the closest church is in the same megasphere but in a different macrosphere.

P3: These people belong to groups that are very, very different from any of the cultural spheres which have an indigenous church. That is, not even their megaspheres have been penetrated.

E0, E.5, E1, E2, E3 ministry. This scale, as mentioned above, does not measure the cultural distance the non-believer must travel to find the church, but the (cultural) distance a believer must travel in order to take the church. For example, P3 people can only be reached by an E3 ministry, by definition. However, many missionaries cross into totally different megaspheres (working at an E3 distance) even though the people they seek to win are already a P1 people, that is, have an indigenous, evangelizing church within their own minisphere. Such missionaries, then are involved in an E3/P1 ministry. Most missionaries today, as a matter of fact, at the end of the Second Era, are either in E2/P1 or E3/P1 ministry, if not E2/P0 or E2/P.5 or E3/P0 or E3/P.5 ministry.

It is of great interest to note that whenever the evangelist goes further than the new believer—when the E number is larger than the P number—there is an inherent waste of effort, even though for other reasons such activity may be justified. An example will help. It is inherently wasteful for an Anglo U. S. citizen to go and try to reach a Hidden People group in Mindanao where there is already a church in a close-by, culturally similar situation. This would be an E3/P2 task that could have been done by a tribal Christian on an E2/P2 basis. Of course, there could well be practical factors preventing the American from working with or through that church.

But suppose an American were to go to the Philippines to the other group where there is already a church, and merely aids that church to grow. This would be an E3/P1 job which is inherently less efficient than for those people to win their own people on the E1/P1 basis. Again, however, maybe that would not happen without outside stimulus. This is the reason we have a single world family of Christians. Note, however, that such observations of "inherent waste" ought not in themselves to constitute criticism but merely encourage mission agencies to make very sure such effort is necessary.

Penetration/Missiological breakthrough. The word penetration plus its associated terms, penetrate, penetrated, has been defined (1978) as whatever activity a Hidden People requires in order to gain an indigenous, evangelizing church or an indigenous Christian tradition within it sufficiently developed so as to be capable of evangelizing its own people without E2 or E3 help. Penetration is, in a phrase, the classical missiological breakthrough, whereby a church in a new tradition is born within the indigenous culture (not borrowed and patched in from another country or cultural tradition). This kind of breakthrough is a more profoundly difficult task than is the task of evangelistic church planting in a culture once such a breakthrough has already taken place. Such a breakthrough classically was Paul's concern, that is, to produce a truly Gentile synagogue. Paul's abhorence of proselyting (requiring Greeks to adopt Jewish culture) encourages us to be very certain that our work is as indigenous as possible lest we also "traverse land and sea to make a single proselyte."

Evangelism/Missions/Regular Missions/Frontier Missions. Employing these distinctions, we have already made it is readily possible to postulate a practical distinction between evangelism and missions—namely, that all E1 work is evangelism, not missions, and that all E2, E2.5 or E3 work ("cross-cultural evangelism) is really missions, not evangelism, and that all P2, P2.5 and P3 work is a special kind of missions to be called Frontier Missions—other mission work being Regular Missions.

This conference has seen fit officially to tie the concept of Frontier Missions to that of Hidden People Groups. Having defined so many terms already, it is possible simply to say that Frontier Missions is the activity intended to accomplish the Pauline kind of missiological breakthrough to a Hidden People Group. Each of these phrases has been defined in the course of the discussions above.

Church. For strategic purposes, as we have seen, the question needs answering whether or not a Hidden People has yet a sufficiently developed indigenous Christian tradition within it to be capable of evangelizing its own people by E1 methods, that is, without (outside) E2 or E3 help. But it is not for strategic purposes important to express a preference for a certain definition of the word church in other contexts. That is, Baptists and some others may continue to avoid ever calling local congregations churches, reserving the term for denominations. Of course, no one objects to that very important New Testament phrase "the Church of Jesus Christ" which apparently does not refer to any specific human organization.

Viable church. The word church in the strategic phrase "A Church for Every People by the Year 2000" must mean a viable church, not just anything someone may call a church, and this emphasis then corresponds to the previous statement: at least that minimum yet sufficiently developed indigenous Christian tradition to be capable of evangelizing its own people without E2 or E3 help. A barely viable church must be understood as a minimal goal. Nothing here should imply that any such church anywhere should be considered totally independent of the world family of Christians, nor that it cannot both minister through and profit from continued cross-cultural contacts and expatriate help. All it means is that the missiological breakthrough has been made. This would seem to require at least a cluster of indigenous, evangelizing congregations and a significant part of the Bible translated by the people themselves.We may also work toward the 20% figure in order to feel safe.

FRONTIER VISION IN GRAPHIC FORM - Ralph D. Winter

I am truly sorry that my highly respected friend from India, George Samuel, is not here to give his address today. In his unavoidable absence I have been asked to discuss further some of the basic concepts of frontier mission vision, illustrating when possible by means of diagrams and graphs. (NOTE: If you haven't done so, we suggest you read FRONTIER MISSION TERMINOLOGY before continuing with this article - Ed.)

THE STRUCTURE OF THE MISSIONARY MOVEMENT

It is often true, even in mission circles, that we get so involved in the details that we fail to see the larger picture. For my first diagram, therefore, I would like to try to picture the entire cause of missions. The missionary movement as a whole necessarily involves more than just those agencies involved in sending missionaries. In my mind I picture the entire enterprise as a huge tree. (See Figure 1)

The branches represent the mission agencies reaching out to the

BRANCHES $\qquad$ $\left(\begin{array}{l}\text{Mission}\\\text{Agencies}\end{array}\right)$

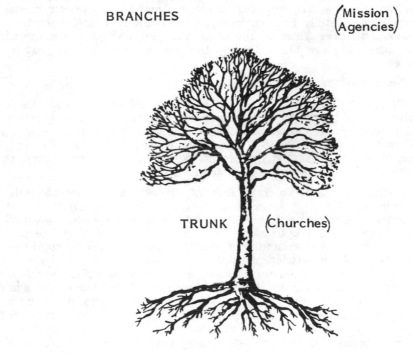

TRUNK $\quad$ $\left(\text{Churches}\right)$

ROOTS $\qquad$ $\left(\begin{array}{l}\text{Campuses}\\\text{Students}\end{array}\right)$

Figure 1   The Three Major Components
of the Missionary Movement

ends of the earth. The trunk represents the supporting churches. The roots represent the students from whose ranks new missionary recruits must inevitably come. Even as the branches of the tree depend upon the trunk, so the missionaries and mission agencies cannot function apart from the prayers and financial backing of the churches. The branches (the agencies) also depend upon the roots (the students) for more personnel, and these students are usually discipled in their faith by the churches, and indeed ought to be sent out by the churches as they come to the doors of the mission agencies.

Thus the structure of the missionary movement necessarily involves all three—the agencies, the churches and the students. The agencies send and do strategic research and planning, but lean on the churches and the students. The churches mobilize financial and prayer support as well as hopefully lead students to the point of commitment to missions, directing them to the agencies. The students are discipled by the church and eventually become the new missionaries sent out by the agencies.

When the Tree Becomes Sick

Only when branches, trunk and roots are all healthy, does the tree thrive. As a result, for the missionary movement to move forward and accomplish its God-ordained task, the agencies, the churches and the students must all have a missionary vision. Just as with a real tree, if any of these major parts of the movement becomes sick, the whole movement will suffer and eventually die.

I will refer later to three Eras of Protestant missions and will mention the transition stage that inevitably occurs during that period of overlap when one era is ending and the new one is just beginning. It is often in this transition period between two eras that one or another part of the structure of missions becomes sick through the application of the mission principles appropriate to the final stages of one era to the early stages of another era. For example, churches can give up mission vision and become become self-centered if the agencies report merely that the job is done, now that the national church is strong. In that case the sending church stops giving and praying and educating its young people about missions. In the U.S.A., what is called "Christian Education" is virtually devoid of any missions content.

The same thing is true in the Christian college curriculum. Meanwhile, the receiving churches may have become ingrown, able to see only their own needs and not those of untouched fields around about them. Then, not hearing the mission challenge in their churches, the students begin to seek to "save their own lives," looking for what is best for their personal careers, rather than to "lose their lives for His sake and for the gospel's." The quality of their discipleship falls as well as the number of recruits for mission. The agencies caught up in this syndrome will lose too. They lose recruits; they lose financial support; and eventually they cannot consider seriously the new frontiers waiting to be reached.

The enormity of this syndrome is seen in the U.S.A. in the statistics of the older denominational sending boards. The churches connected with the National Council of Churches once sent out 75 percent of all North American missionaries. Today they account for less than 5 percent.

A Threefold Cure

To heal such a situation would seem to require a three-pronged renewal effort, serving all three levels at once. First of all, churches must be awakened again to the facts of the massive remaining frontiers, and be made to see that, for example, they cannot go on forever with a Sunday School curriculum devoid of interest in the mission movement. Their participation in the job is still necessary. Secondly, students by the thousands from all over the world must be fired with vision to go. Thirdly, agencies must step out in faith to establish new strategies to reach the new frontiers. All three levels must regain the conviction of those "Haystack" students of so long ago, "We can do it if we will."

THE PEOPLE GROUP STRATEGY IN MISSIONS

We have taken the long view in looking at the structure of the missionary movement as a whole. Now we may examine the microcosm of the missionary task from close up in order to understand the People Group approach, a perspective which is gaining ground. To do this, let us first look at this strategy as it appears in the Bible.

In today's world we tend to think "political entity" or "country" when we see the word "nation."Unfortunately, this is not the concept expressed in the Bible. A closer translation comes directly from the Greek "ethnos" which has not only been translated "nation" but also "ethnic unit," "people", or (as in the New Testament) "heathen" or "Gentiles". In no case does it refer to a country as we think of a political unit today. A more correct usage would be as in the phrase "the Cherokee nation," referring to the tribe of American Indians known as the Cherokee. Even in the Old Testament this same concept holds true. Two words are used in the Old Testament. Gam, which occurs 1821 times, refers to a people, a single race or tribe, or to a specific family of mankind, as in Deut. 4:6 and 28:17. The other word, mishpahgheh occurs only 267 times and is mainly used to refer to family, kindred or relatives. This is the word used in Gen 12:3, "in thee shall all the families of the earth be blessed." The concept of "country" or a politically defined nation is totally absent in both of these cases. The fact that not countries, but rather ethnic units or people groups is what is implied is made even more pointed when in a number of places (e.g. Rev. 5:9, 10:11, etc.) not only is the word "nation" used, but it is further spelled out as "peoples, tribes, tongues, kindred."

It is, in fact, the English language in particular that is the great offender due to the historically recent expansion of the word **nation** to mean <u>country</u>. As a result, the word <u>nation</u> immediately becomes ambiguous for mission strategy purposes.

Every "Nation"

For example, one major mission organization states its purpose as "multiplying laborers in every nation," yet it only keeps track of how many <u>countries</u> it works in, not how many biblical <u>nations</u> it is touching, nor whether such nations already have a well established work or not. Another outstanding mission agency has produced a book entitled <u>The Discipling of a Nation</u>, which speaks of needing one church for every thousand people in a "nation." The thinking of the leaders of that mission is clear, but their words are ambiguous since the book title actually refers to countries, not biblical nations. Yet, strange as it may at first sound, it is perfectly possible to reach the goal of having planted one church per thousand people in, say, the country of India and still not have touched half of the 3,000 different biblically-defined nations in that country.

Are All Chinese Chinese?

Why is this concept of emphasizing a biblical nation or people group a problem in mission strategy? (See Figure 2.) Many Americans in particular tend to assume that all who live in China are racially Chinese, by which they probably mean "Han" Chinese. Or they may assume all the peoples of Russia are ethnically the same. However, even the unity-seeking government of the People's Republic of China recognizes a number of ethnic minorities, that is, distinctly non-Han groups of people who were born and have lived in China for hundreds of years. Furthermore, there are a great many varieties of Han Chinese. There are at least 200 mutually unintelligible varieties of the Chinese family of languages! India we have mentioned—a country of 3,000 nations, only 100 of which have any Christians at all. The Soviet Union also has widely diverse peoples with practically nothing in common except the political glue that binds them together.

The same cultural "mosaic" (to employ McGavran's term) is found in every country of the world today. Probably no country is composed of only one ethnic or cultural unit. This was just not as true in Bible times. But after the Babylonian and Persian empires deliberately switched and scattered widely diverse people groups all over their empires in order to prevent their organizing for rebellion, never again did most of them get back together as an entire people. For example, at the time of Christ there were more Jews still living back in Babylon than had returned to the Holy Land. There were large colonies of Jews in every city that Paul visited, as well as colonies in Alexandria in Egypt and clear over in Spain, and perhaps even in England. Meanwhile, the Holy Land was filled with not only Jews but Romans, Greeks, Phoenicians, and forcibly imported groups from Babylon, and other places called Cuthah, Avva, Hamath, and Sepharvaim, (II Kings 17:24) laying thereby the basis for bias against the Samaritans.   Paul and the Gentiles

Thus it was with mixed amazement and obvious chagrin that after his commission Paul was forced to conclude that God had always wanted to include the Gentiles in His concern. It may, in fact, have taken him three years in the desert to digest this crucial truth fully. It is as if Paul finally said to himself, "It is so obvious; why didn't I see it before?" He came to see that God had always dealt with the Jews as a people, not merely as individuals, and that He now wanted also to reach the Gentiles in the same way. It was not adequate that a number of Gentile individuals had responded to Him, becoming proselytized Jews in the process. For God to reach the Gentile "nations"—the Gentile people groups, like the Galatians—He would have to reach them as a people. Paul spoke of all this as a mystery long hidden, but now made plain. In fact, it was only a mystery because of disobedience and sin; it was never a total mystery to all Israelites, and we see it if we look for it, on almost every page of the Bible.

Homogeneous Unit Principle

In modern missionary strategy this same principle is translated into what is often called "the homogeneous unit principle." Proponents of this principle, with Paul, insist upon the equality of all Christians from every ethnic background. They also appreciate the right of different groups to worship together, if they so desire. And, again like Paul, they also refuse to make the legalistic demand that new converts from Hidden People groups leave their own culture in order to worship Christ. Curiously enough, this is never a problem in areas where a Hidden People group is isolated from other peoples. But when one group is thrown in with another dominant culture, as is often true today especially in the large cities of the world, then the common tendency is for the dominant culture to impose its ways on the minority peoples. In such a situation, proponents of the Homogeneous Unit principle insist with Paul these modern "Gentiles" be allowed, if they prefer, to establish their own church and worship Christ in a way that is meaningful to their own culture.

That is the point where Paul ran into difficulty. And today's frontier missionaries run into the same problem where there are long established (yes, even evangelical) churches representing a majority culture. In all parallel cases today it is still terrifically difficult to see what Paul was doing, and harder still to follow his pattern. Yet if new Christians from a Hidden People group often need their own church, even more so do they need it in order to reach out to the rest of the non–Christians in their same culture—people who, if they were also to become Christians, would have to make both a cultural as well as a religious switch. A few hardy proselytes in Paul's day did this, though they had a hard time. Most Gentiles would never go that far. They needed a Paul to establish a synagogue run by their own people—that is, a Gentile synagogue.

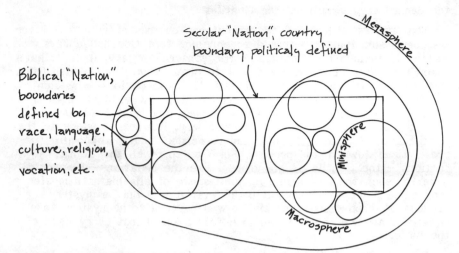

Figure 2, THE BIBLICAL "NATION"

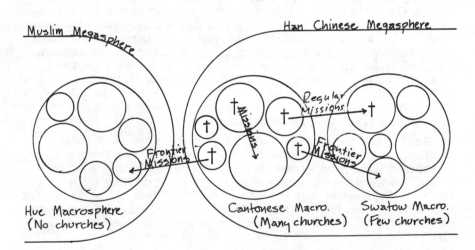

Figure 3, REGULAR MISSIONS/FRONTIER MISSIONS

Thus to look at the world from the "peoples" concept is not only biblical, it is also highly strategic for evangelism and church planting. Moreover, it stresses the need to look at people as part of their own culture, not merely as individuals, and to see them, when converted as individuals, as natural bridges to the rest of their society. To give a diagramatic example of the significance of this for mission strategy, let us look at one small sector of the world.

An Example

In Figure #3, for example, we have three large circles filled with a number of smaller circles. Each large circle represents a "cultural macrosphere"—a group of societies that have certain cultural similarities both within and between them. The middle macrosphere consists of Cantonese-speaking people, most of whom are found in a single country, the People's Republic of China, and they number in the millions of people. The smaller circles I will call "minispheres" represent groups of people which speak divergent dialects of Cantonese mutually unintelligible to each other. People from two such sub-groups can be understood by each other only if they learn a "trade-language" variety of Cantonese. Either the macrosphere or the minisphere could be considered a nation in biblical terms, but note that neither is a country.

Note further that in some of the minispheres—the smaller circles—there is a cross, representing an indigenous church that has been planted within that culture sometime in the past. These churches, if they are vital and witnessing, are readily able to win the remaining non-Christians in that dialect group by normal, near-neighbor evangelism. Some of the smaller circles, however, have no cross. Those minispheres obviously need someone from somewhere else to do the initial evangelizing and to plant the first church. That kind of evangelism from the outside is much more difficult than near-neighbor (or E-1) evangelism, for it requires the evangelist from the outside to learn another language, or at least another dialect of Cantonese. Also, he will find out that some of the cultural assumptions will be different. In other words, ordinary evangelism will not do the task that is required to pioneer in this frontier area.

Culture Shock

I remember once hearing a missionary tell about a Chinese evangelist in the interior of China who was sent from one minisphere on a brief E2 evangelistic trip about fifty miles across the mountains to a different minisphere within the same macrosphere. Weeks later when he still had not returned, the mission sent someone to check up on him, and found him lying face down, almost out of his mind due to culture shock. Yet he was only fifty miles away from home! He had not gone to a foreign country nor had he left his own macrosphere, but he was sufficiently far enough away culturally to suffer severe culture shock. (To the foreign missionary, who had already come a great distance cross-culturally, the relatively small "intra macrosphere" differences did not seem so great.)

The shock would, of course, have been still greater had the evangelist been sent to a different macrosphere. That would have been an E2.5 move. But the severest difficulties in communication and understanding occur when a person moves not only out of his minisphere and out of macrosphere, but even out of his entire megasphere into an E-3 ministry in a totally different megasphere. In such a case he has no clues to language or to culture. Indeed, everything is foreign!

REGULAR MISSIONS OR FRONTIER MISSIONS?

Looking again at Figure #3, you will notice that schematically we show only six of the many minispheres in the Cantonese macrosphere, and that five have a cross, meaning an indigenous church. The Swatow macrosphere, by contrast, has only one minisphere with an indigenous church, and the Muslim Hue macrosphere, which pertains to an entirely different, Muslim, megasphere, has no Christian church at all in any of its minispheres. Each of these macrospheres numbers millions of people; indeed, even some of the minispheres may number over a million people. The job of the ordinary evangelist is to plant churches in his own minisphere. That we call E-1, near-neighbor, evangelism. But where there is no church—no indigenous community of believers—we conclude by definition there is also no indigenous evangelist, since an individual by himself cannot be an indigenous church. In fact, there may be a number of individual believers who (like the New Testament "God fearers") worship outside their culture. There may even be some believers from that group who have left their minisphere and become "proselytized" to another. There still is no indigenous church. In such circumstances it takes a Paul, or someone from outside that language group and culture, to go to that people and plant a church there. Or it takes a Luther within the culture to wake up and go indigenous. In any case, the Cantonese evangelist in Figure #3 who goes to a Swatow dialect where there is no church is doing a missionary type of evangelism. In Paul's words, he is "going where Christ is not named."

A "Missionary Trip" Without Missions

If, however, a Cantonese evangelist goes from his Cantonese-speaking church to a Swatow minisphere where there already is an indigenous church, to help those believers to evangelize their own non-Christian Swatows, remaining in the same minisphere, in such a case he may very well be making a "missionary trip," but he is doing evangelism, not missions, because we have defined as evangelism the activity of reaching out from an existing church within the same minisphere, working to its fringes. The people back home in his Cantonese minisphere may very likely call such a person their "missionary," but technically speaking, even in the biblical and classical sense, he is an evangelist who happens to be working at a cultural distance from his own background. The main point is that winning people into a church that is already within their own minisphere is the work of an evangelist, even if the "missionary" comes from a great distance. We must admit that this is the usual pattern of so-called "missions" today. Most "missionaries," whether from the U.S.A., Europe, Asia or Africa, go from their own cultures to work in another culture where a church is already established. We may have to concede the term "Regular Missions" to such activity, just because of social pressure; in that case we fall back to the term "frontier missions." Some are even incorrectly called "missionaries" when they go to work with Christians from their own culture who have moved to a foreign country. Technically, such people are not even evangelists but rather "transplanted pastors."

THE EVANGELIST'S DISTANCE AND THE CONVERT'S DISTANCE

There are two ways of looking at the evangelism/mission dichotomy. One is from the standpoint of the evangelist. How far, culturally, will he have to go in order to work within a people group to which God has called him? I have called this the "E Scale" and have diagrammed it as follows:

A. Within the same cultural minisphere—"mono-cultural"

E0: The renewal evangelism of church members who still lack real faith.
E.5: Evangelism of nominal Christians on the fringe of the church.
E1: Evangelism of non-Christians who have had no contact with the church.

B. External to one's own cultural minisphere—"cross-cultural"

E2: Evangelism of non-Christians in a similar, but different culture.
E2.5: Evangelism of non-Christians in a similar yet quite different culture, e.g. in a different macrosphere within the same megasphere.
E3: Evangelism in a completely different culture, e.g. a different megasphere.

Let us redraw our previous figure and enlarge it so that these additional details are more obvious. (See Figure #4)

All these categories we have called "evangelism." Some of them — the cross-cultural variety—are, some of the time, missions. That is, by St. Paul's definition ("going where Christ is not named"). However, the E2, E2.5 and E3 activities are clearly Paul's kind of missions only in those cases in which the work is done where there is no viable church. In the same way, even though the evangelist may stay in his own country but go to another dialect within his own macrosphere, if there is no church in that dialect group, he is, technically speaking, doing the work of a frontier missionary. It is clear that this terminology labels certain types of work missionary whether it is performed at home or abroad, but it also denies the term to other activities, whether at

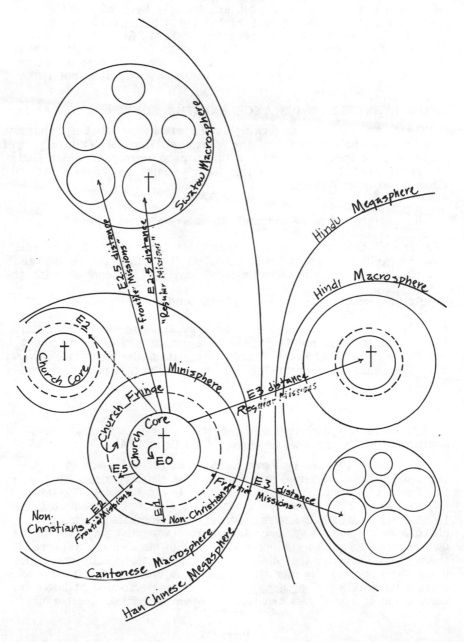

home or abroad.

There is a second way of looking at the evangelism/mission dichotomy. It will help us decide whether, in a given case, E2 or E3 work is frontier missions or not. That is, instead of making distinctions merely on the basis of the cultural distance the evangelist must go, suppose we also make distinctions in reference to the degree of transformation that is necessary for the culturally nearest church to become indigenous to the minisphere of the new convert. Thus it would be helpful to know not only how far the evangelist has gone to take the church, but also how far—the minimum cultural distance—the potential convert would have to go to find the church. To state this in more graphic terms, Cornelius apparently didn't go the necessary distance to become a Jewish proselyte. He attended a Jewish synagogue, but as a "God fearer," he only witnessed a believing group representing a distinctly foreign culture. The cultural distance was so great even Peter had extreme reluctance coming the other direction to visit him. But when the whole household of Cornelius turned to Christ, an indigenous church was formed to which his Roman friends could now have gone a much shorter cultural distance to find accountable fellowship with Christian believers.

The job of Peter, the evangelist, (or rather, the "missionary" in this case), is probably E3 on our scale above. The problem of Cornelius in whose Roman culture there was no indigenous church, would be measured on the "Peoples" or P Scale. It was P3 to begin with, but P1 when the new congregation was formed, if indeed one survived. The family of P distinctions are similar, almost a mirror image of the E scale.

P0: These are nominal Christians, not yet real believers, who are nevertheless participating to some extent in a local church. Yet they face no problem of cultural distance in understanding the Gospel from the closest church.

P.5: These are nominal Christians who are decidedly on the fringes of the church. They are rarely within the sphere of influence of the gospel message; nevertheless there is a church within their minisphere, and they consider themselves part of it.

P1: These people consciously do not consider themselves Christians, but they are, nevertheless, part of the same minisphere within which an indigenous, evangelizing church is to be found, and can thus, on this score at least, be readily won into existing congregations. Note that a Christian community within a minisphere usually forms a microsphere of its own. Over a period of time, if few additional members are won from the surrounding minisphere, and the religious sub-culture becomes sufficiently strange so that strategically whole new congregations must be formed in order win new people, then the earlier church community has to become ghettoized into its own minisphere, and the minisphere from which it has withdrawn becomes a separate, P2 minisphere.

P2:   These people are not the same but only _similar_ culturally to a
       cultural minisphere possessing an indigenous church. They are in
       the same cultural macrosphere, but are part of a sufficiently
       different minisphere so as not to be easily incorporated into an
       existing church.

P2.5: For these people the closest church is in the same megasphere
       but in a different macrosphere.

P3:   These people belong to groups that are very, very different
       from any of the cultural spheres which have an indigenous
       church. That is, not even their megasphere has been penetrated.

In Figure #5 you will notice the horizontal line divides between
mono-cultural evangelistic activities and cross-cultural evangelistic
activity, a distinction I would prefer to call evangelism/missions. The
vertical dotted line divides between work being done where there is
already a viable church, be it evangelism or missions, and work where
the church is not yet viable. For the latter, the phrase _frontier
missions_ is used in order to highlight this all-important type of work.
It may be noticed that Hidden People groups are always a P2 or P3
distance away from a culturally relevant church—that is, they are by
definition unpenetrated minispheres. All along we have assumed that
a minisphere is sufficiently large enough and different enough from
other minispheres so that an indigenous church must seriously be
considered a necessary goal, strategically speaking. Because of the
cultural distance of such groups from any existing church, all
evangelistic effort trying to reach P2 and P3 people groups must be
done at an E2 or E3 distance. That is, while we have noted that there
can be E2/P1 work, there cannot be such a thing as E1/P2 work. In
other words, if a church is culturally close enough to reach out to a
people group in E1 fashion, then that group by definition is P1!

In the case of the P2 and P3 Hidden People groups, while a few
individuals may already have become Christians, until a church of their
own kind can be established within the same minisphere, the dread
possibility is that those few will remain like the God-fearing Gentiles
in the back of the synagogues in Paul's day, and the gospel will
continue to be walled off from people in their group except for those
always rare souls who have the courage to be "different." But for a
church to be planted, a certain number of individuals have to be
"reached," and for a whole culture or a people group to be truly
penetrated by the Gospel, there must be a viable, witnessing,
indigenous church that can from then on reach out in E1 evangelism to
that culture, bringing those people at a P1 distance into that living
fellowship.

Let's suppose for cultural reasons it is not rare but common for
members of one minisphere to want to assimilate (like Ruth) to another

culture. It may still be true that the Gospel will never be fully meaningful to those who assimilate until they return to the culture of their upbringing and establish an indigenous church to which they can win their own people as well as discover the full meaning of the Gospel for themselves.

The Closest are Furthest!

It is well to disclaim any ultimate meaning to all these code numbers. Cultural distance is always important, but it is not the only important factor in missions. Paradoxically, it is almost an anthropological rule that "those who are closest are furthest." That is, culturally-near people can most easily communicate, but often culturally-near people are alienated by prejudice factors. Often the "man from mars" missionary from a distant but highly respected culture may have opportunities which close neighbors lack. Again we see the value of the world-wide family of believers, working together, each doing what he can do best.

Other factors to be considered are 1) receptivity to the Gospel of the individuals in a given society, 2) the availability of cross-cultural evangelists, 3) the knowledge of specific strategies which might or might not be effective in that situation, and 4) the awareness of various mechanisms for mission which could be used. Let us examine this last concept further.

MECHANISMS FOR MISSION

I believe it is possible to distinguish four basic mechanisms down through history which God has used to reach out to the "Gentiles"— that is, those people groups, "nations" which have been outside the community of God. These four mechanisms can be lumped into two main headings: the "going mechanisms" and the "coming mechanisms." (See Figure #6.) In regard to "going," God's messengers have been going to other cultures from the time Abraham went to Egypt. Often those who have gone have been very poor witnesses, as was Abraham when he lied about his wife to the Pharaoh of Egypt. But God had surely intended for him to be a positive witness. If we stand back and look from this viewpoint at the entire 4,000 year period from Abraham's call to the present, we realize that God has always been active in missions, eager to reclaim His lost creation, and that, in fact, His plan to redeem all nations has been in force every step of the way. Walter Kaiser, Jr. Academic Dean of Trinity Evangelical Divinity School, considers the Abrabramic covenant an instance of the Great Commission, and says that we err if we assume it was given to Abraham but somehow did not apply to him but rather was only for future reference.

In Figures #6 and #7, the "Go" category always refers to the believer who is able to take God's message of salvation from a believing community to unredeemed man. Likewise, the "Come" category always refers to the unbeliever who comes to a believing

Figure 5, THE THREE MAJOR TYPES OF EVANGELIZATION

CONVERT'S DISTANCE FROM CULTURALLY NEAREST CHURCH

Evangelist's cultural distance from potential convert

	EVANGELISM AND REGULAR MISSIONS — People being won who have an indigenous church tradition already within their minisphere			FRONTIER MISSIONS — People being won who have no indigenous church within their minisphere.		
	P0	P.5	P1	P2	P2.5	P3
A. MONOCULTURAL-- working in own minisphere	*1. Ordinary Evangelism*					
E0 Inside church	E0/P0					
E.5 Church fringe	E.5/P0	E.5/P.5				
E1 Outside church	E1/P0	E1/P.5	E1/P1			
B. CROSS-CULTURAL-- working in different minisphere	*2. Regular Missions*			*3. Frontier Missions*		
E2 Outside own minisphere in same macrosphere	E2/P0	E2/P.5	E2/P1	E2/P2		
E2.5 Outside own macrosphere in same megasphere	E2.5/P0	E2.5/P.5	E2.5/P1	E2.5/P2	E2.5/P2.5	
E3 Outside own megasphere in different megasphere	E3/P0	E3/P.5	E3/P1	E3/P2	E3/P2.5	E3/P3

Quadrant 1 = Ordinary evangelism, by same-culture worker, where a missiological breakthrough has taken place.

Quadrant 2 = Regular missions, cross-cultural evangelism by a different-culture worker, in association with same-culture workers if possible, where a missiological breakthrough has taken place = Stages 3 & 4 missions, see Figure 9.

Quadrant 3 = Frontier Missions. Here is where cross-cultural evangelism (by a different-culture worker) is essential since no missiological breakthrough has yet been made = Stages 1 & 2 missions, see Figure 9.

(*missiological breakthrough, see page 64 for definition.)

Figure 6   The Four Mechanisms of Mission

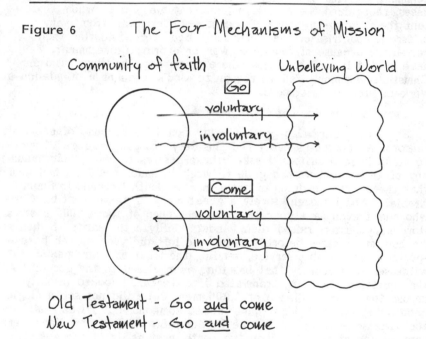

Old Testament - Go <u>and</u> come
New Testament - Go <u>and</u> come

community in which the gospel is resident. The messenger who goes out either goes voluntarily or reluctantly and by force. The unbeliever likewise either chooses to come to where the gospel can be found or is, in some way, forced to leave his homeland and settle elsewhere, where there are followers of the true God. But has God done mission work by force?

If we take a new look at the record, we find that it is not at all uncommon to find God's servants taken away as slaves by a pagan nation. Nebuchadnezzar carried off Daniel and the three Hebrew children. Nehemiah witnessed to a pagan king who was his captor. Celtic and Anglo-Saxon Christians, especially young maidens, were carried off by the hundreds by pagan Vikings. In the early days of American history, the Pilgrims and the Puritans, both Godly communities, fled oppression in England, and only incidentally, in most cases, recognized the American Indians as peoples to whom God had sent them. In our own day, thousands of Christians from many different countries of the world have been forced to flee their homelands because of famine or war or a brutal government. Many have landed in new countries where there are Christians. Those Christians commonly fail to recognize God's mechanism of mission at work in such circumstances.

Christians in Foreign Countries

Some Christians also go to foreign countries because of economic reasons. A few weeks ago I had the very unusual privilege of speaking to 3,000 Korean pastors. I asked those pastors to raise their hands if any of their members had gone to work in Saudi Arabia. I had heard that there were hundreds of thousands of South Koreans in Saudi Arabia. And I thought surely a great many of these must be Christians who might even have gone from the churches of those 3000 pastors. How many pastors raised their hands? Fully a thousand! I then asked, "In how many cases before your people left did your church have a special commissioning service, sending them out as your special witnesses to a country that has long been closed to the gospel?" As that question was being translated into Korean, I looked intently across the entire audience of 3,000 men. But I did not see a single hand being raised. I might have missed someone, but I was really not too surprised—the same is true in the U.S.A. These Christians were sent to one of the places on the earth most needy of the gospel, yet had no realization that perhaps God had a missionary purpose in sending them. The fact of the matter is that neither Koreans, nor Americans nor Christian citizens of any other country are as aware as they ought to be of the four mechanisms that God uses to spread His gospel to all mankind. Lots of Christian Americans have gone to work all around the world for personal reasons, not missionary ones. Indeed, there must be 20 times as many dedicated evangelical believers from the U.S.A. in Africa and Asia than there are missionaries. Oh, that they could awaken to God's reasons for their going! I recall a special convention in Korea in 1978 where "diaspora" Koreans returned to ask what God's missionary purpose for them was. But so far as I know, this kind of a convention has happened nowhere else.

Paradoxically, the voluntary-go mechanism is much more traditional (yet far less common in history) where Christians go away from home, voluntarily, with the primary purpose of evangelizing pagan peoples. Perhaps the only nation as a nation which deliberately tried do this was the Irish between 400 and 1000 A.D. Well, there were also the Pharisees, who, in the inter-testamental period and indeed in Jesus' day, "traversed land and sea to make a single convert." But on the whole, this voluntary-go mechanism has been extremely rare, even today. Apparently God has been forced to arrange for Christians to be taken off by force because they usually have refused to go willingly.

Equally uncommon is the voluntary-come mechanism. Scattered individuals can be cited, as on the chart.But when people have come en mass, as did the Vikings, they thought they were coming for something else, and only eventually and incidentally ended up with the gospel. This is likely true of the thousands of refugees from South East Asia coming to the U.S. today. If Christians in America are faithful, these refugees will also end up with the gospel. Westerners must confront the obvious fact that the large and increasing numbers of non-Westerners flooding into the Western world are not coming by accident but by God's design. Los Angeles public schools at this moment enroll students who speak 88 different languages. Yet paltry attention is being given to this major mission mechanism by the American churches or mission agencies. It could be and should be a major key to "a church for every people by the year 2,000."

THE STAGES OF MISSION

In discussing the various mechanisms which God has used for mission down through history, we have seen that "traditional" missions are included in the "voluntary-go" category. Thanks to efforts of this type, a "national church" can now be found in almost every country of the world today. By God's grace most of these churches are now mature, and incorporate hundreds of well-trained pastors, seminary and college professors, university graduates, medical doctors, etc. They have come of age.

Yet, as we have pointed out, in every country of the world right beside these mature churches there are still many people groups which are essentially hidden from our sight. For them missions as such has not yet even begun. Thus, right in the same country we can often see more than one stage of mission. Let me describe one four-stage analysis. (I first heard the four names for these stages from Geoffrey Dearsley of the SUM fellowship. It is my wife, however, to whom I am indebted for the detailed description of each stage (See Figure #8). The famous church/mission tensions so often discussed in mission circles in the past 25 years almost always occur in the transition between the Paternal and the Partnership stages—so much so that the very word "paternal" has come to be a dirty word. We can compare

FOUR STAGES OF MISSION

Stage		Role of the Missionary
Pioneer	1)	Initiates own assignment, approved by mission board.
	2)	After learning the language, concentrates on language learning materials for others to follow, on Bible translation and on literacy materials.
	3)	E-2 and E-3 evangelism, mostly initial contact.
	4)	Initiates establishment of first church.
	5)	As individuals are won, institutes leadership training courses.
Paternal	1)	Begins setting up institutions (Bible schools, primary and secondary schools, colleges and universities, schools of nursing and medicine, etc.)
	2)	Supervises all institutions and the national church as well.
	3)	Assigned by the mission board in homeland or its contingent on the field. Supervised by mission on the field.
	4)	Has the major voice and a vote in national church assemblies.
Partnership	1)	Assigned by the national church with approval of mission board at home.
	2)	Still in charge of major mission projects involving a great deal of money from abroad.
	3)	Works directly under governing boards composed half of missionaries and half of national leaders.
	4)	Must be invited by the national church to serve in that country. Stays or returns only on approval of national church.
	5)	Never serves as pastor of local church.
	6)	May or may not vote in national ecclesiastical assemblies. His opinion may be asked, but not necessarily followed.
Participation	1)	In the country only by invitation of national church, by which assigned.
	2)	Work budget money directed through national church.
	3)	Role often involves international aspects.
	4)	Works under national director.

Figure 8

FOUR STAGES OF MISSION

Stage	Role of the National Leaders

Pioneer

1) At first there are no national leaders by definition.
2) As individuals are converted, those with leadership gifts begin training under the supervision of the missionary, often on an apprentice basis.

Paternal

1) In charge of all local churches.
2) Involved in leadership roles in mission projects, though usually not as the director.
3) In charge of locally raised funds, but not those sent from abroad.
4) Votes and directs national church assemblies.
5) Begins indigenous translation of scriptures.

Partnership

1) Administrates national denomination as well as local churches.
2) Except in cases of major mission projects involving large sums of money from abroad, the national leaders are in charge of all disbursements from the home board as well as from within the country.
3) Requests and assigns missionary personnel, supervises through governing boards.
4) In charge of all local evangelism and pastorates.

Participation

1) Administration of all former mission-related entities as well as local churches and denomination.
2) All funds (local and from abroad) directed through ecclesiastical office.
3) National church may set up and administrate its own mission agency.

Figure 8

Figure 7, THE FOUR MECHANISMS OF MISSIONS

		O.T. Period	N.T. Period	Early church – 1800	Modern Missionary Period
GO Mechanism	Voluntary	Abraham to Canaan Minor Prophets preach to other nations Pharisees sent out near Israel "over land and sea"	Jesus in Samaria Peter to Cornelius Paul and Barnabas on their missionary journeys Witness of other Christians in Babylon, Rome, Cyprus, Alexandria, etc.	Patrick to Ireland Celtic peregrini to England and Europe Friars to China, India, Japan, America Moravians to America	William Carey and other missionaries of 1st Era Hudson Taylor and the 2nd Era missionaries Third Era to present
	Involuntary	Joseph sold into Egypt witnesses to Pharaoh. Naomi witnesses to Ruth because of famine. Jonah—the reluctant missionary. Hebrew girl is taken off to Naaman's home. Captive Hebrews in Babylon witness to captors.	Persecution of Christians forces them out of holy land all over Roman empire and beyond.	Ulfilas sold as a slave to the Goths Exiled Arian bishops go Gothic areas Christians captured by the Vikings win them Christian soldiers sent by Rome to England, Spain, etc. Pilgrims and Puritans forced to the Americas and to discover their mission to the Indians.	WWII Christian soldiers sent around the globe returned to start dozens of new mission agenciesl Ugandan Christians flee to other parts of Africa Korean Christians flee to less-Christian South, later sent to Saudi Arabia and Iran, etc. to work.
COME Mechanism	Voluntary	Naaman the Syrian came to Elisha Queen of Sheba came to Solomon's court Ruth chose to go to Judah from Moab.	Greeks who sought out Jesus. Cornelius sends for Peter Man of Macedonia calls to Paul	Goths invade Christian Rome, learn more of the Christian faith Vikings invade Christian Europe, are won to the faith eventually through that contact	The influx of international visitors, students, and businessmen into the Christian West.
	Involuntary	Gentiles settled in Israel by Cyrus the Great (II Kings 17)	Roman military occupation and infiltration of "Galilee of the Gentiles"	Slaves brought from Africa to America	Refugees from Communism, Boat people, Cubans forced out, etc.

this transition to that which occurs in the usual family with a teenager. Tensions occur when the child feels it is already an adult, and yet the parent feels it is still a child. Mistakes in correct assessment may occur on both sides. Once the transition is past, and both mission and national church have reassessed their roles, peace can return. By the time the Partnership stage has been reached, missionaries with still a pioneer mentality may find themselves out of place and unable to shift gears. They should perhaps move on to new pioneer fields. Interestingly enough, although in mature fields we tend nowadays to look down on missionaries who must initiate rather than participate, it is the reverse in a pioneer (e.g., frontier) situation. To have only the kind of missionary who knows how to participate but is incapable of initiating would be equally disastrous in the frontier situation. We need both types, and we need to know what type we have on our hands when assignments are made.

Tragically, because most long-standing mission fields are now in the participation and partnership stages, we have tended lately to emphasize, select, and send only that kind of missionary. The pioneering types have turned away or been sent to other endeavors, to the great loss of the cause of missions. Thus, now to start out in new, frontier "Hidden People" areas means we have to learn how to recognize and recruit that kind of first stage (pioneer) missionary again, being careful to send him to pioneering situations while sending his fellow third or fourth stage (Partnership or Participation) type missionary to the fields where we are working with a mature church. We should be careful not to assume that it is easy to shift older missionaries around. Learning a new language in mid-life is not easy, even for the pioneer type. The number of years required for a completely pioneer situation to move into the partnership stage may often be about the ordinary career span of the modern missionary. But this is not always so.

I mentioned earlier that within a given country (and indeed within the work of a single mission, sometimes) all four stages of missions may legitimately be in operation at the same time. Let me explain this further, using completely hypothetical illustrations.

In Nigeria, let us say, work was begun among the Ibos more than a hundred years ago. The Ibo Church is now fully mature, with highly educated leaders and even its own mission board. It is in the participation stage with a few missionaries who perhaps have come to do specialized, highly skilled tasks, such as that of certain surgical specialties. There is now also a Hausa church, but it is very weak, barely out of the pioneer stage. Further to the north in Nigeria, work must still begin with the Tuaregs. Other things being equal, it matters little if it is Nigerian Ibo Christians who evangelize the Tuaregs, or missionaries from Europe and America. Whoever goes there must start at the pioneering level, and will eventually find himself moving through the same four stages in relation to the church that will hopefully result from his work. Indeed, if all goes well, a few years from now, the Tuaregs will have as much difficulty insisting on their Christian maturity when dealing with Ibo missionaries as they would have with American ones. Both may seem at times oppressive, overbearing and paternalistic. Both can work in a pioneer pattern among the Tuaregs only so long as that church is young. As the church matures, the stage changes, and techniques, strategies and missionary personality patterns must also change.

As the church reaches the Partnership and Participation stages, some people talk as though the church should be able to function entirely on its own without any outside help whatsoever. However, the world church is one body, and there will always be the value of a two-way-street fraternal interchange between the various parts of the body. What is true is that a different type of role is performed in each stage.

One other comment needs to be made. As Figure 9 shows, each era of Protestant missions goes through the four stages of mission. This fact is obvious when we stop to think about it. Even as an individual has to be born, grow as a child and a teenager before he can become an adult, so the national church must be first born (Pioneer stage), develop its own leadership (Paternal stage), and reach a certain level of maturity before it can be said to be in the Partnership or Participation stages. No one era of missions can avoid progressing through these four essential stages. The era of the coastlands went through these stages in the coastlands where missions was performed. The era of the interiors likewise experienced these same four stages in the interior of the continents where missionaries were at work. Today in Era Three these same four stages will be necessary. Where work was begun twenty-five years ago, as in certain parts of Irian Jaya, the pioneer stage may now be past, and the paternal stage beginning. Yet that stage also is necessary, as are the two that follow.

THE MISSION OF THE CHURCH AND THE NEW MISSIONS

The most serious problem from the point of view of a Consultation on Frontier Missions is not how or when to replace pioneer missionaries with participation types. There is an even more serious one. National church leaders usually learn very well the message and method of evangelism (E1) within their own cultures. But all too often the missionary working alongside them somehow has never conceived of the need to also pass on a missionary vision to that church. As a result, national church leaders may tend to do one of two things. 1) They may assume that all cross-cultural missionary activity is the responsibility of Westerners. In so doing they lose out on the joy of taking their place as participants in the world-wide enterprise of the Great Commission. 2) They may become so self-oriented, so accustomed to receiving rather than giving, that they even refuse to allow the assignment of missionary personnel from abroad to cultures within their own geographical area but outside their

Figure 9, PROTESTANT MISSION HISTORY
(Four Stages, Three Eras, Two Transitions)

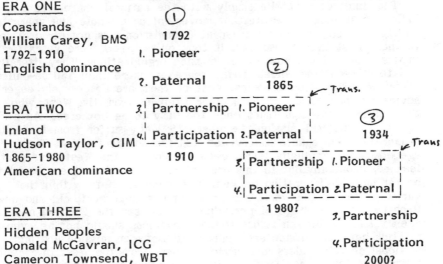

ERA ONE

Coastlands
William Carey, BMS
1792-1910
English dominance

ERA TWO

Inland
Hudson Taylor, CIM
1865-1980
American dominance

① 1792
1. Pioneer

② 1865
2. Paternal

③ 1934 Trans

3. Partnership 1. Pioneer
4. Participation 2. Paternal
1910

3. Partnership 1. Pioneer
4. Participation 2. Paternal
1980?

3. Partnership

4. Participation
2000?

ERA THREE

Hidden Peoples
Donald McGavran, ICG
Cameron Townsend, WBT
1934-2000?
Third World dominance

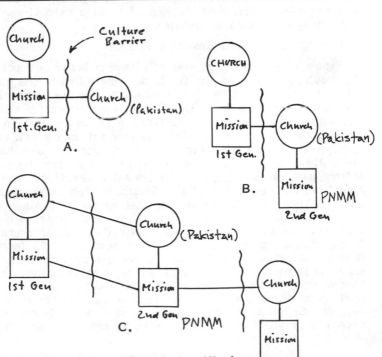

Figure 10, Second and Third Generation Missions

El sphere. Thus they can become not only non-participants but actually barriers to the spread of the gospel within their own country.

The fault does not lie simply with the national church, as I have indicated. It took the Protestant movement as a whole 300 years to be willing to recognize that the Great Commission was not directly solely to those first twelve disciples. It took quite a few more years for Protestants to learn how to run mission organizations. They literally had to reinvent the wheel. Today there are more than 350 so-called "Third World" mission agencies. Most of them are desperately eager for advice on "how to do it" from older agencies from the West, who, to their shame, have sometimes been too busy to be bothered. As a result, Third World missionaries charactistically suffer from inadequate preparation, inadequate supervision and inadequate funding. Those agencies will eventually learn, even as those in the West have partially learned, eventually.But in this present era of missions there ought to be far more collaboration between the agencies, both within the various areas of the world and between East and West, old and new. Perhaps the final stage of participation between the Western mission agency and the church it has founded overseas should not be even a relation between mission and church but between mission and mission. National church leaders and church leaders from the West in recent years have found great joy in getting together for fellowship and consultation. Why should not this be increasingly true of mission agency executives from the West and mission agency executives from the rest of the world? Although the Edinburgh 80 Consultation is the first world-level East/West meeting of mission executives, I pray it will spark many more such interchanges.

Sending Church and Resulting Church

Figure 10 shows the natural relationship between sending church and resulting church on the field.The wiggly line is the cultural barrier which is first crossed by the mission. Then as the national church develops, as in Pakistan in this figure, the mission finds itself increasingly in a less-direct relationship to that church. As a matter of fact, the Church of Pakistan has now set up its own mission agency—the PNMM (Pakistan National Missionary Movement), which Bishir Jiwan is here to tell us about.As can be seen by looking at the bottom part of this diagram, the normal international relationship should be, I believe, that of a Pakistani church to an overseas church, and a Pakistani mission to an overseas mission. In other words, the two missions have as much to learn from each other as do the two churches, whereas to continue to relate the younger church to the foreign mission agency (or the younger mission to the foreign church) is somewhat of an anomaly. As the younger mission reaches out and succeeds in establishing a church within another culture, and as that church grows and matures, the younger (Pakistani) mission will find itself going through the same pattern of relationship with the new daughter church as did the Western mission with its own Pakistani church in previous years. That is to be expected, and that is as it should be.

"Aren't all Missionaries White?"

One other comment. I was talking awhile ago to Bishar Jiwan, who helped to establish the PNMM, and who is a bishop of the Church of Pakistan. He told me that many of the Pakistanis feel inhibited in supporting the Pakistan National Missionary Movement because they can't believe that Pakistanis can be missionaries. Somehow they think that all missionaries must be white people. Let me as a white person just say that all white Christians today are as much the results of missions as anybody else. My own forefathers were a bunch of savages, Vikings, and marauders who killed and plundered and grubbed for roots in the forests of Europe. White Christians are mission field converts too, who then somewhat tardily began to send a few missionaries. Thus all other peoples of the world can become missionaries. They also must share in this task of reaching out to the frontiers and thus fulfill the Great Commission of our Lord.

Today we hear there are already 350 missionary societies in the Third World, with some 10,000 missionaries.Some of these missionaries are not involved in truly cross-cultural work, and those that are may not all be in frontier situations. Nevertheless, I believe that in the years to come, the Third and final era of missions, it will be these Third World mission agencies which will dominate the era.

THE LAST ERA

As I indicated in my first talk, (see FRONTIER MISSION VISION - Ed.) I believe we are in the Third and final era of Protestant missions. I don't think this way because of general turmoil in our world. Many times in history there have been wars, rumors of wars, persecution, famine, distress on all sides. I believe that the most determinative arena of events in the world today is what is happening in missions.Jesus said (Matt. 24:14) that before He would return the gospel would first be preached to every tribe, tongue, and people. For the first time in history it is physically possible for this to be true. Not by satellite—for then all people could not hear in their own language, as this verse implies. For the first time in history it is possible for there to be a church within the language and social structure of every people group on earth, and it can literally be done by the year 2000.

At first glance the task seems enormous—impossible, really! Figures 11 and 12 show the number of individuals in the world today who still need a viable witness. Easily noticeable are the millions of nominal Christians(1,107 million) and non-Christians (660 million) who live in "reached" societies. All of these can be won by E0, E.5 and E1 near-neighbor, ordinary evangelism. Church members in every country can reach out to these people and win them without any specialized cross-cultural training.

The much more difficult task is that of reaching the Hidden

Figure 11, ALL HUMANITY IN MISSION PERSPECTIVE
(Adjusted to Mid-1981 Population Reference Bureau figures*)

FIVE CULTURAL MEGASPHERES (MAJOR CULTURAL BLOCS) | OTHER CATEGORIES

EVANGELISM AND REGULAR MISSIONS

(Individuals, in millions)

REACHED[1] PEOPLE GROUPS		BUDDHIST	HAN CHINESE	HINDU	MUSLIM	TRIBAL	SUB TOTAL	OTHER US & CANADA	OTHER WESTERN	OTHER ASIAN	OTHER AFRICAN	SUB TOTAL	GRAND TOTAL
		20	200	200	30	1,000	1,450	500	500	1,000	2,000	4,000	5,450
Reached[2] Individuals													
1. True Christians, available as a work-force, through Discipleship and Equipping	TCR	2	10	8	.18	18	38	72	67	17	51	207	245
Unreached individuals --may be reached by "monocultural" evangelism needing evangelism)													
2. Purely nominal "Christians" --needing Renewal evangelism E0 to E3. Participating in church	P0	1	1	6	.03	15	23	70	130	16	59	275	298
E.5 to E3, On the fringe of the church	P.5	–	1	6	.03	10	17	83	618	11	80	792	809
		1	2	12	.06	25	40	153	748	27	139	1,067	1,107
3. Non-Christians making no Christian profession but living within Reached Groups --needing E1 to E3 Outreach evangelism	P1	22	256	51	26	22	377	17	191	61	14	283	660
Total Unreached Individuals in Reached Groups		23	258	63	26	47	417	170	939	88	153	1,350	1,767
Total Individuals in Reached Groups		25	268	71	26	65	455	242	1,006	105	204	1,557	2,012

	1,000	2,000	3,000	4,000	5,000	15,000	100	300	550	800	1,750	16,750
UNREACHED PEOPLE GROUPS (Hidden Peoples)	1,000	2,000	3,000	4,000	5,000	15,000	100	300	550	800	1,750	16,750
4a Reached Individuals—True Christians living within Unreached People Groups — TCU	.01	.01	.5	.01	.001	.531	.001	.01	.2	.2	.411	.942
4b Unreached Individuals—living within Unreached People Groups—can only be reached by cross-cultural evangelism												
1) Needing E2 to E3 outreach —nearest church is in a different minisphere — P2	100	652	450	200	35	1,437	8	70	30	10	118	1,555
2) Needing E2.5 or E3 outreach —nearest church is in a different macrosphere — P2.5	110	50	63	493.76	100	817	3	27	30	7	67	884
3) Needing E3 outreach —nearest church is in a different megasphere — P3	0	0	0	0	0	0	1	10	20	9	40	40
Total Unreached Individuals in Unreached Groups	210	702	513	694	135	2,254	12	107	80	26	225	2,479
Total Individuals in Unreached Groups	210	702	514	694	135	2,255	12	107	80	26	225	2,480
PEOPLE GROUPS, WORLD TOTAL	1,020	2,200	3,200	4,030	6,000	16,450	600	800	1,550	2,800	5,750	22,200
* INDIVIDUALS, WORLD TOTAL	235	970	585	720	200	2,710	254	1,113	185	230	1,782	4,492

FRONTIER MISSIONS

Notes

1. For our purposes here the Reached/Unreached distinction when applied to groups simply means the presence or the absence of a viable, evangelizing, indigenous church. This equates Unreached People Groups with Hidden People Groups. The people groups referred to here are minispheres, technically. The megasphere columns break down into macrospheres, which are made up of minispheres.

2. With individuals the reference is whether or not people are truly born again.

Ralph D. Winter, 30 August 1981

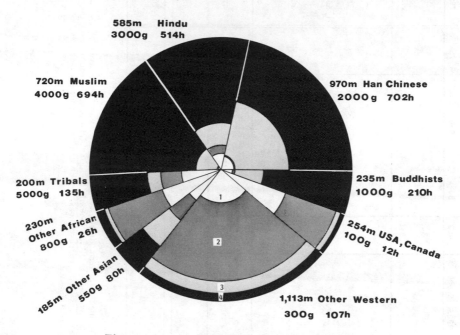

585m   Hindu
3000g   514h

720m Muslim
4000g 694h

970m Han Chinese
2000g   702h

200m Tribals
5000g   135h

235m Buddhists
1000g   210h

230m
Other African
800g   26h

254m USA, Canada
100g   12h

185m Other Asian
550g   80h

1,113m Other Western
300g   107h

Figure 12, THE GLOBE AT A GLANCE

Legend

m = millions   g = people groups

235m = 235 million Buddhists
1000g = 1000 People Groups

210h = 210 million in Unreached
or Hidden Groups

Numbers 1, 2, 3, 4 correspond
to Table in Figure 11

Figure 13

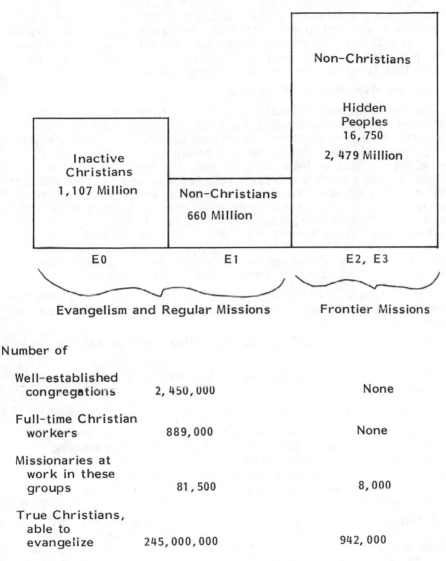

Number of		
Well-established congregations	2,450,000	None
Full-time Christian workers	889,000	None
Missionaries at work in these groups	81,500	8,000
True Christians, able to evangelize	245,000,000	942,000

People groups—those cultures as yet unpenetrated by the church of Jesus Christ. As Figure 11 shows, there are 2,479 million individuals in the Hidden People category still to be evangelized by E2 and E3 methods. Complicating the picture is the fact that most missionaries are not now concentrating on this task. (See Figure 13.) Rather, where the church is well established, missionaries and Christian workers tend mainly to seek to win nominal Christian to a real faith in the Lord rather than to evangelize unreached people groups.

Winning Back Nominal Christians

This fact was very poignantly pointed out to me at the Lausanne Consultation in Switzerland in 1974. I had just come down from the platform where I had delivered an address stressing the necessity of going beyond our own culture and our present mission fields when I met George Samuel of India. Keep in mind now that George is a former nuclear physicist, a brilliant scientist who doesn't make mistakes with numbers. He said to me with tears in his eyes, "Ralph, I have just completed a very careful study of all the evangelizing efforts being undertaken in India, whether by missionaries or by national leaders, and I have concluded that 98% of all evangelization there is E0 and E.5 activity focused upon winning back to the church the nominal Christians. Not even the non-Christians within those same cultures where the church is found receive much attention."

I was stunned, and I finally stuttered out the words, "But, George, what are the 2% doing? Surely they, at least, are working among the unreached!"

"No," he said, "the 2% are reaching within the same societies, doing E1 work."

"You surely don't mean to tell me that no one is crossing frontiers in India," I insisted.

"Well, of course American missionaries are crossing frontiers."

"But is it not true," I answered, "that while they are indeed working cross culturally, they are for the most part not crossing mission frontiers? They're crossing frontiers to get to Madras and to learn the Tamil language. But they're only going where there is already a church. To my knowledge they are rarely crossing any mission frontiers." He agreed.

I believe it is different today, six years later, perhaps partly because of the many voices that stress reaching further out. There are some agencies, the Friends Missionary Prayer Band for one, that are working cross-culturally and in some cases are going into cultures where there is no church. Indeed, we are delighted to see the new book Indigenous Missions in India, which details many others.

In a sense, then, this figure, more than any other, sums up what the vision is and what the strategy must therefore be. The task is not as impossible as it might seem. We must adjust our thinking so that we focus on penetrating people groups and planting an evangelizing, indigenous church. Then instead of needing to evangelize 2.5 billion individuals in Hidden People Groups, we will talk of penetrating 16,750 Hidden People Groups (in which live 2.5 billion people). This approach is much more feasible, and yet will even more rapidly allow for the task of evangelism to the individuals still to be done, now by EI techniques.

Figure 14 makes this point more clear.Even within the Reached groups of people there are vast numbers of non-Christians and nominal Christians who still must be won to a real faith in Christ. But to do this job there are 245 million Christians who live in those same cultures, speak the same languages and are well able to witness to them in an understandable, meaningful way. In the Unreached bloc, however, the proportions are quite different. You not only have vast numbers of unreached individuals, you also have 16,750 unreached societies of individuals for whom there is no witnessing indigenous church of any sort. There may be a missionary or two, and maybe even a few Christians. (There are a million Christians scattered among these 16,750 Hidden People groups.) But there is no automatic mechanism whereby evangelism will automatically, under the guidance of the Holy Spirit, be extended to the rest of the people in that culture. A church still must be planted before the task of normal, near-neighbor evangelism can begin.

16,750 Recruits Needed!!

If we were to assign one missionary to each of these unreached people groups, we would need at least 16,750 recruits. Some frontiers involve millions of people, and obviously require more than one missionary or one couple. Yet today we have the potential of missionaries from all parts of the globe.

A Spiritual Task

The job is large, but not too large for the church around the world. We are in a new era. Now every church in the world ought to be involved with the frontiers. New missionary recruits cannot come just from the West, nor just from Asia, Africa or Latin America. We must all work together to do this task.

But let us be warned! More than the sheer weight of numbers, this task is difficult because it is a spiritual task. Satan will oppose it on every front, with every kind of strategm. He will make it seem impossible. He will make it seem unnecessary. He will make it seem ridiculous. He will oppose it through ungodly governments, through ungodly individuals, and, yes, even through the church itself and through godly individuals. Let me give an example.

A couple of months ago I received through the mail a huge new reference Bible. It is beautifully bound. Many of its pages are tinted in yellow ink, referring to massive notes at the bottom of each page. The day it arrived I stayed up until midnight starting in Genesis and

Figure 14 **The Challenge of the Frontiers**

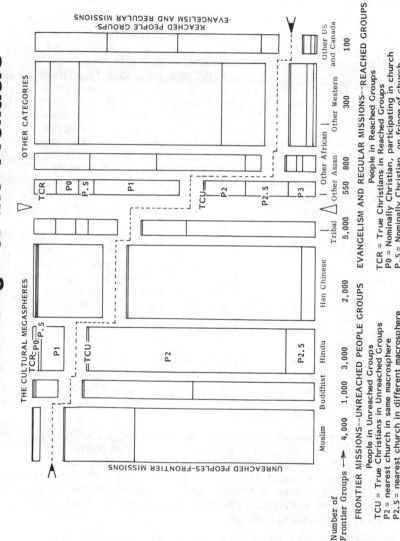

THE CULTURAL MEGASPHERES

OTHER CATEGORIES

REACHED PEOPLE GROUPS-
-EVANGELISM AND REGULAR MISSIONS

UNREACHED PEOPLES-FRONTIER MISSIONS

Muslim   Buddhist   Hindu   Han Chinese

Tribal   Other Asian   Other African   Other Western   Other US and Canada

Number of
Frontier Groups ⟶   4,000   3,000   1,000   2,000   5,000   550   800   300   100

TCR   P0   P.5   P1
TCU   P2   P2.5   P3

FRONTIER MISSIONS—UNREACHED PEOPLE GROUPS
People in Unreached Groups
TCU = True Christians in Unreached Groups
P2 = nearest church in same macrosphere
P2.5 = nearest church in different macrosphere
P3 = nearest church in different megasphere

EVANGELISM AND REGULAR MISSIONS—REACHED GROUPS
People in Reached Groups
TCR = True Christians in Reached Groups
P0 = Nominally Christian, participating in church
P.5 = Nominally Christian, on fringe of church
P1 = Do not claim to be Christian

pursuing every missionary verse in the Bible.None—not one!—was commented on in the notes.Finally, in despair, I jumped over many passages to Matthew 28:19-20 thinking, surely this, the Great Commission of our Lord, would merit some comment.Sure enough, those two verses were tinted in, and I looked with eagerness at the lengthy comment at the bottom of the page.

This was the note: "When your children grow up and leave home, and the house seems empty, loneliness may overtake you. But just remember that Jesus said, 'Lo, I am with you always.'" The paragraph was titled, "How to Conquer Loneliness." That was the only comment on those important verses: "Go ye therefore and teach all nations, baptizing them in the name of the Father and of the Son and of the Holy Spirit, teaching them to observe all things, whatsoever I have commanded you. And lo, I am with you always, even unto the end of the earth."There seemed in this particular Bible a great willingness to have the Lord present, but also a great indifference to His conditions—"Go!"

I tell you, it is perfectly possible to use the Bible heretically, and this is, I believe, an example.

Putting Feet to our Vision

It is up to us, therefore, who have caught the vision to keep it burning bright and to pass it on. Will we be true to it? Or will we play games with it until the Lord removes it from us, and at the same time also removes his blessing? The two go together. God intends that the nations be won. It is not merely a desire of His; He will see that it is done, one way or the other. But, as He warned the vacillating Children of Israel standing at the entrance to the Promised Land and afraid of the dangers they might have to face, this thing He intends will be done. But if we do not participate with Him in obedience to His commission, neither will we participate in the blessing that accompanies it. As some have so pointedly said, "The 'Lo' is only for those who 'Go'!"

FRONTIER MISSION STRUCTURES
Dr. Petrus Octavianus

1. PREFACE

First I want to put the subject of "mission structures" into the wider context of movements of the Gospel, especially in Asia, more specifically Indonesia. God is reaching out for Christians in Asia to build them up for the task of serving the Gospel. This movement is like completing a circle with Asia included in the plan for reaching the world. This is evident from the great miracles God is doing in several countries in Asia. In the completion of His saving plan for the world, God has returned to working through His existing church in these last days. He has raised up and anointed His apostles here and there, who are travelling around with the Gospel. There are three ways in which He is working:

The Holy Spirit has been poured out upon His church. Christians who have been lukewarm for a long time have been revived and are now shouldering the responsibility of witnessing to their own people of Asia. There are churches that are no longer able to accommodate all the people who want to hear the Gospel. Church buildings in certain areas are having to be enlarged. In many places extra meetings have been arranged for prayer in the homes of believers. The movement of the Spirit among high schools and universities has been outstanding.

The Holy Spirit has brought into being evangelistic teams comprised mostly of peasant folk who have experienced the anointing of the Holy Spirit. These teams often travelled hundreds of kilometers taking the Gospel from village to village and island to island without feeling tired. Thousands upon thousands of people have repented and received Jesus Christ as their Saviour through the ministry of these teams. Everywhere churches have been cleansed from the powers of darkness through the power of the Holy Spirit manifested through these teams.

The Holy Spirit also worked with people of other religions. God met with them through dreams, visions, healings and through their hearing something about Jesus Christ. In many instances, they repented and followed the Lord Jesus without the counselling or help from any other people. In other cases they met with the leading personalities of other religions, who had become followers of Christ. This inspires us with hope for the evangelization of Asia at the present time and in the days to come. In this respect, I am in complete agreement with Dr. Abdul-Haqq. He says, "The old, traditional methods of propagation of the Gospel in India and Southeast Asia are being replaced by new ways."

2. INTEGRATION AS A MODEL IN MISSION STRUCTURES

At a consultation on missions in Indonesia held in Batu, East Java during September 1980, a considerable range of mission agencies were represented with approximately the following division: 50% were agencies with clearly foreign roots, about 30% represented independent, indigenous churches which have come into being through mission agencies, whereas about 20% were agencies which have sprung up within the movement I described above. The Indonesian Missionary Fellowship in Batu, who sponsored the consultation, represents a combination of at least two kinds of agencies represented, yet it also is a further development in itself. It is an agency which sprang up within the movement of the Spirit in Indonesia. From its inception the principle of integration has developed and given the IMF its particular identity. In this way it has been able to draw on the spiritual strength of that which God is doing in Indonesia and also on the spiritual heritage contributed through foreign members of the team.

The concept of integration can play a vital role in the

development of structures which are appropriate to present day conditions. No nation can afford to ignore other nations and no part of the Christian church can afford to ignore other parts.

2.1 Political and Missions Background.

Political background

In these last 35–45 years about 100 Asian and African nations gained independence.

They want to express their capacity to stand on their own feet. That in itself is something positive. But the way of expressing it may look negative. It comes out in explosions and eruptions.

In the course of independence being gained, the governments took over churches or church institutions, stressing that leadership must be handed over from the missionary to the national worker. Needless to say, a transitional period is a period of crisis. The important thing is that we do our best to minimize these crises.

How important it is for the missionary to be sensitive to the mental attitude, thought pattern and philosophical outlook of the national churches and institutions.

Herein lies the reason that through integration the internal tensions can at least be minimized. The cross has a place to operate.

Historical background of missions

In 1810 William Carey proposed the First International Missions Conference to be held in Cape Town. Had these plans been carried through, it would have been evident that what was meant was in fact a First World Missions Conference, because at that time missionaries going out from their own countries were mainly from Britain and Europe. At that time Second World (North American) Missions were just starting. A hundred years later, John Mott succeeded in bringing about the First Missions Conference in Edinburgh. At the time, Second World Missions played the most important role, and still are. (Statistics in 1978 show that, from a total of 55,930 missionaries, 50,200 (88.3%) come from the First and Second Worlds, while 5,780 or 10.1% come from the Third World).

The understanding of International Missions in 1910 was still confined to the First and Second World, while the Third World (Latin America, Africa, Asia) was represented by less than 2% out of 1200 delegates, and therefore, had little to say in missions.

In 1974 at the International Congress on World Evangelization it was shown that, in these last thirty years, a considerable number of mission societies from that Third World (Latfricasia) have come into existence. Therefore, in inter-mission relationships, like partnership or integration, the Third World must be taken into consideration.

2.2   The Biblical basis for integration

The Biblical basis for integration is seen in passages of Scripture like the following: John 1:14; 20,21; Acts 4: 33-35; 1 Cor. 9:19-23; 2 2 Cor. 8:9; Phil. 2:1-8.

There are three important aspects to the identification of the Lord Jesus with mankind: He was willing to (a) empty Himself, (b) become like men, (c) suffer for men.

In 2 Cor. 8:9 Paul also stresses the fact that Christ who owns everything was willing to become poor that we may become rich. Here we see that Christ's ministry results in His identification with mankind. Paul himself proves that he integrated with those whom he serves (1 Cor. 9). So great is his sacrifice that he is willing to lose his rights, which are lawful to him, so that he might by all means save some.

The foundation for integration as a living relationship is found in the willingness to (a) leave something behind, (b) become like your fellow worker in some aspects, (c) suffer for others. These aspects are made possible in the life of the Christian/missionary only through the power of the cross of Christ. As we further look at the passages in Philippians, John and in Acts we notice three important factors:

a) Integration means that we do not hold on to and defend ourselves and our interests in relation to others. This has to be applied very widely within an evangelistic fellowship. Everyone has his own identity relating to doctrine, to level of education and social status. Yet integration is the motivating force for him not to hold on to himself and his identity for the sake of developing and promoting the ministry together in fellowship with his brethren.

b) Integration means that we seek to identify ourselves with those to whom we minister (compare John 1:14). This identification is very important and is one of the conditions for effective communication between the one who ministers and the one being ministered to. And it is as important in relationships between members of different identities within one fellowship or evangelistic group.

c) Integration means that the common needs, the common fellowship and the common ministry is more important than the individual interests of each member.

Webster's dictionary defines integration as "to put or bring together parts into a whole, unify." The important aspect is that "unity is in the whole." The Latin word "integratus" has three main meanings: (a) "to make whole or complete by adding or bringing together parts." The whole consists of the parts, but is different from the parts; (b) "to put or bring (parts) together into a whole, to make unity"; (c) "to organize various traits or tendencies into one harmonious personality". The main point is "the whole, the unity" where the parts have a vital function and develop TOWARDS perfection within the whole.

2.3   Integration as a mission's identity

Within the development of missions we meet with three main forms of cooperation between foreign and national groups: (a) Partnership, (the most widely practiced form); (b) Workers being on loan for a limited time and for a specific task; (c) Integration.

We have to look upon each of these different forms as a particular gift from the Lord for a particular mission or church body. Beware of regarding any particular form as the ONLY and best, the others as inferior. It is necessary to have a genuine appreciation toward ALL the different forms.

At the same time it is necessary to obediently enter into the specific form which the Lord gives to a particular mission. In the IMF we hold to integration as the God-given line for us. The members of our fellowship come from very different backgrounds, denominations and nationalities. If we start to separate ourselves according to our differences and tend to emphasize our individual uniqueness rather than seeing the whole, then we are surely in for difficulties. For us that is important not only in relation to the members who come from abroad but also in relation to the Indonesians among themselves. The people from Minahasa for instance are quite different from the Javanese, or the Batak from the Timorese. They each have their own way of thinking and cultural background.

Concerning the development of the IMF into its present structure I want to underline three identities:

a. The international character of the IMF. Of course, our mission is a national body in the sense that it is not a branch or representative of any foreign mission. However, the IMF dates back to the combined initiative of Indonesians in fellowship with Westerners. In 1964 when the Lord gave us the word from Isaiah 45:2,3 as a foundational promise, it was received in one night by two people of different national backgrounds.

b. The interdenominational character of the IMF. Our members come from various church traditions and join forces in pursuing our main goal, namely the propagation of the Gospel.

c. These two mentioned characteristics can only be worked out through integration as a form of living, working and ministering together.

I want to mention eight aspects in the outworking of integration in the life of a mission. Much, of course, is based on the experience within the Indonesian Missionary Fellowship, but I believe they have a wider application in missions.

2.3.1   The aspect of theological conviction.

All who join IMF hold to the same conviction as to faith in the Bible as the Word of God, the importance of the New Birth and the

Commission to propagate the Gospel. In that there is no problem.
But besides these common convictions each member has his/her own
"pluses", according to the teaching within their individual denomination.
And whenever someone promotes his individual conviction without due
appreciation of another's view, there are surely problems. I am
convinced that the weaknesses of the one denomination can be
complemented by the strengths of another. Within the IMF we have
room for the various "pluses", however we must never regard our
differences more important than our common convictions.

2.3.2   The cultural aspect

In addition to the various tribal backgrounds represented already
from within Indonesia, we have so far received 11 different nations
into the ranks of our mission. There is the tendency with us to bring
our customs and culture into the propagation of the Gospel, and this
can cause troubles. Therefore, in integration, the cross of Christ has
to be applied. And the Holy Spirit checks as to every custom and
cultural form. Only on that ground is it possible to accept each
other. Each of us has to be open and willing to receive help from
another. Within the IMF we do not disregard the "pluses" from the
cultural background, but we accept that the Lord wants to form us
and shape us and sometimes this happens in a hurting kind of process,
and we are convinced that the Lord wants to give us lines of conduct
which are commonly acceptable. Therefore, we cannot afford to think
that we have individual freedom to just do as we used to, without
regard to that which others are used to. Integration can be a help to
us in order to accept that which the Lord wants to do for us as
individuals in the midst of our felt differences.

2.3.3   The educational aspect

Within a fellowship, differences in educational background can
create difficulties. In our mission there are those who have received
advanced theological training, there are those who have received
education of an intermediate level and also those who do not have full
theological education. Every member receives the same financial
allowance without regard to his educational standard. Differences of
financial allowance can create tensions and divisions within a
fellowship. But the line of integration helps us to overcome those
problems. We recognize that education can be a plus, but that which is
the uniting element for us is the fact that we are together in a
service and ministry.

2.3.4   The cooperation aspect.

Within our mission, integration is the basis for cooperation. As
to leadership position we do not favor any particular national,
educational or social background, but the decisive factor is the proven
ability and gift of the individual concerned. (Of course, this cannot be
separated completely from the educational factor.) The foreign worker
does not HAVE to be in the lead if there is an Indonesian capable of

exercising leadership. On the other hand, if the foreigner is able to lead, why should he be rejected?

2.3.5 The aspect of leadership in an integrational structure.

Here again we do not heed national, educational and other differences. We equally regard, appreciate and give place to every member in accordance with the ability and gift proven. In the history of missions in Indonesia, the western person had to be the leader, or the one who held the power. This was possibly because Indonesians felt that westeners were superior. Of course, there are the strong points to the foreign worker - education, financial strength, riches of experience. But these are not the decisive factors. The most important is the ability and the gift.

Every person who is called of the Lord to be a leader will surely be given authority and power. From the human side, a leader needs forming, training, maturity, skill and experience. In a work of the Lord this is not enough. He needs the special endowment from the Lord. A fellowship has to be able to say with conviction that this is truly the leader chosen of the Lord.

A leader has to: (a) understand the personality and the spiritual condition of the members and give personal counsel; (b) Orderly arrange the financial matters of the fellowship; (c) Have a prophetic vision - to look ahead and see possible developments when the other members do not see anything of that yet; (d) Be able to think through the problem of continuity for the work, in case someone drops out or moves to another place; (e) Be able to rejoice with those that rejoice and feel the grief of those who are grieved.

The political development and the signs of the time demand a leadership consisting of national brethren. This does not mean that we refuse the leadership of foreigners, but it does mean that we have to give attention to the need for strong motivation to be given to the national brethren who will carry on the leadership. On the other hand our brethren from outside the country have to be able to accept and appreciate the leadership exercised by the national brethren. The line of integration can ensure a harmonious relationship there.

2.3.6 The aspect of ministering together.

We have experienced something very beautiful in working and ministering together. There is no impression that our foreign members are the ones who hold the power, even if they are in leadership position. On the contrary it is obvious how we all, irregardless of national, educational or other background, can work together and minister together. We also have witnessed how it is possible for the gifts to develop in ministry even though the one who has the gift may not have the same educational standard as someone else. For this we want to give glory to the Lord.

2.3.7 The financial aspect.

In Acts 4:33-35 we notice two things. First, that the believers brought the money gained through selling their property and laid it at the feet of the apostles. Secondly that money was distributed among the believers according to need. The amount gained through the sales was brought together and then distributed. Within an integrational structure we need a financial policy which reflects something of this principle. Of course, also in financial matters there are the individual "pluses". Spurgeon once said that the effort to equalize finances completely is contrary to Scripture, as differences form a very part of the Lord's creation. But we need a certain common standard in order to safeguard against there being those who suffer want side by side with those who enjoy abundancy. And we also need to feel near to each other, being willing to bear one another's burdens, in that those who have plenty feel responsible to share with those who suffer want. The line of integration can help us to live in that direction.

The way to follow is that of pooling the money for the common allowance. Tied in with this is the consequence that national believers are being motivated to contribute to the Lord's work, because they will trust the system of leadership if there is the common standard. And the members do not feel that they receive as individuals from individuals, but that they receive together from the Lord, the money being available is seen as the result of being together in prayer and trust to the Lord for the supply of it. This is a very important factor for Asians who are prone to strong feelings of owing gratitude and of feeling obliged to repay in other forms. This then can cause reservations as to openly criticize where it is necessary. After a time, as mistakes which go uncriticized have accumulated, it may cause an eruption and some kind of rebellion because of the feelings which were suppressed too long. Then feelings often will manifest themselves in rather nationalistic-looking reactions. Another consequence can be that the national worker suddenly cuts the relationship, as the only way out for him because he cannot bear the suppressed feelings any longer. Therefore it is of such vital importance that the financial aspect be handled in a way where the money is genuinely regarded as being received together.

2.3.8 The aspect of living together.

We consciously seek to avoid the development of, for instance, Germans only fellowshipping with Germans, Norwegians only fellowshipping with Norwegians, the Eastern people only seeking fellowship among themselves, etc. Something like this would easily show up in little islands being formed where they each live on their own campuses. So various workers coming from different nationalities are put side by side, and relationships are being strengthened. We have to practice the line of integration in the daily activities together. The individual has to be willing to come to know and understand something of the etiquette, customs and cultural background of others.

In our fellowship, missionaries coming from abroad go through a time of adjustment together with the newly applying members from inside the country. They live and learn together, learning of language, fellowship regulations and culture. In this way the missionary can experience the most natural initial adjustment to the culture, and make himself familiar with the constitutional foundation of the country and the overall situation of the churches. He can then develop a sensitivity towards, and appreciation and understanding of, the situation in the country and existing church life.

This period lasts for two years and is decisive regarding acceptance into the fellowship.

3. EVALUATION OF SOME MISSION STRUCTURES

The observations here are mostly founded on Indonesia, though I have visited other mission centers and areas in other countries.

3.1   The tradition of missions and the young churches

Every mission is bound to formulate certain principles of life, faith and working policy. In the course of development these principles change into the tradition which is then firmly held onto, both by missions of denominational as well as interdenominational character.

In every tradition we meet with positive and negative elements. Therefore it is of great importance that every principle and tradition be re-evaluated from time to time, so that it may not turn into a hindrance in regard to reaching the highest goal - the propagation of the Gospel and the leading of Christians to spiritual maturity.

3.2 Pioneer missionaries who lack orientation as to the existing church and local culture.

Missionaries are pioneers, to a large extent. It is the foremost task of a missionary to seek access to new areas. The typical pioneer missionary is a person of strong character and individualistic outlook.

Many missionaries lack a wide orientation concerning churches, the cultural context and the political structure of the country. This may be because they seek to enter the interior to where they are called as soon as possible, and that they spend nearly all their time there or that they seek to establish the concept of their mission or their mother church in the place where they find themselves without giving due attention to the local situation, nor the whole cultural context. (compare Arthur Glasser "Missionary Preparation" in his paper "Timeless Lessons From the Western Missionary Penetration of China", The All-Asia Mission Consultation Seoul 73, Chaeok Chun ed.).

It can be of real help to missionaries if from time to time they visit other parts of the country seeking to spend time and having contact with the leaders of established churches seeking an understanding of the development taking place in the country as a whole, including the development of the political scene.

Missionaries often lack an understanding of the local culture. This may be due not so much to the fact that they are not open to the people around them but that they do not look for any deeper fellowship with national brethren who would be able to give helpful and needed advice in this regard. An attitude of being willing to learn the national Christian's way of thinking, in the context of their culture, is of great help to missionaries in the effort to build bridges of real understanding. Christians of a more simple background will generally tend to admire the missionary and not feel free to openly criticize him. Therefore it is my suggestion that missionaries who work in more backward areas make the definite effort to seek fellowship with national Christians from other, more progressive areas, who would be mature enough in their own outlook and sufficiently removed from denominational or mission background to be able to give constructive advice.

3.3 Mission structures and the emergence of national leadership

The difficulty is that often two leaderships are being exercised side by side: (a) leadership of the mission, and (b) leadership of the national church which has been established by the mission. The mission has its own program besides that of the church. In regard to organization and responsibility the two work separately, though they may from time to time meet for consultation. To this system there are positive and negative sides.

The positive sides are: (a) Each can decide on their own program. (b) Each can safeguard unity among themselves. (c) It is easier to avoid misunderstandings which can arise between the missionaries and the national church leaders, even though these are usually temporary. (d) There is no need to seek to overcome the differences in life style, financial policy, culture, way of thinking, way of working etc.

The negative sides: (a) The fact that the mission makes its own program usually causes annoyance on the part of the national church leadership. This can be suppressed temporarily, but from time to time it will come to the open, especially if the national church leaders are already able to critically and rightly analyze the way of life and leadership of the mission in question.

(b) There is lack of knowledge and understanding towards each other's burdens because they are not being dealt with together.

(c) There is an obvious relationship of superior to inferior. Where the missionary is addressed as "sir" indicates that it is not a relationship of equality.

It also creates the unhealthy relationship which lacks openness and becomes a hindrance to the growth of fellowship in the life of the body of Christ. The kind of fellowship which may be there may very well become superficial and false, being far from the biblical concept of 1 John 1:7 or Ephesians 4:15. Where can there be the experience of the power of the cross of Christ if each side closes itself off so as to avoid misunderstandings? Compare the view by Marlin Nelson in the book, "The How and Why of Third World Missions, an Asian Case Study" page 36. "We are not to work OVER or UNDER the national Christian, but WITH him".

(d) With two organizations and two leaderships existing side by side, it is very difficult for a true national leadership to emerge which can develop towards maturity and capability.

Here it is necessary to state the qualifications for a church leader in the Third World.

The foremost aspect is that his life is being controlled by the Spirit of God and richly rooted in the Word of God, together with a deep personal devotion.

Besides this there are aspects and proofs to be met of leadership in: (a) the mission, (b) one's own church, (c) relation to other churches, (d) relation to the government.

A national brother may be appointed leader in the mission because of his spirituality and his understanding of and obedience to the mission. But this may not automatically mean that he can take his stand as a national church leader. In the mission he always exercises his leadership at the side of another leader. His responsibility for a mistake can still be shared with the other leader, but as a leader in his own church he has to take full responsibility.

The efficiency and authority of a leader is very much dependent on his understanding of other churches. Also a national church leader must have an understanding in the field of sociology and be familiar with the national scene in his country. Whether we realize it or not, most of the (national) leaders of churches which have been planted by missions are very limited in their leadership, mostly to fulfilling the demands mentioned under mission and spirituality. Missions have been weak in developing the kind of national church leadership which would fulfill the five aspects mentioned before.

As a result there are three dangers which have to be faced: (a) The leadership of the national church looks stable and efficient only as long as the missionaries are still present. (b) Both missionaries as well as national leaders are narrow in their way of thinking and decision making, (Western or non-Western.) (c) The leadership of a particular church is only oriented towards the leadership of the particular mission, and with that, towards the church from which the missionaries originate, without there being the development of an independent leadership.

Therefore the mission has to continually give attention to the upgrading of the national leaders so that the work will not come to a standstill when the missionaries have to leave, but rather continue and enlarge.

If there is the willingness on both sides, (especially of the missionaries) to enter into the "body life" of the national church which has come into being through the mission, the weaknesses mentioned before can be overcome through:

(a) The WILLINGNESS on the part of the missionaries to be led by national brethren.

(b) The working out of a joint program with a common goal, by the missionaries and the national leader. They can look together at various factors, both from the point of view of the mission as well as the national leader and in accordance with the local conditions and situations. In this way much misunderstanding and mis-communication can be avoided. In sitting and talking together the concept of something being forced by one or the other side can be avoided and much of tension taken away.

(c) The gulf of separation becoming less and less, because the misunderstandings can be overcome in the grace of the cross of Christ.

(d) The kind of fellowship which is true and deep and beautiful, and not just limited to worshipping together in a church building.

(e) The willingness of the missionaries to more effectively support and strengthen the national church leadership and build strong bridges.

4. MISSION STRUCTURES AND SHORT TERM WORKERS

The short term missionary takes an ever-increasing part in today's world mission movement, and might soon equal the force of career missionaries if the present rate of growth continues. We find the short term missionary both in agencies which specialize in that kind of arrangement as well as in agencies which make room in their structure to accommodate short term personnel for a specific task and a limited period. Or there is the situation where short termers fill gaps in missions. (Compare "A Statistical Study of Short Term Missions," by Thomas W. Chandler.)

Among the reasons given for this of development are the growing awareness of young people concerning the world as a whole, as well as the fact that the development of methods used in missions result in an increased number of opportunities where people can be of help even if they come for a limited time.

4.1 Short term personnel in specific situations.

There are specific situations where the contribution of short term workers is of invaluable help. The relief work in Cambodian refugee camps has greatly profited through the willing service of short term volunteers, even student nurses from Bible colleges, who are willing to enter into difficult situations like that.

We, in our fellowship, experience help through so-called associate members who come for a limited time in order to contribute their specific skill and knowledge. We have greatly profited through this in the erection of our radio studio, especially on the technical side of things.

4.2 Short term personnel and the existing structures.

For situations which constitute emergencies, (like the above-mentioned refugee camps,) we need to use all available forces in whatever form possible. Yet in relation to existing mission structures, the evaluation needs to take into account other factors, not just the immediate need.

Studies show that the people of the country entered were least convinced about the effectiveness of a short term ministry. As to evaluation of motivation the people had mostly gained the impression that it is a kind of adventure and a "tourist"-like understanding. The missionaries who had experienced help by short termers were much more enthusiastic as to effectiveness.

Effectiveness, in a mechanical sense, is a valid criterion in evaluation, yet the matter of establishing relationships is a different and often much more relevant criterion in many cultures. In evaluating mission structures on the whole, much boils down to the matter of relationships. Therefore, to serve the short termer, the existing agencies need to give attention to that aspect. We should continue to receive the short termer but should also realize that we serve him best and can channel his pioneer spirit in the right way if he sees the reality of lasting relationships and knows in which direction to go in his learning. The openness of youth and the fact that young people of today often have experienced the rapid changes of culture in their own life time, may help to make the short termer a true learner. Yet we and he must realize that lasting structures are not built through a commitment limited from the start, but that it needs the long range commitment. And if we do expect that, from among those who come for a short term assignment, there will be some who decide to commit themselves more fully, we must be able to show them the value of lasting relationships.

5.   COMBINING EFFORTS.

The question as to ways in which agencies can best help each other in their pioneer endeavors is a very important one. No doubt we need each other and no doubt we need to learn from each other.

5.1   Assessing one's strength and weakness.

The matter of frequent consultation in openness and willingness to admit our failures and seek for ways of complementing each other is of fundamental importance. We have to seek to assess our own strengths and weaknesses rightly. An example: We have a missionary family from Indonesia working in Brazil. An outside observer drew the conclusion that, because they come from a context of church growth,

they have from the start expected to experience church growth. In
this they could rightly be an inspiration to others who find it difficult
to really expect that churches do grow, perhaps because in their
background they are lacking this experience. Of course, it is necessary
for others to be willing to receive inspiration, as it always needs the
openness and humility to receive each other's contributions. This also
applies on the level of inter-mission relationships.

One of the fundamental helps, therefore, can be to assess the
strength rightly and seek to contribute where that strength is needed.

We have often experienced that the fact of a team which consists
of different races, different nations and different denominations, yet
able to minister together, has helped to resolve tensions which existed
in the situations we entered and of which we were often not aware
beforehand.

5.2 Seeking ways of contributing and of receiving contributions.

I am convinced that through consultation we can join efforts, (a)
on a short term basis, as in the case of teams being formed whose
members could come from different agencies, and in ministering
together enrich each other; or (b) on a long term basis where workers
can be received on equal terms between agencies. In some cases this
is already being done, but there is much more room for cooperation
and passing on of experience in a practical way.

6. MISSION STRUCTURES AND SOCIETY.

In his book, "The Gospel and Communism in Asia and Africa", Dr.
Verkuyl writes a chapter on "Critique of Western Missions". This may
be worthy of thoughtful consideration. He draws conclusions from
the writings of various ex-China missionaries before the communist
take-over: "That which happened in China is also a judgment of the
Lord on all the shortcomings of Western missions in China. Of course,
the whole country and society was hit in this judgment, but the church
and the mission was hit too." Some of the failures and practical
examples given refer to society, like the following:

(a) The policy of missions in the field of politics, culture and
society was felt as an invasion of Western culture rather than
awakening responsibility on the part of the Chinese Christians to
strive for renewal of their society.

(b) The missions failed to give due attention to government circles
and failed to influence the macro structure of society in the same way
as the micro strucutre.

The question is how can we reach out with the Gospel in such a
way that there will be an impact made on society?

6.1. The concept of "tentmakers" in specific situations.

We in the IMF see our task in serving the existing churches with
the evangelistic message and vision. Together with those who are

themselves being renewed and remain within their churches and positions, we are reaching out to the unreached peoples. In this way an effective outreach has also developed through people who hold influential positions in secular agencies in areas which are otherwise difficult to reach. There are one or two areas in Indonesia where the actual outworking of freedom of religion, (ensured by the constitution), is somewhat being qualified by the strength of tradition. In such a situation, "tentmakers" in the above-mentioned sense can be very effective, even sometimes the only effective way of witness.

6.2 Outreach to the macro structure of society.

A chain reaction has developed in some cities in Indonesia where people in influential positions reach out to their equals. Bankers, lawyers, even government officials who are personally being ministered to, then seek to reach out to their level of society, (through luncheons in hotels or other ways), with a burden to reach the unreached. Of course, unreached peoples can be found in every stratum of society.

The question then is whether our vision and concern are also directed towards the macro structure of society and whether we use all the possibilities there are for that.

In developing countries, people are longing to learn English, the language which connects them to the world at large. Through the medium of English classes right up to university level, people can be reached with the Gospel. This avenue is by no means used to the full yet.

Thus it is, through people who remain in their original profession and have an effective witness to the saving power of the Gospel, that an impact can be made, both in specifically difficult areas as well as in relation to higher level of society. What we, as mission agencies, can do is to look for openings in order to reach out to key people like that and be concerned for the whole of society.

7. CONCLUSION.

We are all concerned to find structures that are:

- effective in terms of reaching the goal - realistic in terms of taking into account developments in our present world - adequate for the individuals who constitute the material from which these structures are built.

Integration answers the above-mentioned aspects in that it:

- helps us to join forces while being directed towards the common goal - takes into account the situation especially in developing countries with sensitivity to national identity and equality - gives room for the power of the Cross of Christ to work in and through individuals who make up the structure. In that sense it is adequate.

While it is right to hold on in firm conviction to that which is entrusted to us by the Lord, we want to remain open and recognize that God is never bound to a pattern but chooses to work differently in different situations.

The challenge is: are we willing for the way He wants to work in and through us?

FRONTIER MISSION PERSONNEL - Panya Baba

1. DEFINITION

In Romans 15:20 Paul describes the frontier field as "not where Christ was named." From this point of view, frontier missionaries are those pioneers who evangelize among unreached peoples to whom Christ's name has never been mentioned nor fully enough understood in order for them to make the decision either to follow or reject him.

2. INTRODUCTION

The three quarters of the world who are yet to be reached by the Gospel have become a great challenge and concern to us. If, during the life of our Lord Jesus the crowd in Palestine alone could move his heart with the kind of compassion that led him to call for more prayers, send his disciples as missionaries and eventually sacrifice his life at Calvary, how much should we as ambassadors of Christ do today in order to reach the three billion people who are hopelessly waiting for the judgment? As the world population increases, how many more missionaries should we send out?

3. CALL FOR FRONTIER MISSIONARIES

The call to the church today is still a frontier missionary call. "As the Father has sent me, even so I send you," John 20:21. "Three billion people still unreached, and two billion non-Christians separated from Christians," (Reaching the Unreached by Edward R. Dayton) makes it clear that the era of frontier missionaries has not yet ended.

"There is also the frontier of the encounter with other faiths such as Moslem and Buddhist societies. There is the encounter with the independent, separatist churches in Africa, who seem nominal Christians but who practice syncretism. There are people of subcultures in every land around the world to whom little witness and ministry are being offered," (Beaver, Consultation of December 1972). The question is not whether we need frontier missionaries, but where shall we get enough to send? "How shall they hear without a preacher? (Romans 10:14)" For example, research shows us we still have 85 unreached tribes in middle and northern Nigeria. There is no way to reach these frontier people unless we send pioneer missionaries among them. There is a wide open door for national missionaries to evangelize these tribes.

Although evangelism may be more easily done by national missionaries, missionaries from the West can still participate and supplement what is lacking. The only problem is visa restriction. This can be solved in some cases by arrangement with the national church, provided the missionaries are willing to sacrifice their own identity to work with the national missions. In areas prohibited to foreign missionaries, there is no reason why national missionaries cannot penetrate further. "The real issue of world missions is not moratorium, but the problem of how to build right and normal relationships between the new and the old forces in missions," (E. Frizen, AMA, Jan. 1979). It is high time for third world churches to catch the vision of reaching the world beyond their boundaries and for the older missions also to renew their vision to penetrate and mobilize forces to reach the millions of unevangelized frontier people.

4. NEW RESOURCES FOR PERSONNEL:

World evangelization is a gigantic work which cannot be accomplished if we depend on one type of missionary. "There is no church in any one nation which has all the adequate resources and full time missionary personnel needed for the job," (G. D. James, AMA Bulletin, Jan. 1979). Therefore, all types of missionaries should be sent into the harvest. These categories are:

(1) - EMIGRATION OR MOBILIZATION OF CHRISTIANS to settle among the unreached peoples, either geographically or culturally.

(2) - GOVERNMENT AND PRIVATE WORK MISSIONARIES who are employed by the third world countries.

(3) - VOLUNTEER SHORT TERM MISSIONARIES.

(4) - FULL TIME PROFESSIONAL MISSIONARIES.

The great commission was not given to only half of Jesus' disciples but to ALL of them. Our Lord Jesus saw the harvest plentiful but workers few.

The motto of COWE Conference was, "How Can They Hear?" The Bible shows clearly that they hear by having a preacher. Therefore, the failure of reaching two-thirds of today's world population is not closed doors but the lack of missionaries. There have never been permanently closed doors for the Gospel. The door can be closed in one country while open in another. We need to encourage all those whom the Lord of the harvest has called to go to the field.

CATEGORY 1: EMIGRATION OR MOBILIZATION OF CHRISTIANS TO BECOME MISSIONARIES should be encouraged. This was the method of the early church. Christians were first tempted to do evangelism only in Jerusalem and Judaea. It was not until they were mobilized by persecution that they began cross-cultural evangelism. (Acts 8:1-4)

Missions in Category 1 are less expensive to support. Since cross-cultural training takes time and produces few workers, why should we depend only on Short Term and Full Time missionaries? What we need today is to motivate Christians to settle among the unreached frontier people in their local areas. This can be done after a very simple and crash training programme on cross- cultural evangelism suited to the local unreached areas where they will work.

For example: Christians of Southern Zaria in Nigeria number over 70% as the result of the mobilization of the early believers who settled in each village, became farmers like the villagers, adopted the life style of the people and became witnesses to the non-Christians. They overcame the problems related to isolated compounds, different style of dress, etc. These were replaced by identification with the people.

This method also is now being applied by EMS to reach Hausa Maguzawa people. We cannot meet the demand if we depend on and wait for full time permanent workers. There are also fewer cultural problems involved for the Maguzawa converts to work among their fellow Hausa Moslems than for missionaries who come from the southern part of the country. What the local people of the Hausa Maguzawa need is a very simple method of approach to the Gospel which is related to their cultural background. Seminary graduates with their academic theological background may not fit their need. But the type of missionary used among the Maguzawa may not fit for the Hausa people in Ghana where another cross-cultural approach has to be considered. Bible college or seminary graduates are mostly needed there.

We need to emphasize our call for missionary mobilization more than for permanent residential missionaries. We should avoid the temptation of the early church of being settled permanently in one place until they were scattered by persecution to mobilize. A frontier missionary can be stagnant and become a hindrance to the young church mobilizing for evangelisim if he resides too long in one area. We should learn from the early missionaries, Paul and Barnabas, (Acts 14:21-23).

During the COWE Conference someone expressed his deep concern saying, "How many Americans are willing to leave the United States to settle in Mexico? How many Asian Christians in the West are willing to go back to settle in the China Mainland?" A similar question can be asked based on our own country or tribal background. How many of us are willing to mobilize and go?

One of the ways Islam spread in Nigeria, apart from being forced by the sword, was through this method. There were no full time Moslem missionaries but traders who emigrated to settle elsewhere and took their religion with them. They demonstrated their faith wherever they lived. Why shouldn't Christians be encouraged to do so also, for the sake of the Gospel?

Billions are still unreached and will probably be still unreached unless we discuss more concerning this method of missionary mobilization. For example, it is the policy of EMS of ECWA in Nigeria to send a missionary to plant a new church in an unreached area. As soon as the church is planted, leaders will be appointed and the young church will be joined with the nearest older church for growth and pastoring. The missionary moves to a new area. Therefore, the EMS missionaries continually mobilize to reach out into new areas. But we need more helping hands of Christians instead of depending only on 460 full-time missionaries who are Category 4 type workers.

CATEGORY 2: GOVERNMENT AND PRIVATE WORKERS EMPLOYED BY THE THIRD WORLD COUNTRIES should also be encouraged and upheld in prayer. They are also a strong force, especially in countries where the door seems closed. God has been using these missionaries in some resistant areas. Their services prepare people to be open to the Gospel. But it is unfortunate that information of what God does through them is not adequately presented to our churches in order to motivate more to go and to appeal to Christians to pray for them as well as for those in Category 3 and 4. They need more recognition and backing as missionaries who follow the steps of the early missionaries who were rather self-supported (II Thessalonians 3:8,9). Some of our new churches in northern Nigeria have been planted by missionaries like this.

For example, an Indian Science teacher in Nigeria, Alexander Rajon, is making a great impact on the Church in Nigeria. Also, Mr. T. Wilmot, an English businessman, has contributed tremendously to evangelism and church growth in Nigeria. Others also play a great role. On the other hand there are those expatriate Christians who need encouragement and could even be commissioned by their own church before they leave their countries so that they will be more effective. Tentmakers also should be put in Category 2.

CATEGORIES 3 AND 4: VOLUNTEER SHORT TERM AND FULL TIME PROFESSIONAL MISSIONARIES are need in special areas where Category 1 workers would not fit because of inadequate training or qualifications. They need a longer training period and need to be qualified before they can be sent. Therefore, we need ALL TYPES of missionaries who feel called and who are willing to go and identify themselves among the frontier peoples.

5. PREPARATION BY TRAINING

A. NEED FOR TRAINING. An army officer once said, "Give me the WELL TRAINED soldiers to fight. The blood must be shed, but the victory should be ours." I emphasize "well trained", because it does not matter how many soldiers are sent, but how many are qualified and disciplined in order to get the victory. Abram conquered four kings and their multitude of soldiers with only three hundred trained soldiers from his household (Genesis 14:14).

It took Jesus three years to train His disciples for the work of evangelism. Even then he commanded them not to start, "But stay in the city until you are clothed with power from on high," (Luke 24:49). In spite of the urgency of the work, there is the need to wait and be trained. The disciples needed to be well equipped in order to avoid discouragements when encountering problems. We also need to be prepared before we are sent. Training is not only needed but very essential, especially for cross cultural evangelism.

B. MODELS OF TRAINING. There are two methods of training: theoretical and practical. Our Lord Jesus used both ways to train His disciples. Sometimes He opened His mouth and taught them, (Matthew 5:2). At other times, He took them along with him to see and observe. He also asked them to take part in doing and even sent them to put into practice what they had been told. "When he had called unto him his twelve disciples, he gave them power against unclean spirits, to cast them out and to heal all manner of diseases," (Matthew 10:1). When a mistake was made, Jesus corrected them, (Mark 9:28,29; 38-39). We need both in order to have adequate training.

We have different models of missionary training schools today. Some emphasize theories to provide graduates with higher qualifications on a degree level and ignore the practical side. Others give more attention to the practical side. For example, it is my understanding that:

(1) All Nations Christian College in Ware, England trains new missionaries by bringing them together with old missionaries. It helps the older ones to study new ideas while they share their experiences with the new ones. The past experience of the old missionary staff also makes a tremendous contribution. As a result of this, the training in All Nations Christian College is both practical and theoretical.

(2) The Indian Evangelical Mission Fellowship trains their missionaries in Bible school for one year. Then they are sent to spend 6 months in field work with an older missionary before they complete their 3 years training in seminary; then they are finally sent to the field.

(3) The Friends Missionary Band of India first trains its workers in Bible school for 2 years. Then it sends them for practical training for 6 months, usually under an older missionary. They spend another 6 months working with their supporting church before they are sent to the field as permanent missionary workers.

(4) The Indonesian Mission Fellowship trains its missionaries for a total of 5 years, which includes both formal and practical training.

(5) The Evangelical Missionary Society of ECWA in Nigeria trains its workers 4 years with 3 months out of each year spent on practical training.

One of the factors for our failure to penetrate the frontier people is inadequate cross-cultural evangelism training. Most of the frontier people cannot be reached except by cross-cultural missionaries. There will be no cross-cultural evangelism without training workers. An example from my home area will emphasize this. In years gone by it was the practice of our people at the death of an elderly person to slaughter an animal. The blood was placed on the top and sides of the door just as at the Passover in Egypt. This was done to "open a way for the deceased to enter the world beyond." This practice still takes place in a few of our areas.

We owe gratitude to God for the early missionaries who sacrificed their lives for the sake of the Gospel. We must salute and imitate the courage and sincere love of those early pioneers. However, had they received cross-cultural training to search for things like this within the culture, it would have been much easier for them to communicate the Gospel. Had they learned of this custom they could have used it as a bridge. It would have made the Gospel easier for our people to understand and accept, instead of introducing Christianity as an entirely new religion of the white people which naturally produced antagonism and resistance.

The similar idea of using the cross had been practiced among other tribes in the northeastern part of Nigeria such as Kilba, Jukun and Buchama before the pioneer missionary came (Christianity in Northern Nigeria, Crompton). The sacrifice of a "peace child" in Papua New Guinea relates to our own reconciliation to God which was made for us by Christ. This is another example of how important it is to learn about the culture in which one will work.

We need to follow the Biblical pattern of Paul as he preached in Athens (Acts 17:31). He preached and taught the people according to what they already knew and then took them on to the full knowledge of the Gospel. But he approached the Jews on their own cultural background and beliefs (Acts 13:16-43).

The essential call today to our Bible schools, colleges and seminaries is to modify their curricula in order to teach cross- cultural evangelism and produce the right kind of missionaries who can go into the field to plant new churches among hidden peoples. If the frontier people are to be reached, then the right frontier manpower must be produced whether from the West or Third World countries. We should not think of sending or receiving countries anymore, but rather encourage the idea of cross-fertilization for personnel and support. For the whole world is God's parish.

C. THE URGENCY OF THE TRAINING. The urgency of the task raises the need for establishing the following: 1) MISSIONARY TRAINING AND RESEARCH CENTRES. It is important to provide these centres also in Third World countries where more nationals can be taught more easily and more cheaply and also in their own cultural background. Ideas, methodologies and know-how can be pooled. This type of training may take time in order to produce enough workers. Therefore, we need to discuss the possibility of the second kind of training which I call,

2) CRASH TRAINING PROGRAMME. This training can be done either through seminars or summer courses where subjects taught are those related to the local situation. For example, the growth as a result of evangelism among the Maguzawa in Nigeria has caused the problem of a lack of workers. We prepared a simple training programme called the Branch Bible School (first introduced by Rev. G. O. Swank) These are taught for three months during the dry season. The subjects are well prepared, simple enough to teach new converts the Word and to prepare them as Category 1 missionaries, bringing them up to a standard whereby they can become missionaries among the unreached people in that local area after completing two sessions. Those found capable of continuing with the four-year training programme may prepare themselves as Category 3 and 4 missionaries. It takes a longer time before workers are produced from a full-term Bible training programme, while the Branch Bible Schools produce local workers every year. That helps us to recruit more missionaries. Additional practical training is done in the field by holding seminars for them.

D. POLICY - QUALIFICATIONS. The reason for training is to qualify a person for a job. Therefore, qualifications are essential if:

1) They help to get some missionaries into countries where the government demands paper qualifications before it will issue a visa.

2) They help to give more opportunities for missionaries to serve in some ministries which seem impossible without qualifications.

Although educational and paper qualifications are needed and important, spiritual qualifications are far more essential (I Corinthians 13). There are many professionals who have left their countries for business, to make money, or to gain popularity. However, they do nothing to satisfy the many hungry souls. On the other hand, there was a missionary who was not accepted by a certain mission. They told him he was not qualified. But, having a burden and sincere love in his heart, he decided to sell his possessions and pay his own fare by labouring on the ship to Africa. When he arrived on the field, he was accepted by the same mission because they could clearly see his Christian life demonstrated. Many Moslems gave him the nickname "Almasihu", meaning "Christ Himself". To them, this man practiced his preaching.

God used him in wonderful ways. He planted many new churches including my hometown church. When he died, hundreds of Moslems attended his burial and confessed that, "If this man 'Almasihu' will not see God, no Moslem or anyone else will see God at all, for we believe he was really a man of God." The stone he used to stand on to preach in the centre of Jos City market was marked and protected by Moslems.

The best training is the transforming work of the Holy Spirit. The love of Christ in a person cuts across every cultural barrier.

Paul said, "We are the ambassadors of Christ," II Corinthians 5:20; "For I decided to know nothing among you except Jesus Christ and Him crucified" (I Corinthians 2:2). He also said, "Consider your call, brethren, not many of you were wise according to worldly standards " (I Corinthians 1:26).

It is useful to be qualified both educationally and spiritually, but the spiritual qualifications are far better. Acts 4:13 says, "They perceived that they were uneducated, common men; they wondered and they recognized that they had been with Jesus." We need to produce not only more missionaries, but missionaries who are men of God.

6. FINANCIAL SUPPORT: Some Third World missions have more personnel than they can support. Others have received a vision to send missionaries out of their country but foreign exchange restrictions allow only a limited amount to be taken out of the country. Because of this, the number of missionaries sent out by emerging missions has been limited. According to the Five Year Plan of EMS of ECWA in Nigeria, by the end of 1985 we would have increased the number of our FOREIGN missionaries up to ten couples (an increase of about 150% over our present number), Although there may be personnel, permission has not yet been granted to transfer money out of the country to pay the workers.

On the other hand, the older mission societies from the First World countries which have more support, face the difficulty of trying to obtain visas for their missionaries to enter some of the Third World countries.

The second problem is the rapid rate of inflation in all parts of the world. Some supporters can hardly afford to keep up with the regular increase of the missionary support. This delays the recruitment of new missionaries. I am in hopes that the Edinburgh Consultation will bring relevant suggestions as to how these problems can be solved.

Rev. G. D. James in the AMA Bulletin wrote that "Cross-fertilization (of personnel and money) can help overcome the monetary exchange problem." The time has come to establish a missionary co-operation or exchange programme. For example:

(1) CO-OPERATION BETWEEN THE FIRST WORLD AND THIRD WORLD COUNTRIES. An arrangement could be made between two mission bodies to exchange their missionaries according to the need of certain projects. The emerging missions may require professional or expatriate missionaries from a society in the First World to work with them. While the Third World mission society may not be strong enough financially to support the missionary, it will be able to obtain visas for those from the First World mission societies more easily than having an outside mission society doing this. The First World, or older mission society, may require a missionary from an emerging mission in the Third World country who may be sent to work in the field of evangelism to reach the hundreds of Third World immigrants or

refugees who settle in the First World countries. Again, some emerging missions are not financially strong enough to support their missionaries in First World countries and they may not be allowed to transfer money even if they did have adequate finances. However, there is no reason why these missionaries cannot be accepted and supported by the older missions there in the First World countries. The whole world is God's field and the resources are His, whether personnel or finances.

(2) CO-OPERATION BETWEEN EMERGING MISSIONS IN THE THIRD WORLD COUNTRIES THEMSELVES. A missionary from Central Africa Republic could be supported by EMS of ECWA in Nigeria while a Nigerian missionary could also be supported by a mission society in Central Africa Republic if a good arrangement is made. The same could apply to the missionaries in Brazil and Argentina, or Thailand and India.

The best way to avoid the support problem caused by inflation is to encourage the use of missionaries from Category 1 and 2. The churches will support them for the first and second term until they have settled in their new countries. Then they will become self-supporting for the rest of their time of service, or they may be partly supported, as some of our EMS Missionaries are in Nigeria. This method will help churches or mission bodies to carry on with the burden of suppporting the full time, permanent missionaries which will still be needed for certain jobs which the others would not be able to cope with.

There is a tremendous opportunity for the expatriate pioneer missionaries from the West within the national frontier boundaries or the emerging frontier missionary movement. Their professional jobs have a great role to play in helping to cross bridges and open doors for evangelism. The emerging missions may be limited in professional manpower though they can better carry on with evangelism with fewer cultural barriers and problems. However, the whole total Gospel will not be presented if physical needs of the people are entirely neglected. There is need for co-operation in order to accomplish the work.

7. RECRUITMENT: There seem to be two ways in the Bible of recruiting missionaries:

A. By the call of the Holy Sprit to an individual who then volunteers to go. We have many examples of this. In Isaiah 6:8 we read where Isaiah responded to the Lord's call saying, "Here am I, send me." Jeremiah also answered God's call. Ezekiel was sent by God to the nation of Israel.

In Matthew 4, we read that Jesus said to Simon and Andrew, "Follow me" - and immediately they followed him. James, John and Levi were also called individually and answered the call. The angel of the Lord spoke to Philip telling him to go down to Gaza, and he went and ministered to the man from Ethiopia.

B. There is also the call of the Holy Spirit to the entire church to send out the gifted missionaries in the church. In Acts 8:14 Peter and John were sent by the church to do a certain work. Acts 11 gives us the story of the church at Jerusalem sending out Barnabas. Acts 13:2 tells us that the call came to the whole church to "separate for me, Barnabas and Saul, for the work whereunto I have called them."

The missionaries were there in the church and they had specific gifts but somehow were hidden. No one was doing the outreach work until the Holy Spirit called the entire church to fulfill its role of evangelism and send out those who were gifted.

To recruit more missionaries we must follow both methods. We must challenge individuals to listen for God's call and be ready to accept it when God speaks to them. And, we must challenge and motivate churches to take up their responsibilities for identifying those gifted for specific kinds of work, including that of evangelism.

How can a church identify those who should be sent? By prayer and fasting, seeking the mind of the Holy Spirit just as was done in Acts 13:2,3. The significant thing is that the best missionaries were discovered and sent to the frontier. We need to encourage more missionary conferences whereby adequate information could be given to congregations. There is need for an Urbana-type conference for Third World countries.

Over the past two years, as ECWA churches became aware of their responsibility for mission work, EMS of ECWA in Nigeria has recruited about 140 couples. The churches began to search for the hidden-gifted missionaries and they were willing to release them to be sent to the fields. The Holy Spirit has enriched our churches with missionaries as well as pastors and other church workers.

Since God is the Lord of the harvest, and it is His duty to provide the workers, we are told to pray for Him to do so. I believe that He is faithful. He has done His part by giving churches gifted missionaries even for cross-cultural evangelism. THE PROBLEM IS WITH US. Are we ready to seek His mind to find out those among us who are gifted, to encourage them to go and help them overcome their fear of lack of fellowship and support?

The three billion hidden people today need hundreds of frontier missionaries. God is seeking them one by one (Ezekiel 22:30). Where are they? What can we, as mission leaders, do to better plan for the work? What can we do to help identify those who should be missionaries? How can we motivate our churches to do this?

We also have yet much land to possess, many people to be saved. We can only achieve that by co-operation in strengthening and enlarging our efforts together to spread the good news of our Lord Jesus Christ to all nations throughout the world.

5
HIDDEN
PEOPLE
AMONG
ANIMISTS

Page 125

REACHING FOLK RELIGIONISTS -- Don Richardson

There are probably about 215 million tribal people in the world. Of course all of us were tribal people at one time, whether we originated from tribes living in the forests of northern Europe or an area of India. But notice these figures that compare the number of tribal peoples with the numbers of the large religious flocks of the world. Christianity claims approximately eleven hundred million adherents, Islam about 700 million followers, Hinduism 600 million, Buddhism 500 million, (See Chart). I have another heading called, FOLK RELIGIONS. These are the religions that the tribal people adhere to. They have not been propagated by any missionary force, but have just sprung out of the common soil of humanity, as it were. These folk religions claim about 3,200 million adherents.

CHRISTIANITY	1100 million
ISLAM	700 million
HINDUISM	600 million
BUDDHISM	500 million
FOLK RELIGIONS	3200 million
WORLD POP.	4400 million

You'll see a discrepancy in the figures. There are about 4.4 billion people in the world, but if you add these figures they come to 6 billion. What's happened? Simply this. Many of the Christians included in the 1100 million are really folk religionists. They are peoples who are not fully committed to the Christianity that they claim to follow. They still adhere in their daily lives to the basic tenets of the folk religion that they had before they became nominal Christians. The same is true of the majority of the Muslims, Hindus, Buddhists, and so on. Tribal peoples, folk religionists, really have more in common with the rest of mankind than you would think and the evangelization of the world requires reaching 3,200 million people who, in their basic presuppositions, are not actually Christians, Muslims, Hindus or Buddhists, but folk religionists.

CHARACTERISTICS OF FOLK RELIGIONS

Folk religions around the world tend to have certain things in common. They all have a body of traditions that explain creation, man's relationship with nature, animals. Secondly, they all tend to have a system of taboos. Thirdly, they have different ways of making offerings to the spirits to appease them. Fourthly, most folk religions also have a sorcery component which could be called spirit manipulation. Our fifth component is something you would not expect to find - an incipient monotheism, a basic belief that over and above this fog of evil spirits that the animist sees himself moving in, there is shining like a bright sun, a supreme god! A scholar from Germany,

Dr. Wilhelm Schmid, compiled all of the instances of monotheistic belief found among the various cultures of mankind. To his amazement it took six volumes totaling 4,500 pages to detail all the examples of monotheistic belief, (belief in one supreme creator) included among these thousands of folk religions from every possible part of the world. So then we, as Christians seeking to fulfill the Great Commission, need to realize that the basic tenets of folk religions are the main religious adherents of humanity.

REACHING FOLK RELIGIONISTS

How are we going to reach Christians who are not truly Christians in heart but only on the surface, having a veneer of Christianity, but underneath still basically holding to folk religion tenets? How are we going to reach Muslims who are in the same situation, and Hindus and Buddhists? Obviously, we have to understand not only the beliefs that go with that veneer but also beliefs of the animistic peoples as they really are deep down. Here are some examples of how an animistic people's monotheistic presuppositions have opened the door for the entrance of the Gospel.

THE SANTAL OF INDIA
"God has not forgotton us after all."

In 1867, a bearded Norwegian missionary named Lars Skrefsrud went to India under the Santal Mission. He found himself in the midst of two and a half million people who called themselves the Santals, and adhered to a folk religion of India. Lars learned the Santal language; soon he began to preach the gospel as best he could, praying, "Oh, Lord, how many years may it take before these Santal people who have never heard the gospel before, who have never had any contact with the beauty of Christian traditions, will even show an interest in the gospel, let alone open their hearts to it?" To his surprise, however, the Santal almost at once manifested interest in the gospel. Soon he heard them exclaiming to one another, as he was preaching, "What this stranger is talking about must mean that Thakur Jiu has not forgotten us after all this time." "Tharku Jiu, who's he?" "Oh, stranger," replied Santal men, "Tharku Jiu is the god you are describing." "Do you mean that you already know about him?" "Why, of course, he's the god that our forefathers used to worship, when we lived long, long ago in a land far to the west of India." "You obviously don't worship him today. What happened?"

"Well", they said, "our forefathers, in one of their ancient migrations, came to a lofty mountain range, and failed to find a pass through. They thought that Tharku Jiu had deserted them, so they called instead upon the spirits of the great mountain, the demons that they believed were blocking their way. They offered sacrifices and promised the spirits that if they allowed them to pass through the mountains they would serve them. Almost immediately they found a pass (it may have been the Khyber pass) and the Santal people broke through into the plains of India where they settled. From that time forward, they saw themselves as remaining subject to the spirits of the great mountains. But through passing centuries, the Santal still remembered the name, Thakur Jiu, the god that their forefathers used to worship. And they used to exclaim wistfully to one another, around their cooking fires, "Oh, if only our forefathers hadn't made that grievous mistake, we might still know Thakur Jiu today and everything would be so much better. He's probably written us off and won't have anything more to do with us." But when the Santal heard this preaching of Lars, hope revived. Using Thakur Jiu as the name for God, which in the Santal language means the genuine spirit, he named Jesus Christ as the son of Thakur Jiu. It sounded awfully strange to his own ears the first time he said it, but after a couple of weeks the strangeness wore off and it sounded just fine. You can be sure it sounded just as strange the first time that someone ever said Jesus Christ was the son of Deus, or the son of Theos, or the Son of God, because these were all originally pagan names.

Before Lars Skrefsrud knew what was happening, he had about 15,000 Santals standing in line waiting to be baptized. He sent out a cry for help, and other missionaries rushed in to help him reap the fast-ripening Santal harvest. Within a few more decades, that increased missionary force had still another 85,000 baptized believers among the Santal people north of Calcutta.

THE KAREN OF BURMA
"Our forefathers lost the book."

Let's go back further to 1828, when a colleague of Adoniram Judson, a man named George Dana Borgman, and his lovely wife Sarah, went to the Karen people in the Panhandle of Southern Burma. They expected it might take many years before the Karen people would show an interest in the gospel. However, Borgman and his wife did not know that the Karen people had a tradition dating far back into antiquity, which said that their forefathers used to walk in fellowship with the true God whom they called Y'wa. (That sounds almost like Yahweh, the Hebrew name for God.) In the distant past, said the Karen tradition, Y'wa, the true God, had given their forefathers a book with His writings, His will, His law. But the forefathers lost the book. And the Karen said, "Ever since, we have been living in this world, wandering through it without the law of God to guide us." But their traditions also claimed that one day Y'wa, the true God, would send a white brother, (not a white master), to restore to them another copy of the book their forefathers lost. When Borgman and his associates walked into Karen villages and opened their Bibles, saying, "Here is a message from the true God," the Karen people were electrified. They came by dozens, then by hundreds, then by thousands, later by tens of thousands, to inquire about this message from a book that was being restored by these white brothers. Within a few decades, the number of Karen believers who were baptized multiplied into many tens of thousands.

That was only the beginning. There was another people, numbering 500 thousand, the Kachin in the northern part of Burma, who also had a tradition of a book from their god that their forefathers had lost. And now probably half of the Kachin people in northern Burma are members of Christian communities.

THE LAHU AND THE WA
"You must be the man we've been expecting."

In the eastern extremity of Burma, two other peoples called the Lahu and the Wa used to wear cords around their wrists so that when people asked them they could answer, "We wear these cords as a symbol of our bondage. We used to know the true God, but we lost contact with him. Our forefathers lost the book that He provided, and ever since we have been wandering in the world without true knowledge of God's law." In the late 1890's, William Marcus Young and his two sons, Howard and Vincent, went among the Lahu people in Burma. In the market place one day as they were preaching, holding their Bibles open, strangely garbed Lahu tribesmen gathered around them, like moths drawn to a lamp, exclaiming, "You must be the men who we've been expecting from time immemorial. Now you must come to our villages." From 1904 to 1936, he never baptized less than 2,000 Lahu per year, and in one year he baptized about 4,500 for a total of 60,000 people who came virtually stampeding into the kingdom of God because of a monotheistic tradition in their own folk religion that had prepared them for the coming of the gospel.

THE MOTILON OF COLOMBIA
"Where is the banana stalk?"

Bruce Olson, a missionary among the Motilon Indians of Colombia, South America was having a rather hard time getting the gospel through the Motilon resistance to new ideas. One day a Motiloni said to him, "Bruce, you say you are trying to bring the message of God to us, but where's the banana stalk?" He said, "What does a banana stalk have to do with me bringing God to you?" The Indian cut a section out of a piece of banana stalk, pointed to layers of white fiber inside and said, "Our forefathers told us that one day, Sama Dajera, the true God will come out from between these layers of fiber." As Bruce Olson looked at the layers of fiber suddenly they began peeling open. He reached into his pack, grabbed his Bible, held it up beside the piece of severed banana plant and began letting the pages flip, one at a time, just the way the layers of fiber were opening. He said to them, "My friends, do you see any resemblance?" They saw. Then a Motiloni man reached out his hands, caressed in utter awe the layers of white fiber inside Bruce Olson's Bible and said, "Bruce, do you know how to let Sama Dajera, the Creator, out from between these layers of fiber?" Bruce said, "That's what I've been trying to do all of the time". They said, "Oh, why didn't you say so?" That Motiloni belief in Sama Dajera, the Creator, the Supreme God, served as an ally to the Gospel, and it reduced Bruce Olson's cross-cultural communication problem among the Motiloni people to a manageable size.

THE INCAS OF PERU
Who is the True God?"

There were a dozen or so Inca rulers who reigned during the length of the Inca Empire. The 9th Inca Emporer, Pachacuti, was a devout sun worshipper. He worshipped Inti. He even refurbished the temple of Inti, in the capital city. But later he came to doubt the credentials of his god. He observed that Inti never did anything as far as he could tell except rise, shine, cross the zenith and set. He said to himself, "Surely if Inti is God, he would do something original once in a while, but he never does." He noticed also that any passing mist could dim the light of Inti. Surely if Inti was God, he reasoned, then nothing could dim his light. And so he tumbled to the realization that he had been worshipping a mere thing as his creator. He was brave enough to ask the inevitable next question. If Inti, the sun, is not truly God, then who is? He recalled a name of a god that the forefathers of the Inca people used to worship called Viracocha, and tradition said that Viracocha was really the creator of everything, including the sun. There was just one altar left, in the upper valley, where people still paid homage to him.

Pachacuti decided to call an assembly of the priests of the sun. In this council, one of the great theological conferences of history, (a pagan equivalent of the Nicene Council if you like), he stood up before the assembled priests and explained why Inti couldn't be god after all. Then he said, "Now you tell me who the true God is," and they all hung their heads in shame, and one by one acknowledged, "The true God is Viracocha." "I, as your king, command that from this time forward you address the sun as kinsman only. Prayer and worship must be directed to Viracocha." Truly that must have been the optimum time in the history of the Inca people for the gospel of Jesus Christ to come over the horizon. You know of course that it did not come. Instead came the conquistadores rampaging through the Inca Empire, smashing, burning, pillaging, destroying and the Empire went into eclipse. And along with sun worship, (which of course still continued among the common people), the conquistadores destroyed also a monotheistic belief in Viracocha which could have opened the hearts of the entire Inca people to the gospel of Jesus Christ, if only there had been some one on the scene who could have recognized that.

THE KOREANS
"They know more about our god than we do!"

In 1884, the first Protestant missionary arrived in Korea. Soon, other colleagues followed and the study of the Korean language and culture began. Someone discovered that the Korean people already had an amazingly clear concept of one supreme god who was above all other beings. And they called him Hananim, the Great One. The Protestant missionaries decided that the name Hananim did indeed qualify as the equivalent of Yahweh. So they adopted the name. They proclaimed to the Korean people that Hananim, (whose name they knew but almost nothing else) had not been idle over the past many centuries. He had given mankind a written revelation, He had sent His own Son into the world to redeem mankind, including Koreans. Wherever they went, Korean people who were already curious about the name Hananim, were amazed. They said, "Here are people who know more about Hananim even than our king.

Korean people came out of curiosity to learn more about this god, who up till that time had done nothing to involve himself in their lives and in their history. Koreans by the dozens, then by the hundreds, then by the thousands, became Christians, began to study the Word of God, and learned to pray, to worship and to witness. Now, almost a century later, the number of baptized believers has grown from zero to almost 22 percent of the population. Some of the largest churches in the world are in the capital city, Seoul. One church there is believed recently to have passed about 110,000 members, and new churches are being opened in South Korea at the rate of about 10 a day to accommodate the still rising flood of new converts. South Korea, which was basically a nation of folk religionists at the turn of the century, may become the first entire nation in the world to have more than 50 percent of their population enrolled as members of Christian churches by the year 2,000 if the Lord tarries.

VANISHING TRIBES
"Can't we leave them until later?"

Some people say, since the pure tribal peoples number only about 200 million, (a comparatively small part of mankind) perhaps we can leave their evangelization until we have finished bringing the gospel to the hundreds and hundreds of millions of nominal Christians, Muslims, Buddhists, Hindus, and so on. There's one thing that we need to keep in mind. Many of the tribal peoples are being threatened with extinction. Some tribes are rather small in numbers. Some live in forests coveted by lumber companies, or in mountains where prospectors expect to find valuable minerals. Some live in lowlands where farmers want to drive them out so that they may farm the land for their own profit. Every year probably five or six minority tribal peoples are passing into extinction, toppling over the brink. The lights go out. Every last man, woman and child is dead and buried; an entire culture gone forever. And with that culture, the language, the lore of a people vanish, with not a single person left to hear the gospel. For many of these endangered tribal peoples, we are the last generation that can bring them the gospel.

John Heming, in the book Red Gold, states that from 1900 until 1957, 87 entire Indian tribes vanished completely from the face of the earth in Brazil. That's an average of one and a half per year in just one nation. D. C. Bates, in "The Passing of the Aborigines", tells of the extinction of entire Aboriginal tribes in Tasmania and Australia. If you know of endangered minority tribal groups in your part of the world, please do not think you can wait for another generation to evangelize them. They may not be there!

May God bear home upon the hearts of every one of us, a sense of the need of the world's tribal peoples who often are illiterate and cannot read literature distributed in mass distribution campaigns. Nor can they listen to radios, because radios do not broadcast in their tribal languages. They have to have missionaries who will go in on the ground, live among them, learn their languages, understand their culture, ferret out the monotheistic beliefs that may still remain among their traditions, and then build upon that monotheistic base the communication of the gospel of Jesus Christ as a revelation from that God of whom they already know.

REACHING NORTH AMERICAN INDIANS - Black Buffalo

My name is Black Buffalo. This is a real name. I am a Cowlitz Indian from the State of Washington. My brother is currently chief of the tribe. You have probably read and know more about Cowlitz than you realize. For if you have been reading about Mt. St. Helens in Washington State, that is our mountain. That is our land, or rather it was our mountain, it belonged to our people first. A man came to our school when I was in the first grade. He shared Jesus Christ with us. As he talked to us from Romans, I learned that no one could take the love of God from me. Not even death. (I had watched a friend of mine die not too long before that.) I asked Jesus Christ to come into my life and live in me; He has never left me. That was a very real day in my life. From there on, many things happened in my life. But it wasn't until after I had grown up and went back home to minister to our people that I finally realized that many of our old people had sat in church for Sunday after Sunday, year after year, and had never heard that Jesus loved them. It wasn't because the minister or the missionary did not preach it. It was because he preached it in a language that they did not understand. You see many of our Indians in America still speak our own language. There are still 150 of these languages today. And it was then that I determined to take the gospel to my own people in their language. We began working with Gospel Recordings. (I'm not a part, officially, of Gospel Recordings, but I encourage you to read about them.) There are more languages under the roof of Gospel Recordings than any other building, I believe, in the world. And it's all the gospel message of Jesus Christ. And from there on, we have begun reaching, from our own people, out into other tribes, and God has blessed in many ways.

Rather than go back into the animistic teachings of some of the old polluted religions, I would like to verify one of the things that Don Richardson said tonight, - that if we look, we can find parallels to present Jesus Christ. One of the sad things in the history of America has been that the missionaries came, not trying necessarily to make Christians out of our Indians, but to make American-cultured

Christians out of our Indians. I am glad the missionaries came, but sad to say, most of them came without trying to find out what our Indian people believe. Perhaps what I share with you tonight will help you in the various parts of the world where you are working or where you go to work, in the ministry of Jesus Christ. I never say anything against our old Indian religion. When I go into a particular tribe, if there has been anything written, anything recorded, I study as much as I can. If there is not, then I sit down with the oldtimers of that tribe and try to find out as much as I can about their ways. Among our own people of the Northwest, I would like to share just a couple of things with you.

I had gone into one of our longhouses, - that's one of the worship places for the old Indian way. It's also a meetinghouse. Many years ago, our people lived in the longhouses. The cooking and ceremonial area would be in the center with families living on the sides, in a communal-type situation. I came into this particular longhouse in British Columbia, for the first Christian meeting to be held there. The tribal chiefs wanted an Indian evangelist. As I was standing in that longhouse, I looked on one side and there was a giant thunderbird and on the other side, a very large butterfly - symbols. Totem poles were holding up the corners of that great longhouse, a beautiful place. I stood there praying, "God, how am I going to be able to relate to the people." I sang a song in their language, which is the trade language for that whole north area, and I knew the old-timers would understand it. I sang, "Are you washed in the blood of the Lamb?" But it comes out a little different in the Indian. It says, "Has your bad been made good by the good heart of Jesus." I kind of like that way anyhow.

Then I related to the butterfly as I looked at it. We were always told that if we lived good in this life, in our next life it would be beautiful like the butterfly, in the place that is called the Indian Heaven. I used to say, when we go to the old men and say to the old men, "How do we know what is good?" "Oh," the old men would say, "you just do what I tell you to do and everything will be all right." And so, we would go to the old lady and say, "How do we know what is good?" And she would say, "Don't listen to that old man. You just do what I tell you to do and everything will be all right." Well, needless to say, it left us confused, but I want to tell you that I was able to stand there in that longhouse and say, "Now I can tell you how you can know that everything will be all right, how you can know that you will have everlasting life; that when you die, you shall rise again." Then I looked at the Thunderbird, and I said, "In most of our Indian tribes of North America and clear down into the Indians of Panama, you'll see the design of the Thunderbird. And among most of them, the Thunderbird literally means, the sacred or holy bearer of happiness. They use the bird, not in a worship sense, but in a relationship. It was like the eagle, soared the highest of all the birds. The thunder and the lightning was like the voice and the eyes of God seeing us. We're reminded that He was always there. Our word for God was Saghalee Tyee. He was always there. But one day, Saghalee Tyee would send to us the sacred bearer of happiness, and there would be peace upon this earth forever." And I said, "I can show you who He is. I remember the day I used to ask who He was, what was His name. No one knew. But today I can tell you who the sacred bearer of happiness is; that is Jesus Christ our Lord and our Savior, who one day is going to come in the same manner as He went away. And He offers to you and to me a relationship with Him that means that we will be part of His family that can live forever and ever." And in the next few moments as I stood there and said, "Who would like to know Jesus, the Son of God, the sacred bearer of happiness," over 80 people, beginning with the old chief Jimmy Seaward and his wife, came forward to accept Christ on that day.

On the northwest coast of the United States, a number of years ago, one missionary after another had come to a particular tribe of Indians, up the peninsula from Olympia and tried to share Jesus Christ, but the old chief would not let them come on the reservation. He said, "That's the white man's religion and the white man has brought us disease, mistrust, alcohol, jails. We want no part of that." One missionary after another tried to share the message of Jesus Christ, and the chief would have them removed from the reservation. (A reservation is the Indian land that has been granted through treaty rights.)

One day a man came. He said to the old chief, "I want to tell you a story." Indians like stories. The old chief said, "What is the story?" The man said, "It is a story about Saghalee Tyee." Saghalee Tyee in our language literally means, "The God over all." And I like that one, too. The old chief looked at him and said, "Saghalee Tyee I know. I know all the stories, I teach the children. Never heard that Saghalee Tyee had a Son. Maybe He could have a Son, tell me." This man in his wisdom began with the Creation. Almost all of our Indian beliefs tell that the God of the sky, God overall, the one God, came down to earth and took from the earth and made man and that's why we call the earth, Mother Earth. That's why the Indians do not believe in cutting the forest, because they said, "Who has the right to cut our mother's hair?" This man told about God taking from the earth and making man, and the chief said, "Ah, I know." Then he moved quickly on into the flood, and how that God who had made man, had watched men do so much badness, decided to get rid of them, brought the flood, but said He would never do it again after saving the one. And the old chief said, "Ah I know." Almost all the old Indian religions have a story of the flood. Then the man went on through and finally came to God looking once more and seeing that man was living bad, had done so many things wrong. God in His heart must have said, "How can I talk to them?" Then he said, "I know, I will send my Son. He will talk to them and show them the things I want them to know." His Son came as a baby, and grew, and lived among the people and then told them what God wanted them to know. But some people did not like to hear what He said, and so they took Him and they killed Him and they put Him in a cave. And they put a stone over the front of the cave, which was the same way these people buried. But He had said that He would not stay there. They could kill Him but He would not stay dead. He would prove the resurrection, because He would come back to life, and in three days He did so. And He said that whoever believed in Him should not perish but have everlasting life. The old chief looked at that man and said, "I believe, I believe Saghalee Tyee, who made the land, who made the mountains, who made the streams, and all the beauty that is in this world, I believe that Saghalee Tyee could have a Son, but who is He? Tell me His name, so I will know who His son is." This man, looking at the chief, knew that when anyone said the name of Jesus, they were thrown off the reservation. This was the test. As he looked at the chief, he said, "His name is Jesus."

At that moment, tears began to run down the cheeks of the old chief, and he said, "No one ever told me that Jesus was the Son of Saghalee Tyee, and I have kept the Son of Saghalee Tyee from my people. Why didn't anyone ever tell me that Jesus was the Son of Saghalee Tyee?" That man went on to be one of our great Indian preachers, unable to read, yet a tremendous prayer warrior among our Indian people on the northwest coast of Washington State.

ANIMISM - Dr. George M. Cowan

Nature bears a powerful and universal testimony to God's wisdom and power. Animism is natural man's attempt to relate to that revelation, but without the enlightenment of the knowledge of God as revealed in Jesus Christ.

"Since the creation of the world God's individual qualities - His eternal power and divine nature - have been clearly seen, being understood from what has been made, so that men are without excuse, but ... (they) exchanged the glory of the immortal God for images made to look like mortal man and birds and animals and reptiles ... they exchanged the truth of God for a lie, and worshipped and served created things rather than the Creator ... " ROMANS 1:20,23,25

ANIMISM — A DEFINITION

Animism may be broadly defined as the belief that inanimate objects and natural phenomena possess a soul and supernatural power. Animism is MORE than worship of the created but falls short of TRUE worship of the creator.

ANIMISTS - AN EXAMPLE

I lived and worked among the Mazatecos of Mexico over 20 years during which time we recorded and translated hours of the shaman's chants and rituals. They worship the sun and moon as their forefathers did who built the pyramids to the sun and moon. They invoke spirits of 53 sacred rocks, rivers and plants. They use hallucinogenic mushrooms to divine and establish communication with the spirit world. They consider themselves Catholics but in major crises they go to the shaman, and may even hire him instead of the priest to pray to Catholic saints. The shamans in turn have added elements of Catholic ritual to their chanting.

ANIMISM IS A WAY OF LIFE

For many adherents of the so-called world religions, faith consists of a set of doctrines and rituals without much relationship to moral conduct. But for the animist, every aspect of life is dominated by the spirits. Some anthropologists have spoken of religion as a glue that holds all elements of a society together, in a more-or-less unified world view. For the animist this glue is of a definitely spiritual character. The Australian aborigines considered the outsiders, even the missionaries, unspiritual as compared to themselves. The outsider paid attention to his God only one day a week and sharply distinguished between religious and secular activities. For the aborigine, every activity had spiritual implications and obligations. The words of Paul to the Athenians fit the animists of the world quite well (Acts 17:22ff), "I see that in every way you are very religious." Paul proceeded to present the Saviour who manifested love, overcame the powers of evil and offered eternal life, beginning now, in this present world. What is offered is a new and alternative way of life. It is a life-changing decision the animist must make.

An anthropologist studying the 50,000 Tzeltal people of Mexico added a special supplement to his description to say that 1/4 of the people did not fit it. They were still Tzeltal, spoke Tzeltal, dressed Tzeltal, but unlike other Tzeltal, they now willingly obeyed their own civil authorities when requested to donate time and work to village projects. They no longer drank liquor. As a result they had money to buy clothes and for the first time owned their own domestic animals. Their villages were notably cleaner and more progressive. For every school the government built, they voluntarily built a second, if the government would supply a teacher. They paid their past liquor debts and refused to deal with traders who had exploited them. They had their own churches, were eager to learn to read their own language and Spanish, ran their own health service and were much more open to new farming methods. They had found a new way of life and it had affected all of life and the only explanation he could give was that they were now Christians. While the anthropologist gave no indication he believed the Gospel, as an objective researcher he felt obligated to point out that his description of Tzeltal culture was true of only the other three quarters of the people.

RESPONSIVENESS OF ANIMISTS TO THE GOSPEL

Animist peoples are among the most responsive to the gospel. A high percentage of people movements in recent years have been among animists. For most of them spirits are evil and unpredictable. Life is a bondage of fear and uncertainty, and they see no way out except appeasement of the spirits. If you offer them an alternative - especially one that focuses on a helpful good Spirit - and can demonstrate that He is able to make a difference to THEM in THEIR culture, not just to YOU in YOUR culture, many are interested. The Scriptures document Christ's power to overcome and cast out evil spirits and to set at liberty those who all their lives have been subject to bondage - this is GOOD NEWS indeed. Listen to an actual case of deliverance.

The Deliverance of Gunday

"My thinking WANTS to be crooked," declared Gunday with a trapped-animal look. Her dark eyes were full of hate and terrror. Her husband Ulgi spoke up apologetically: "She's shredded all her clothes and I don't have money to buy more. I have to keep her tied up. If I didn't she'd not only hurt herself but attack others."

Gunday had told Helen Johnston that demons had attacked her several times as a child. This was not uncommon among the Cotabato Manobo people of the Philippines. Ulagi and Gunday lived only 20 yards away from Clay and Helen Johnston. On one occasion when they were away, Gunday had forcibly entered their house, ripped the padlocked door from its hinges and smashed everything. It took seven men to capture and tie her down. The Manobo church leaders gathered around her daily and prayed. She began to improve. But this was not dramatic, so Gunday's parents put pressure on Ulagi to call in the traditional medicine men who administered native medicines and worked over her, but she only became worse. The church elders decided against further personal contact. Clay and Helen could hear when Ulagi tried to bathe her dirty body or comb her matted hair. Gunday would spew out foul language. Her laughter was loud and mirthless. Her condition was horribly depressing to everyone.

"What Can I do?"

Helen's thoughts kept returning to Gunday. "What can I do for her, Lord?" she asked. Suddenly a strong impression came: "Read her the Scriptures." "Just READ to her? What good will THAT do," she thought. "The Word of God is living and powerful... piercing... dividing... soul and spirit ... " But could His Word go directly to the heart of a human being like Gunday? Could it bypass her twisted, tortured mind and speak to her innermost being? With a burst of faith Helen declared, "It can, Lord, it can!"

So armed with the recently translated Gospel of Luke she went over to Gunday's hut. There she sat, alone. "Gunday, would you like me to read you God's Word?" Helen asked. Gunday just nodded her consent.

As Helen read from Luke 4, verse 18 leaped out: "He sent me to proclaim release to the captives... to set at liberty those who are oppressed..." Gunday became restless and inattentive. Disappointed, Helen left. She had expected an instant miracle. But she was able to read twice more with Gunday before she and Clay had to leave. "Gunday, call on Jesus to deliver you," Helen pleaded. Gunday's response was a silent, belligerent stare.

"When Did You Begin to be Healed?"

Four months later the Johnstons returned. The news was good: Gunday was well and telling everyone that Jesus had healed her. Helen asked: "When did you begin to be healed?" "When you began to read God's Word to me." Others filled in the amazing story. Only two days after the Johnstons had left, Gunday began to quiet down. In three days they were able to untie and set her free. God had used His living and powerful Word to deliver her!

RESISTANCE OF ANIMISTS TO INNOVATIONS

Animist societies can also be very resistant. They are often limited in size and close-knit in their relationships and social groupings. The individual is deterred from making an independent decision by group pressure or threats. Where the group as a whole, or its recognised leaders, make decisions, the implications must be thoroughly discussed before a decision is made.

Among the Chamula of Mexico for any member of the group to deviate was to die. Yet some believed. They had to flee for their lives and live elsewhere until their numbers increased and they dared return.

Today there is a strong Chamula church and Christ is a valid option for all the Chamula people. At the public dedication of the Chamula New Testament in January this year 3,000 people were in attendance. Men stood in a line a block long to get a copy. The first edition of 500 copies was sold out that day. A rerun of 2000 more was ordered. Animists will respond as the Spirit of God uses the Word of God in the language of the people.

COMMUNICATING WITH ANIMISTS

How should we communicate with animists? In their own language. To the animist words have power. Language is not something in a book. Most of their languages are still unwritten. It is not a subject to be studied. Animism as such has no formal schools but one learns by living and observing and mimicking the previous generation. Language is like the air we breathe. It makes everything live and function. Objects, activities, relationships, attitudes and values – all are encoded, talked about, made overt and experienced in terms of language. This is true whether the language has been written down or not. It has well been said that "Language is the shrine of a people's soul."

As no other element of culture, language serves as an identifying and a distinguishing factor in determining and reaching the hidden peoples of the world. Those who speak the same language recognize each other as linked together at the deepest levels of life. They also see those who don't speak their language as outsiders, even though living in the same country or village.

Cross-cultural communication must take seriously the language of the people whom we seek to reach. To refuse to learn it, is often to leave them without an opportunity to know Christ. To belittle their language, is to belittle the people who speak it. To strive to learn it, is to declare the people who speak it of worth and to identify with them. Around the Mazatec area is a no-man's land, across which Spanish-speaking Mexicans never used to pass without arms for self-defence against the Mazatecos. I was asked one day by a Mexican why I didn't carry a gun. A Mazatec answered for me. "Oh, he doesn't need a gun. He speaks our language." In the market place, they will charge foreigners exorbitant prices. When they discover we speak their language they will cut the price down to what they charge their own people.

Trade Language

But what about the trade or national language we already know and speak? Can't we reach them in that? Some of them know a little of it? Perhaps - but by no means as well. When did God make learning another language a condition of salvation? To the contrary, when He revealed Himself to the Hebrews He did it in Hebrew; to the Greek-speaking world He revealed Himself in the everyday Greek of the common people. Jesus Christ learned and preached in the Galilean dialect of Western Aramaic, lowly regarded by the Jews of Jerusalem. On the day of Pentecost the Holy Spirit so empowered the disciples that each of the world travellers in Jerusalem heard them speaking in his own language. Jesus Christ spoke to Saul on the road to Damascus - a man fluent in Aramaic, Hebrew, Greek and perhaps Latin. Yet Christ chose to speak to him not in the language of the educated, nor of religious conservatives and Pharisees, nor of the political power whose citizenship he proudly claimed - but in Aramaic, the language he had learned at his mother's knee. And Paul never forgot it. Seventeen years later as he testified before Agrippa he considered it an important element in his conversion. "O King Agrippa, when I heard a voice saying in the Aramaic, Saul, Saul... "

Thus God has gone on record concerning His preference for the use of the mother tongue. Why then do we refuse so often to learn it - or think somehow we can do the job some other way? The history of missions is eloquent that the communication of the Gospel to any people is far more effective in the mother tongue than in any other language. Dr. Kenneth L. Pike has written: "It is a burden for the uneducated to struggle with another tongue. Should we deliberately force them to struggle to learn about Christ in our language simply because it is hard for us to learn their language?" A Cakchiquel Indian of Guatemala responded to a witness to him in Spanish, the national language of his country: "If your God is so great, why does He not speak my language?" God does not become my God until He speaks my language and I can speak to Him in my own language. Otherwise He remains the foreigner's God. So - How are we to communicate with animists? In their mother tongue.

WHAT DO WE COMMUNICATE TO ANIMISTS?

Are we to communicate to animists God's own revelation of Himself as recorded in Scripture, or our summary statements of it, our favorite doctrines selected by us from it, and our own cultural and ecclesiastical form of applying it? Under the guise of church planting we are exporting denominationalism wholesale to many parts of the world. While talking of indigenous churches, we fail in too many instances to give to the church the Scriptures in their own languages, leaving them dependent on foreign training in foreign languages, dominated by foreign teachers and theologies.

We have made disciples too much in our own image and too little in His. Our Lord commanded His disciples to make disciples of all peoples. We are to teach them to obey all things Christ commanded us. Note that He did not say that we are to teach them all the things we obey and ignore the rest. The planted church as well as the planting church is to declare the whole counsel of God. But these things are impossible without the Scriptures in the language of the people. How is the Christian convert in an animist society to live "by every word that proceeds out of the mouth of God" if we, who have it all in our language, do not give it to him in his? And if he doesn't need it, then I don't either. But if I need it, then he does too.

We must pledge ourselves to provide God's Word in vernacular translations until every people has it available in a language they can understand. Otherwise we are not providing for the churches what God and Christ repeatedly emphasized as absolutely essential for the early New Testament Church. And we have left the Holy Spirit without His preferred instrument to do His work in human hearts - the sword of the Spirit, which is the Word of God, with a sharp and penetrating edge in the language of the people. So - what do we communicate to the animist? The whole counsel of God, the Bible.

How Many Have the Bible?

Am I making much about little? Let's look at the facts. On the computer list before you there are listed, by name, 5,103 languages spoken in the world today. Let me ask, Why have so many hidden peoples been bypassed until now? One reason is they speak a different language. But languages can be learned. Training is available. This is no longer, nor was it ever, a valid excuse. And what about the Scriptures? The United Bible Societies tell us that as of December 31, 1979, only 273 languages have whole Bibles, only 472 more have at least a whole Testament, and 940 more have less than a Testament, but at least one book. The rest have nothing at all. The Bible is not a luxury to the church you belong to or to the church you plant. It is the one, indispensable, authoritative foundation upon which Christ said: "I will build my church." We ignore the clear teaching of Christ and the lessons of history if we continue to plant Bibleless churches.

Ralph Winter said this morning: "A vision that is not precise is not a vision that can be obeyed." As research on the world's languages and bypassed peoples has progressed, and the number of known languages has increased, some have seen it as discouraging. In our experience, the more specific the information, the more compelling and obeyable the vision. Forty years ago we thought there were only 500 languages needing Scripture. Then the figure became 1000, then 2000, and now nearer 3000. But God's people have responded and now there are Bible translation organizations in Korea, Nigeria, Philippines, Papua New Guinea, Brazil and increasing numbers of such organizations in the United States.

WHAT IS THE CHURCH AMONG THE ANIMIST PEOPLES LIKE?

Can God raise up a vigorous church that can carry on all the ministries of the church, including evangelizing its own people and sharing in frontier, cross-cultural missionary church planting? Our experience is that He can. If we provide them what they at first can not provide for themselves, the Scriptures, and if we teach them to read and obey the Word of God, to trust God and not be dependent on us.

Let me illustrate. The Tzeltal believers, guided by the Holy Spirit, believed that no one should learn more truth until he was obeying what he already had. So in their Sunday School they remained in the same class week after week, studying the same lesson, until they had memorized it word perfect and were living it - on the testimony of their neighbor! Is it any wonder that this church multiplied. The first rows in the churches were reserved for the people whom they had just won to the Lord. These, they said, needed to hear everything clearly, since they know so little. Those who had won them and knew more of the Christian faith could sit at the back where it was harder to hear, or even outside to listen through the windows. Today there are 18,000 believers in over 500 churches. In one instance recently everyone in a new village but the village president himself accepted Christ and a new church was born. The Tzeltal have been instrumental also in starting a gospel witness and now churches have resulted in 3 or 4 neighboring tribes. The Reformed Church missionaries in the area, providing training for the pastors and leaders, reported last month that the church is growing at a rate of 12% annually.

We do the churches among animists an injustice when we believe and act as though they were incapable of carrying on worship, evangelism, and missionary cross-cultural outreach. We do them no service if we excuse them from any command of Scripture or from claiming every promise of Scripture. But why should they have to do it our way, with all the complexities and excess baggage of centuries? Why can't they do it their own way?

"We Should"

Hwacha, a recent animist convert from the jungles of Peru spoke to his people when they received the Scriptures for the first time in their own Piro language. He read to them the words: "Go into all the world and preach the Gospel to every creature." "Whose language is that in?" "That is our language," they replied. "Who is it speaking to then?" "It is speaking to us." "Is it speaking to the foreign people in our country, the missionaries and traders?" "No. They don't know our language." "Is it speaking to the Spanish-speaking people who run our country?" "No. They don't know our language." "Then who is it speaking to?" "To us, the Piros." "Then who should do what it says, and go?" "We should." And so they organized their own missionary outreach team for the cross-cultural project of reaching adjacent tribes, some of whom had been their enemies.

Among the Navajo of the United States, once they had the New Testament in their language, some of the very ones who had learned how to translate on that project, formed the core of a Navajo team that continued on, with Bible Society and mission personnel as consultants, to finish the entire Old Testament in their own language. Today, where churches have sprung up without the Scriptures available for either pastor or people, we are training some of those very pastors and people to translate into their own language. Believers who are former animists are able to help themselves, given the basic tools and training.

This Missionary-Built People

In the Philippines, among the 80,000 Ifugao, when the linguist-translator began and the first few came to Christ, they asked him when he was going to build a church building like other missionaries they had heard of did. He said he didn't come to build a building, but to give them the Word of God. So he continued on translating and building people instead. Numbers grew and while he was away on furlough, the local group finally outgrew the home they were meeting in, so they built their own church building. Today there are over 400 churches, (groups of believers, not buildings) and over 3000 believers among the Ifugao, worshipping, evangelizing and starting new churches, with the Ifugao Scriptures.

Jesus said: "Upon this rock, (God's revelation concerning His Son as we have the inspired record in the Scriptures today) I will build my church." I believe He will do it among every animist people. God grant that by the year 2000 there will be at least one such church, with all its potential for reaching its own and other peoples, in every animist people group.

6
HIDDEN
PEOPLE
AMONG
MUSLIMS

AN ATTITUDE CHANGE -- Don McCurry

What we would like to achieve tonight, believe it or not, is an attitude change. I think all of us for the last 1400 years have been preconditioned by our heritage, by our history, by the sad story of war between Muslim and Christian nations, and because of that there is in us a subtle, a deep, and almost constant stream of prejudice against Muslim people. I can remember one of my students coming into his church and seeing there at the entrance of the church inside the vestibule a picture of Khomeini. Filled with anger he started to go up to that bulletin board to snatch that picture right off the wall, and then he read these words underneath,"Have you prayed for this man today?", and the truth is that Jesus Christ has asked us to love our enemies, to bless those who curse us and to pray for those who despitefully use us. We may be on our knees sometimes in front of Muslims, and they have the whip hand over us. Jesus was knocked down, remember? Jesus bore a cross, and it's only as we see the love of Christ coming through suffering, and it's only as Muslims see it, that they'll understand what the love of God is all about.

For those of you who are filled with the love of God for Muslims, I apologize for implying that you weren't. For those of you who have yet to really enter into a friendship with Muslim people, I would encourage you to pray that God would give you the opportunity to befriend a Muslim. We have discovered that as soon as you pray, God begins to arrange for things to happen to you that have never happened before. I've invited four men who have been involved in one way or another in contacts with Muslims to share their experiences.

When I visited Dr. Petrus Octavianus in Eastern Java, I heard the story of a man who had spent seven years in obscurity preaching among Muslim people, learning many lessons. And then when I asked questions about his Bible School, I heard some amazing things. And I'd like him to tell you some of them.

MUSLIMS IN INDONESIA - Dr. Petrus Oktavanius

Let us open the word from IIChronicles 7:14. "If my people which are called by my name shall humble themselves and pray and seek my face and turn from their wicked ways, then will I hear from heaven and will forgive their sin and will heal their land." Dear friends in Jesus Christ, after seven years having preached not the gospel but politics, sociology, philosophy, I came to the Lord Jesus Christ in a wonderful, wonderful way on November 20, 1957. At this time I was the principal of the International Teacher's Training College. I was also in politics and we used to stay in big cities. But after two years Miss Joy Ridderhof from Gospel Recordings came to Indonesia. After being converted I started every day preaching the gospel to the students. At the time I had about 2000 students under my supervision. Students from Muslim background turned to Christ and were baptized in several churches.

Joy Ridderhof of Gospel Recordings spoke from John 10:9 "I am the Door, if any man enter in, he will be saved, go in and out and will find pasture." After she spoke to our students, I asked one of our missionaries from WEC, so I'd like to say that I'm influenced by two important missionary socities. One is from Gospel Recordings, Miss Joy Ridderhof, and the second man is that nice gentleman, a WEC missionary, from Germany, and when I talked to him I said: "You know that this is a very important task that I have as a principal of the Teacher's Training College." Then this man said to me, "Brother Octavianus, you need to know the will of God." And after Joy Ridderhof left I resigned from my position as the principal. I had to leave the big city, leave my position, leave politics and I went around the country preaching the gospel in the streets. The first nine years I preached the gospel to the Muslims from market to market, from village to village around Indonesia, 12,500 miles. We moved to a Muslim village, there was no single Christian in this village. There we started our work. The first years in this Muslim village were hard. One time our house was broken, windows were broken into, but the Lord spoke to us to stay, "This is your call, give your life to this nation." The beginning of revival started in 1957. Five people started to pray, two Indonesians, two Indonesian Chinese and one WEC missionary. "If my people humble themselves, and pray, and seek my face, and turn from their wicked ways, then I will hear from heaven and will forgive their sins, and will heal their land."

At the time our country was under the influence of communism and because we started to pray, the Lord added more people to this prayer meeting from day to day. It grew up to 300, 600, 900 people joined together every morning at 5 o'clock to pray. We just started here and there. After 7 years staying in my village, God came in in a wonderful way. On Christmas Day, I invited all the Muslims to attend our Christmas meeting. I told the Muslims to repent, to accept Jesus Christ. I just said, "Come and stand up and receive Jesus Christ". All of them stood up, about 300 people. I said, "Please sit down, you don't understand me, please sit down. I have to make it clear. You who will freely accept Jesus Christ, you have to leave behind you the old allegiance, to become Sons of God, to have fellowship with God."

Now I have no time to talk about how to preach the gospel to the Muslims, because it was the first place that Dr. Mooneyham came to Indonesia, visiting me and we went to the villages.

In 1964, our dear brother, Leslie Brierley (who is sitting here) from WEC mission, London came to Indonesia, and spent three days praying on a mountain, waiting on the Lord. God reached out, "Nothing is impossible with God, come and speak to us to reach the whole nation with the gospel of Jesus Christ," and God came at 1 o'clock at night, and spoke to me, and spoke to him, both of us received Isaiah 45: verses 2 and 3, "I will go before you, make the crooked ways straight, I the God of Israel. I will give you treasures in the darkest places, I the Lord God of Israel." And then the next morning, he went down the mountain with the promise of God: then we started to go to the whole nation of Indonesia. Seven years ago no one was a Christian. We have baptized more than 300 Christians today. All the Muslims around my house have become Christians, and some of them are elders in the church today. Praise God.

———

Now do you believe all things are possible with God? They are, and here's a living testimony of a man who lived it out for you and is doing it. God wants us to be encouraged to believe him for great and mighty things.

———

MUSLIMS IN NIGERIA - Rev. Panya Baba

It was my privilege to meet another brother at a mini-consultation on Muslims in Thailand. He is a very modest man, he was just sitting there and I knew he was attractive and nice looking, but I didn't know what an important person he was, until he was introduced to me and they told me some amazing things about him. Now I'm going to ask Panya Baba to join me———

Don: "What is the name of your church in Nigeria, Panya?"

Panya: It is ECWA, stands for Evangelical Churches of West Africa.

Don: "And does this church have its own missionary society?"

Panya: Yes, it does, it has a missionary arm called EMS,

Evangelical Missionary Society.

Don: "How many missionaries or missionary couples are there in Nigeria going over different parts of Africa."

Panya: We have today 230 missionary couples in the fields.

Don: "Now among those 230, do any of them have a call to work among Muslim people?"

Panya: Most of them work among the Muslims, especially in the northern part of Nigeria, in Niger public, part of Dahomy and Ghana.

Don: "That's fantastic. Do you believe that Muslims are going to come to Jesus?"

Panya: God has power, and His power exceeds any other power in this world. Two years ago we were invited to reach the Hausa speaking Muslims in Acroura, some 70,000 people, and during this past two years, two young Hausa speaking churches have been established.

Don: "Now do you believe all things are possible with God? Among a people who are supposed to be resistant the church is now being established! Pray for these men, key leaders in other parts of the world who are pioneering for the Lord, showing us how, encouraging our hearts. Praise God.

One of the things that people say to us is: "Why don't you try to do in America the things you are telling other people to do all over the world." And so we tried. David Cashin, who is on the staff of the Zwemer Institute took up the hard work of what we call Stage One. Because the love of God was really flowing into our hearts, that love impelled us to go and search for Muslim people where we live. It was hard work. And I want David to tell you what he got involved in, and about the report that came out of it.

STAGE ONE: FINDING OUR MUSLIM FRIENDS - David Cashin

Somtimes we tend to think of researchers as rather obscure people who inhabit the bowels of great institutions of higher learning and who only emerge to show rather un-understandable charts and maps and transparencies. But really I think that every good missionary is in essence a good researcher. Research is not merely statistical delineation of people groups and where they are, but it's seeking to find what are the deeper needs, the heart throb of this community, the point at which the Gospel begins to become relevant. Dr. Max Kershow challenged us almost two years ago to undertake a survey of the Muslims in Southern California, and I suppose when I first started the project I wasn't quite aware how difficult it would be. I owe a lot to Don McCurry for keeping the fires of vision burning at times of discouragement. We went out initially just to run around to the various mosques, and our project was merely finding the people, counting the bodies, if you will. That was startling enough in itself! We took a look at Los Angeles, a city of 8 million people, with hundreds of different communities.

We wondered where to begin, so we decided just to go through the telephone books, looking for everything that had to do with Islam in its title, or some other Muslim related word. Eventually we were startled to find about 19 different mosques and somewhere around 100,000 Muslims. We found a Black Muslim community that was not only active, but growing. And we were startled to see that Islam was not only present, but it was a very growing phenomenon right there in Los Angeles, behind the backs of the Christians. Christians living right next door to a mosque, who wouldn't know the slightest thing about the people who are right next door.

So we started to see a little bit about Islam, but there was something missing. It was the personal factor. I had many Muslims give me their testimony about how they'd become Muslims, but there was still a little bit of uneasiness. Who was this American who bopped in with his beat up old Buick, and comes walking around asking us all these questions. There was suspicion - the role identification wasn't proper, and that's when my frustrations began. But the Lord knew my need, and so he raised up two people in particular who were to play a very significant role in the more in-depth information gathering of that survey.

One of those fellows was Dr. Mohammed Mobin Khan. Mobin was a great encouragement to me when he heard of my struggle. He pulled out his Muslim clothes and said, "Let's go down to the mosque. And he put them on and went running into the mosque," and he was just completely at home, relaxed, and the Muslims were immediately at ease. And I well remember the day when we went into the black Muslim Mosque, where one of the fellows commented "If you'd come in here 5 years before, we would have killed you." They took us to the back of the mosque, and there we met a fellow from Ghana, who was a missionary leading blacks into Islam, and helping those who had become muslims to understand their faith more deeply. This man opened his heart to the whole breadth and depth of that Muslim community, their needs their struggles, their victories. And the vision within our hearts began to burn. And I well remember Mobin saying again and again, "This is a shame for you. This is a shame for you." But he was so burdened himself to see that the Muslim community was growing up and no one was doing anything about it.

Eventually this survey was produced. But I owe it to another Muslim who had become a Christian to give me the vision that Muslims can become Christians. This fellow was an Iranian who had met Christ about 8 years ago. And with two other Iranians and a few Americans, my wife, and myself, he began a Muslim fellowship for converted Iranians. In about a year 6 different Muslims found Christ and got baptized. We began to realize that not only is there a Muslim community in Los Angeles, not only can we discover its needs, but if we witness to this community, share the love of Christ with them, if we really open our homes in a manner that's appropriate to them, without all kinds of designs in the back of our minds, but just desiring to share the love of Christ, God can break through, and yes, indeed, Muslims CAN get saved. And we thank God for that truth.

Stage two is finding our Christian friends. That is, those that can help us minister now to all of these Muslims that we uncover. Paul Ford has been recruited to help us locate churches and parachurch organizations that existed around mosques. He has been working with us now for a few months, and has visited somewhere in the vicinity of 80 to 85 churches. Paul, share your impressions of what you've been finding in these churches, and some of the things that we're trying to do to bring attitude change and commitment to the unfinished task of bringing the love of God to Muslims.

STAGE TWO: FINDING OUR CHRISTIAN FRIENDS - Paul Ford

Before I do that, I would like to make several comments on what has already been said. I was in Regents Park Mosque this past weekend, on the way to Edinburgh, there met a Western Muslim from Kansas - the middle part of the United States, who said outright "If you fight the Muslims, we will grow, like you have never seen." Perhaps we need to humble ourselves. For I believe that what Muslims most want to see is whether or not they are really loved by Christians. Secondly, Dave mentioned that there were 19 mosques when he did the survey in Los Angeles. Now there are 21. Two new mosques in Los Angeles since February of this year. There's growth in North America Islam. But, on the positive side, could it be that God has indeed given Christians an unbelievable opportunity and the open door to reach Muslims from closed countries? In Los Angeles I believe He has.

Think of it this way. Each one of us here represents many many people from back home. So it is with these Muslim students and immigrants in Los Angeles who do have and will continue to have contacts back in their home country. Many are average everday Muslims. But many potential future leaders from their own countries are there. We have come to Edinburgh to catch a fresh vision to take home to share with our brothers and sisters. So can we also pray that many Muslims in Los Angeles and elsewhere will catch the vision of Jesus as Lord and Savior. And then take that home with them in their hearts to be shared. We have a fantastic opportunity.

We have three premises from which we have developed our plan of action. The first is this. We have confidence that God has already placed a foundation of witnesses to the Gospel in strong churches as well as in many campus fellowships, throughout the Los Angeles area. Our second premise is this: That the spirit of God is already out ahead touching the hearts of many Christians to be open to love, to reach out, to meet Muslims right where they are. And thirdly, and very important, Muslims in Los Angeles need and want American friends. A poll was taken at a university in the Los Angeles area of students, (mostly international.) Half of them were Muslims. Guess what they desire most during their time in America? An American friend. They would like to find an American who would really care for them. What an opportunity!

What are we seeking to do to motivate Christians to reach out to these Muslims? I set up meetings with pastoral staffs, missions committees, campus ministers, and so on. We talk about three basic things.

First of all the basic facts about Muslims. Mulsims seem to be coming to Jesus Christ in unprecedented numbers. My two brothers have already shared that. Also did you know that there are more Christian workers among 400,000 people in Alaska than there are Christian workers in all of 750 to 800 million Muslims in the world. A rather important fact. Secondly we talk about the needs right in Los Angeles. And mainly what I do there is simply share the Los Angeles Muslim survey. It speaks very well for itself, as Dave has already shared. This of course is most effective with people who live where there are large numbers of Muslims. Thirdly comes the response The most important part, the most challenging part. Sometimes the process ends with education, with the facts right after step two. And that's O.K. because we need to know the facts so that indeed the Holy Spirit can convict us more deeply by those facts of the great need. But more often though, there has been dialogue on how can we then reach out to Muslims. In many ways I have been encouraged by the number of Christians in Los Angeles excited about reaching out to Muslims.

We had some very exciting specific results in fact. Between 80-85, churches, have gotten a vision for reaching out to Muslims as individuals. There is a pastor here tonight who can tell you the joy that a Christian couple within his church body has found by opening their home to the Muslim who is living with them. Really loving sometimes costs a great deal. They are finding great fruit. Most exciting to me is that nine churches have already decided to begin reaching out ot Muslims. I say exciting, because I believe that many of those church folk are aware of the cost involved. There is a great cost. There is time. (It is very hard for Americans spend time building personal relationships) And lastly, within several church bodies, or because of several of these task forces, Muslims have indeed come to Jesus Christ. So our work has not been in vain, but I must say again in closing, PRAY. Think of it this way, if we don't reach Muslims in our own backyard, how will we be able to reach them in closed countries. PRAY. We have an unbelievable opportunity.

HIDDEN PEOPLE AMONG MUSLIMS

LOVE MUSLIMS! — Don McCurry

One day when I was traveling from Rawalpindi to Lahore I asked if God would allow me to share my faith with some Muslim beside me on a train. I was on a reservation-only train, and people were trying to get the empty seat beside me, making all kinds of offers to the conductor. And we pulled out of Rawalpindi station and that seat remained empty. And I wondered what in the world I had done wrong that God was not letting any Muslim friend sit beside me. Well at the next station I found out. A high government official, a young man sat down beside me. And sure enough we began talking about the things of Jesus Christ. And as we talked, I sensed a softness in him that I had not often found in initial conversation with Muslim people. "Nasim, you seem to have heard something or have been touched by Christians or the love of God somewhere before. Would you mind telling me about it?" He told me the following story:

> "One day my friend and I were walking in a summer resort town high in the Himalayan mountains. It was at the peak of the tourist season, and the streets were very crowded. Along the side two Catholic sisters were collecting funds for the building program. Both my friend and I felt contempt for these Christian nuns, and my friend in order to show contempt leaned over and spat in the outstretched hands of one of those girls. Very quickly she reached into her sleeve and pulled out a handkerchief, and wiped the spittle off of her hand, and extended her hand again, and looked right in the eye of my friend and said, 'OK that was for me, now what are you going to do for Jesus Christ.'"

I turned to look at Nasim, and tears were streaming down his cheeks. And I said "Nasim you know that you are not very far from the Kingdom" and he said "Yes, I know." I tell you this story tonight to encourage you to be willing to make that second effort if you feel rebuffed. For often it is that gesture of love against all efforts of rejection that break the heart of a person who has been fighting against God.

7
HIDDEN PEOPLE AMONG HINDUS

THE HINDU WORLD - Rev. N.J. Gnaniah

Hindu people love stories and I would like to tell you a story, a very sharp study which we read in one of the great Hindu epics. There were five princes and they were taught to shoot arrows. After the training was over, Dronah, the teacher, wanted to test his students. So he took the five students into the jungles, and called them one by one. The first one came and he said: "Aim at the hidden bird in that tree." And the teacher asked the student, "What do you see?" He said, "Sir I see a bird." "What else do you see?" "Oh, sir, I am seeing some nice flowers in the tree." "What else?" He was telling so many things. So the teacher said: "You are not a good student. You were not aiming so go away." Then the other students came one by one. All were telling, "I see this thing, that thing, this thing, that thing," apart from that hidden bird. And finally the great archer came, and the teacher asked, "What do you see." "I see a bird, a hidden bird, and I am aiming at it." "What else do you see." "Teacher, I do not seeing anything else except that bird." "You are a good student, you are aiming at only one thing." And we have gathered here in Edinburgh to aim at one thing. If we see so many things, we are not good students.

I come to my topic, the Hidden Peoples among the Hindus. A few weeks back in a seminar a short paper was given entitled "Reaching the Hindus of our Age." I will read a few lines. "As we take a close look at Hinduism, we will find that we cannot really define it. Great men find it difficult to define Hinduism. Somebody has described it as a great river on its way to the sea being fed by its tributaries. It is really true. There are so many small and big divisions inside

Hinduism. The common talk in our country about the number of gods and goddesses in Hinduism tell that there are 340 million of them." I think it is a point to note in this consultation. The number may not be correct. It does denote that there are so many different people groups worshipping different gods of Hinduism. The COWE consultation in Thailand this year had a mini consultation on Hindus. That group classified the Hindus in the following 7 categories - religious Hindus, popular Hindus, mystic Hindus, tribal Hindus, secular Hindus, philosophic Hindus and also Hindus of the sects.

Where are the Hindu people living? They live mainly in India, but also in nearly more than 25 countries. 600 million Hindu people making the 13% of the total population of the world, need our attention this evening, I would like to read the countries, 27 of them, starting with India, Nepal, Bangladesh, Sri Lanka, Pakistan, Burma, Bhutan, Afghanistan, Indonesia, Malaysia, Fiji Islands, Singapore, Hong Kong, Arabian Gulf countries, Mauritius, Kenya, Tanzania, South Africa, Zambia, Rhodesia, Great Britain, Holland, Guyana, Trinidad and Tobaga, Surinam, United States, and Canada.

As the majority of the Hindu people live in India, it is natural to talk more about India. Before doing so, I want to give some time for the other countries where the Hindu people live. We are privileged to have two people who are living outside India but working among the Hindu people. Dr. Chris Thomas will share a few things about the Hindus in Singapore and also about many, many lands. He is the Secretary of the Fellowship of the Southern Asian Christians. So he is the right man to tell where the Hindus are living and what type of work is going.

HINDUS IN SINGAPORE - Dr. Chris Thomas

God called me 23 years ago to go to Singapore and I left for India. saw many, many Indians there, but I could not reach any of them. I went to work among the Chinese in Singapore. And within a year, I baptized more than 55 Chinese, those who come from Buddhism or Confucianism, or some other religion. But I baptized only one Indian. So Indians were very hard to be reached in a foreign country. The people always labeled them as unresponsive people. So I did not reach them. I prayed for them many times. I cried unto the Lord. And then when I went around the world, the Hindus came to listen to me. I was in Guyana; hundreds of Hindus came up to that meeting because an Indian came from India, not because I was preaching Christianity or Christ. Trinidad, Jamaica and Canada, U.S., United Kingdom, and many parts of the world, wherever I went, many Hindus came to listen to the Word of God. And then I felt that I'm leaving Malaysia and Singapore but I want to reach these Hindus with the gospel, so I went back with a special program to reach the Hindus. Those were supposed to be unresponsive people. But I felt that they needed to hear the gospel because nobody preached to them. There was only a handful of Roman Catholic churches among the 2,000 large rubber estates which each has 500 or 600 people. In the last five years, more people have accepted Christ among the Hindus in Malaysia than in the last hundred years. And there are more than 35 new churches planted, and in a six months' campaign, we baptized 463 adults, 98% of them from Hindu families.

So then I found there are more than 20 million Hindus who live outside of India. But these people need to be reached with the gospel of Christ. These Hindus are not all laborers like Malaysians or those of Guyana. Some of them are well educated, in universities. Many are engineers, doctors and professional men. The high caste Hindus, Brahmans, vegetarians, live a very righteous life, and they criticize the so-called Christian people because they live a very loose life. So we felt that we need to reach these people for Christ, all over the world. And we had a Congress, The Overseas Indian Congress on Evangelism in Singapore just before the COWE Congress. There were 16 countries represented and we didn't pay for their fare. Every one of them paid for their own. Many of them are professionals, and many of them are working among this people of South Africa and African countries, U.K. and Europe, and Canada, United States, and in Guyana and Caribbean. They all felt the great open door to reach the hidden people outside of India, the Hindus.

A testimony was given from a Hindu who was in New York, in Syracuse University. He was sent by the Indian Government to study there on a special assignment. But because one Christian family was interested in him, and adopted him, showed him love, and affection during that time, he found Christ. Not because of preaching, not because of debating about Hinduism and Christianity, but just because they showed Christian love, this man came back to India and he is still a Christian. And I can also tell you many, many stories how God has saved many of His people. And still there are hundreds and thousands of them untouched by the gospel. I pray the Lord will help us to remember these hidden people around the world.

These people took their religion with them and in Malaysia, Singapore. They kill their bodies, they walk through the fire, they poke their bodies with hundreds and hundreds of hoops. I never have seen them in all my life in India where I live. But in Singapore and Malaysia, they make a big show and Indian idolatory is a Hindu religion. They do not believe in religion as such, but they want to show they are Indian. They want to compete with the Buddhists, in a fire-walking ceremony or a Muslim religious ceremony, but in reality they do not have any religion. These are third and fourth generation Hindus, living outside of India, are very, very responsive to the Gospel of Christ. Dear friends, if you find a Hindu, don't close the door to him, please invite him, adopt him, pray for him, shed tears in the presence of God for him, and he may come to know Christ. The Indians have migrated to many, many countries. They live there. They adopt a new country as their own country, but the people are not accepted in their own country. I have seen many, many places, you go to some Christian church which has predominantly other races, they'll say, "Thank you for coming, but don't come back next week." He might be a new Christian, a Hindu, recently accepted Christ, but there's not a church to go to. So I believe that it is a challenge to us. Bring them to Christ, but also give them a place of worship and give them Christian nurture.

Recently, there was a girl who brought a letter from India. She said she was born and raised in Kenya, of a Hindu ancestry, but God had saved her. God has called her as a missionary to go back to India to do missionary work. Isn't that wonderful, isn't that a scriptural thing? God calls people from all over the world. Hindus can be reached, and they can go back to their own country, or any part of the world to reach them.

The Hindus have an old slogan, "Do not go to a town where there's no temple." So wherever they go, they take their idols, images, with them. In New York City, in London and many other big cities, the Hindu temples are there, but they did not bring it immediately, they brought only small images and put a little worship place in their home. Now thousands of dollars have been poured in to build Hindu temples, and the Hare Krishna movement became such a missionary movement, the Hindus living outside became revived in their religion and also many of the rest of the nation have accepted this movement. So dear friends, Hindus who are not reached with the Gospel should be your concern. I pray that these people will be a great resource for evangelism. Pray for these people and accept them in your church, and love them in your family.

Rev. J. Paul will share his experiences in Malaysia. J. Paul is from India, and he is a missionary to the Hindus and also to the Muslims in Malaysia.

HINDUS IN MALAYSIA - REV. J. PAUL

I come from South India, and I was born in a Christian home. My parents used to take me to evangelistic meetings in a jungle area, and speak abut Jesus. Then I went to the Bible college to study about Jesus. As I was doing my third year, one day I was sitting in my hostel, and the gardener of the Bible college began to worship the Sun. That moved my heart. I ran to that man. I yelled, "Sir, what makes you worship the Sun, the creation, instead of the Creator." He told me, "Unless someone tells me, how will I know." That challenged me, I began to cry to God, "Lord, use me." And the Lord began to use me in India itself. After my graduation in 1968, for seven years I was serving the Lord in a Hindu city. I used to spend my time teaching the Bible school as well as preaching the Gospel in various places, conducting Sunday school, and doing personal evangelism, always with tracts. One man came from Singapore to study in my Bible school. I took him house to house; finally he invited me to come to Singapore. We went house to house. God gave us souls, the Lord opened the door to preach on the radio, sing. The principal of Malaysia Talmud

Bible Institute asked me when I could come and help. I said unless God tells me how can I come, I don't want to go. The next time I went to Malaysia I met with an accident. I was about to die but the Lord saved me without any injury on my body. Then when I went to preach in other places, I found that the need was to go to the Indians and the Chinese people. Then the Lord brought me to College in Singapore to do my Master of Divinity. I finished my studies, and I was planning to do my Master of Theology. One day Dr. Thomas came to me and said, "I am not allowed to stay in Malaysia. I feel that you are the right man to come to Malaysia and be in the Bible school to train students who will become teachers, evangelists, and pastors." And I said,"If the Lord wants, I will obey." The Lord made a conviction in my heart, "You have come here many times, why don't you go and become a missionary." I went back to India, I was praying. My wife told me, "The Lord will be taking you to Singapore and Malaysia." And the Lord began to confirm it through words from the Bible, and so forth. Finally I took a decision. I came to Malaysia as a missionary in 1978. I am teaching in a Bible institute in Malaysia. We have over 20 students. Malaysia is a Muslim country. The state religion is Islam. 53% of the people are Malays. They believe in Islam. 34% are Chinese, and the remaining people are Indians. We are more than 1 million people. Out of those one million people, 800,000 are Tamil speaking. They are living in 2,000 estates. And now we are staying in the estate where there are hundreds and thousands of people. We have so many black cobras and other creatures, yet we have Jesus with us. Every weekend I travel to various places to preach the Gospel. I do personal evangelism.

The Lord has given me a burden, and as I was coming here I found a group was praying in London for Malaysia, Africans, English people, Malaysiam Indians, and Chinese. Praise the Lord, and you pray for us, and we are praying for you, because Jesus loves everyone.

I call upon Mr. P. M. Thomas. It is a joy to present him before you. He's a man for missions. He was born in the southmost state, that is Kerala, and he studied in the center of India, in Maharashtra, and now he is in the northmost part, Kashmir. When he wanted to go to Kashmir, people said, "You are from south and you cannot live in that north Himalayan country. It's like Scotland, shivering cold. You will die!" But God is still on the throne, and He helped him to visit us, to share his heart for the Hindu people in Kashmir. Now Mr. Thomas.

HINDUS IN KASHMIR - Mr. P. M. Thomas

I come from the extreme south of India, from a Christian family. I was a schoolteacher, saved in 1944 at the age of 14, and from that time the Lord gave me a burden for missionary work. I remember days and nights when I could not sleep because of the burden for souls. I wanted to go as a missionary, but I did not know how. The more I read the Bible, I found the pattern for missionary works should be the pattern of the prophets and the apostles. I had indication from several foreign organizations and established institutions to join them, but I knew that my call was very definite, the pattern of the prophets and the apostles: trust in the Lord alone, and not wait for any salary. And I did not know how to proceed because north India was far different from my culture and my language. I did not speak their language. I come from a very hot country, South India. We have only 3 seasons in south India, hot, hotter and hottest. So I did not know how to go to the north, especially among the Himalayas. I waited upon the Lord and the Lord gave me the courage that if I believe, He would be faithful. I joined as a teacher because of the doubts I had. I postponed for 7 years, and I remember the Lord told me, very clearly, "I am calling you." Many nights I could not sleep, but I did not have the courage to resign my job. In 1954, I resigned my job, and without knowing anything, with my wife and little baby, I moved to the north. As I was going, I had nothing at all, no promise, no money, no mission, no church, but I knew the Lord was calling me, so I proceeded towards the north and all the way I could see people waiting with food cooked for us and warm clothes for us, and by the time I reached Kashmir, we had enough warm clothes and more than we could carry. On reaching Kashmir, our support was quite uncertain. I did not know how to pass each day. I remember a day when I did not have a glass of milk for my little boy, who was only 7 months old. And a father can starve, but to see a little boy starving is more difficult. I said, "Lord, now things are going to be very serious. Within two hours you must give a glass of milk to my boy before he dies." Within 2 hours, I saw the Lord giving me enough money for a glass of milk. I remember food was uncertain another time and my wife and I prayed. A Hindu neighbor brought cooked food in front of us, and it was a surprise to us. That increased our faith, and the Lord helped us several days, many people were converted over there, and opposition started. Our lives were in danger. Many Hindus were so angry and bitter, and few nights we thought we are going to be burned inside the small mud hut where we were living. But the Lord stood with us. Many prayer groups were formed all over south India, mostly in Kerala, to pray for us and support our work. And many people who were converted through our ministry joined us as missionaries. Today we have 150 missionaries in 3 organizations and over 1,000 converts.

From north, we go to west India.

HINDU WOMEN - Miss. Manjula Shah

I am working with Operation Mobilization in India. I was born in and brought up in Kenya, and then my family moved to India and from there they migrated to England, and I have been working in India ia, based in Bombay. Starting from first of December, we have had a very special program in Maharashtra. This is a very special effort because many different churches in Maharashtra, plus several different organizations, plus O.M., are all coming together to have a main thrust in the land of Maharashtra. We have been doing a lot of groundwork , programming, and spying out the land in the last years. And for the 3 months from 1st December to the end of February, all the O.M. teams, plus a lot of local Marathi people are all coming together to reach every home in Maharashtra. The program is called "Love Maharashtra." Maharashtra means, "Great Nation."

This is a consultation in which a lot has been talked about many different hidden peoples, about reaching Muslims, Hindus, but one thing in which we have failed, is to realize that women may also be called the hidden peoples, especially in Muslim and Hindu lands. When you look at slides of open air meetings, how many times do you see women standing to listen to the gospel? I personally believe that especially in eastern countries, it's only women who can reach the women. In O.M., very often I have gone door to door and found out that the best place to reach a Hindu woman is right inside her home, sometimes even in her kitchen, where I can go and talk to her about the Lord Jesus Christ. Many times, even if the men are educated, maybe know a lot about Jesus Christ, women often know very little or nothing about Christ. Someone was telling a story this morning about the Stewardess who did not know if Jesus Christ was in the plane. Sometimes we go to house and ask, "Do you know anything about Jesus Christ?" Very often the women say, "He doesn't live in this neighborhood. Maybe he lives in the next village." The kind of work that my heart really bids is to train the women in India who would be willing to go and reach the women in their neighborhood. They need to learn the balance between being a Mary and a Martha. Women in India are very hospitable people, and they would do anything to serve you. They would really lay down all that they have before you, even if they come from very poor families. But I feel that the Indian Christian women need to learn to know how to speak and how to witness. Because even though our land is ruled by a woman, there are many women who are still very, very much in the home.

"When I requested Manjula to come and challenge she was so hesitant, because she thought only a few women are here. I hurriedly counted 43 ladies and they will take up your challenge.

Now, we go to the east India, and I am happy to introduce Rev. Lunkim from Manipur. He will be talking about the Hindus, especially in Manipur."

HINDUS IN MANIPUR - Rev. T. Lunkim

The Word of God says that "with God, all things are possible". Impossible things are possible for Him. I was converted at the age of 25 after marriage. I started preaching to my own people because of the urge that came into my heart. Many people became Christians, but to my surprise I was asked not to evangelize. Why? Because I was not literate and I was not officially appointed by the church. I began learning privately without the knowledge of the churches, and so I was able to read the Bible and continue preaching. The churches were divided. I questioned them. They say, "You have no Bible training." "That's why you question me. If that is the case, I'll go to college." I spent 4 years, got my Bachelor of Divinity, came back home. I was forced in a way to translate the whole Bible from Genesis to Revelation. With the help of the Bible Society I finished it in 1971. It was released, and in circulation. A man who has never gone to school is now standing before you as a witness to the Word of God saying, "Impossible things are possible".

I come from Manipur. This Manipur has been forgotten for years and years. We are not really look-alike with our Indian brothers and sisters. But we do not say that we are separate. Two hundred years back, the people were forced to become Hindus by the King of Manipur. So I am representing before you this people numbering about 900,000. They want to revive their old religion and not to continue in Hinduism. What can they do? This people are waiting for the churches to come and evangelize them. If we do not do it, they will go to Communism. Will it not be a shame to all of us? We are on the border of China and Burma, so if that part of India becomes Communist dominated, then this will be a danger to the Government of India. We are really happy that the Government of India gives maximum freedom of religion to that area. We continue preaching. People are willing to hear the Word of God. The non-Christians say, "Do not plan denominations, but make us Christians. We don't want to be divided into churches, but we want just to become Christians." So this is a big burden.

The second group that I would like to tell you about is the plain people in Assam. A big group of people realize that they are not really Hindus, so they want to revive their old religion again. This segment of the people there are fairly receptive right now. If they do not win this big segment of people, at any time, they may join communism and then this whole area will be shaken up again. This small area is now divided into 7 states. We have never been discovered by even the churches in India. This is a very strong area where the churches are working indigenously. We do not depend on foreign churches. We have organized one mission society, and then we depend on our own resources. If you come here, you will discover churches are beautifully built, stone buildings, big buildings are there. And then you will be amazed that there is a church, but in the heart of these churches, you would see the Meitei people, and the Boro people who are nominally Hindu, but they want to get out of it. Which way will they go? To Communism or to Hinduism, or to Christ?

REACHING HINDUS: THE CHALLENGE - Rev. Gnaniah

There are 3,000 people groups in India. And out of them only 22 have feasible Christian populations, and 50 more have tiny congregations here and there. This being the case, the remaining case in India will be to establish churches in more than 2,900 people groups. The Holy Spirit is moving in India, and I could see it in my own experience of church-planting for the past 5 years. Nearly 75 missionary agencies, Indians, indigenous, are working in India. The Lord is working among the people groups, in the State of Gujarat. People movements are taking place among the peoples called Bihl. In the State of Andra Pradesh, so many conversions are taking place among the high caste Hindus. Though persecution is going on in one side of Aranachal Pradesh, conversions are taking place on the other side. Many people groups are becoming responsive or receptive to the gospel. I come from South India. In our state lives a particular people group who have travelled all the way from Gujarat, 1000 miles away, and have settled in big numbers in my state. And nearly 450,000 people are living there. Recently, they showed a responsiveness to the gospel. Now there are many earnest seekers in the community, and last month I had the joy of baptizing the first convert of our Indian Church Growth Mission. I could give more reports about the receptive people groups, but there is no time. One thing is sure that God is at work, and many people groups are ready for the harvest.

In Acts 16:8-10. "So they passed by Mysia and went down to Troas. During the night Paul had a vision of a man of Macedonia standing and begging him, 'Come over to Macedonia and help us.' After Paul had seen the vision, we got ready to leave at once for Macedonia, concluding that God had called us to preach the gospel to them." I stand here as a representative for the Hindu world to call for help. Just as that man from Macedonia begged Paul, I do want to beg all of you here to help Macedonia. I stand here asking for the Hindu world. Those who have ears let them hear what the Holy Spirit wants to tell them. Here is the challenge to the mission leaders. Will you consider the hidden people among the Hindus for your mission? Will you pray, plan to send missionaries to the needed 2,900 people groups in nearly 27 countries? Let God speak to you. Will you take some partnership with some Indian missions here, which are doing the work and could very easily expand its borders if it gets help. Let the Holy Spirit guide us all in this consultation in the days to come.

Secondly, the challenge to the students. Will you consider going to India or to some other country where the Hindu people live? How I wish and pray that more missionaries should come to plant churches from the student consultation groups here. I will not forget that evening I was standing in front of a tomb in a small town. That tomb belonged to the missionary called Ragland. Ragland came from England. He was a professor of mathematics in Oxford, but came to my country, leaving his big position, and lived as a bachelor boy, preaching the gospel in many different villages with difficulties, without proper facilities. He died there, a missionary pioneer. Now because of his work, so many Christians have come. Is there a Ragland here, who will say I will go to India, to the Hindu people? May the Lord guide the young people here. The Macedonian call comes to you, personally. Will you obey the Lord?

HIDDEN PEOPLE AMONG HINDUS

Thirdly, to the Scotland Christians the challenge comes. I stand here in Edinburgh, in this historic consultation as a product of missions. I am not a Hindu convert, but my father was. Missionaries from Scotland, from England, from United States of America, came to my country and did their work. And the work that has to be done in India is great. As the product of their work, we stand here now to speak about missions and also about our need. The work which we do needs partnership. Will the Christians of Scotland once again get the missionary vision, and also especially for the Hindu people?

Someone said this afternoon to me, From next week to the year 2,000, we have 1,000 weeks exactly, and we have 2,900 peoples. So we need 3 churches every week for the Hindu people. Amy Carmichael, the great lady missionary, who came from this land to south India, had a dream, and in that dream, she was seeing some blind people going, falling down into great pits. They were blind. At the same time, some people near them were playing and singing, and when the blind people were falling into the pit, they shouted, "Oh, I die, Oh, I die." So many Hindu people are dying. Do we see them? The Hindu world calls for action.

8
HIDDEN
PEOPLE
AMONG
CHINESE

Introduction by Dr. Danny Yu

Tonight we look into two hidden people groups out of the many Chinese people groups. One group is a Hakka people. Dr. David Liao wrote a book about them entitled: "The Unresponsive - Resistant or Neglected?" We have a Hakka with us, and we would like to have him to share with us about reaching this, one of the most difficult to reach, people groups in Taiwan. Rev. John Hsieh is the Taiwan director of Asia Evangelical Mission, and will speak in Taiwanese, translated by Rev. Chuck Sanders.

HAKKA PEOPLES - By John Hsieh

I'm very happy that so many of you are concerned about my people. This is from the Lord. My people all over the world have a desperate need to hear the Gospel of Jesus Christ.

Recently in Taiwan we had a big evangelistic outreach. Every place received gospel tracts. We praise the Lord that this was completed. We reached out to the Hakka people in an area. Those people have a desperate need to be emphasized and to be worked amongst. The Hakka people have customs and feelings that are a lot different than the normal Chinese. They are very, very conservative. And they respect their ancestors much more than all other Chinese. They need somehow to relate to these ancestors and we need to find a Christian way of relating to ancestors to help the people to come to the Lord. If we are going to reach these people, we need to have more people understanding them and cooperating in reaching out to them. Their thinking is very good. They will believe in the Lord.

They will not change, they will always have this thinking. Amongst the plain people, there are Taiwanese and Hakka people mixed together, and we labor to reach them in the area where we are. I ask you to pray for the Chinese, and especially the people that need to be touched, the Hakka, who are resistant or possibly neglected. We would ask you to come and help in reaching Hakka. —————————————— Next we move our perspective to the Chinese in Mainland China. Mrs. Leona Choy will share with us one of her burdens: a people group in China, the intellectuals, especially those who are under 30. Leona is the editor for Ambassadors for Christ. She is a popular writer on China issues, and has written a book for tourists going to China. She has a special burden and vision for special ministries to peoples in China.

YOUNG PEOPLE IN MAINLAND CHINA - by Leona Choy

We have made four trips into China during the last 12 months. Three I made as a foreign tourist, on an American passport into different directions in China. On the 4th trip, I went in as a Chinese with my husband. Not everybody can change their identity in this way, but I have done so legally. The Chinese people, one billion of them, have been a hidden people for much or all of your lifetime. And the hidden people for whom we are especially burdened are the 600 million youth. They have been hiding behind a flag, a political idol. But that which we thought was impossible, the removing of the great stone of Maoism, has happened. According to Daniel 2:20, God changes the times and the seasons in answer to your prayers. Through these decades of an impossible situation in China, God has changed the times and the seasons.

Even now, China is still in the throes of de-deifying Chairman Mao, and saying, "You have no more a great redeemer. In fact you never had a savior." Suddenly, instead of a waving fist, and a push for Marxist ideology, we find a smile and a welcome among a disillusioned 600 million youth under the age of 30. Idols are being removed from their pedestals, and off of the posters. We find nobody reading the little red book. I had a hard time to find a souvenir copy in China, in all of those trips. They don't want us to learn their language. In fact, we are accosted on the street by their wanting to learn English. "Please may I practice a little English with you." So the impossible has become possible. The 600 million youth under the age of 30 now have the possibility of close encounters of the spiritual kind.

The Service Entrance

We may enter China today, but not in traditional missionary approach. God is very creative. He has given us many other possible approaches. Many times when we can't enter a front door of a building, we find a little placard along the side, "Deliveries by the service entrance." So the Lord has given us a beautiful opportunity as tentmakers today. We may go in at the service entrance, and what better entrance, as ambassadors of Christ, entering with the humility of a servant. We may go in as technicrafts, as teachers of English or other areas of expertise, as tradesmen, business people, and we can go in as tourists, which is one of the areas that we have been developing for Christians. Actually there have been 2 million tourists to enter China in the first half of 1980. 200,000 of them have been foreign tourists, among them many, many Christians. So there is an opportunity for us to touch China today. We must be very, very careful to go in the mind and humility of Christ, touching the people carefully, in discernment, as Jesus Christ would have us. We have the opportunity to form personal bridge relationships, friendships with the people in China, who warmly and eagerly welcome our help. They don't welcome our political system, they don't welcome our religion at this point, but they are open to the outside world.

Worshipping with Christians in China.

On the fourth trip into China with my husband, I had a Chinese visa, and we were able to go into areas looking for the family of God, the household of faith. My husband was born in China, left as a youth, grew up in Hong Kong, with his seminary and higher education in the United States. He is exploring the possibilities of penetrating China even as an overseas Chinese Christian. We went into China for a month with Mao jackets and baggy trousers, identifying with the people as we could, looking for the Body of Christ, asking the question, "Christians, are you still there?" Was the missionary mandate that was carried out for 150 years of missionary work a success, or did the seed die after all? It was a marvelous, life-transforming time as far as my own viewpoint is concerned. We found the people of God, not only in one area, but on a wide base throughout China. One group of Christians led to another. We visited the house churches on a very broad level. We worshipped with Christians, and I'll never be the same.

They were Praying for Us!

Brothers and sisters, the church was there! In fact, while we were asking, "Did the church in China make it," they were praying for us, and asking, "Did the church outside make it?" This was their one concern for us. When the seed was planted by the missionaries through all of those years, of course the seed grew. It doesn't have to have the presence of missionaries. After the farmers sow the seed, we don't see them. They have done what they ought to do. And then God does His thing. He sends the sun and the rain, and the seasons. We don't plant missionaries, and we don't clone ourselves as emissaries of the gospel. We plant a seed outside of ourself and that seed reproduces in the power of the Holy Spirit. We found the church of China all over, and the joy and spiritual emotion of seeing that God was faithful. Through persecution and adversity, His church stood. And not only stood, but 70 to 80% of these thousands of believers worshipping in the house churches, were youth Chairman Mao's revolutionary youth, disillusioned with all the promises of the system and seeking something, someone, and turning to Jesus Christ. Not through mass evangelism, not through structured churches with all the things that we consider so essential for the propagation of the gospel, but person-to-person witness. The church grew under persecution.

They Have Never Met a Missionary!

There was one question that my friends asked when we came out of China: "Did the brothers and sisters in the house churches ask how soon the missionaries will come back?" They never thought of asking us that question. Most of them never met a missionary. It was a spontaneous spread of the gospel. These Christians in the house churches actually were evangelizing, witnessing, training, reaching out like any vital, healthy, witnessing church. All of the gifts of the Spirit were evident throughout China in the groups with which we worshipped. Thank God. The church in China now needs a normalization of relations, not political, but with God and with the church outside. I am afraid that perhaps we are obsessed with the doorway. We still are focussing our prayers somehow, "Lord, let us get in and have a piece of the action." Well, perhaps we may have that opportunity. Perhaps God has bigger and better creative plans for the evangelization of China. I would suggest that we pray for the church inside of China, and ask the Lord to loose her from the restrictions in which she is bound, and then by the power of the Holy Spirit she may spread the gospel throughout China. Perhaps the Lord will use Third World Christians to supplement the spread of the gospel in China. Perhaps the Lord will give us the opportunity to have the Chinese Christians come back over that bridge and show us how to live triumphantly in Jesus Christ, under a restricted society.

Brothers and sisters, keep praying for China, in this critical hour, for a normalization of her relations with God and for the normalization of her relations with the total body of Christ outside.

Rev. Thomas Wang is the general secretary of the Chinese Coordination Center of World Evangelism. (CCOWE). He is also a member of the Lausanne Committee, and a member of the WEF Missions Commission. We are very privileged that he can share with us a message deeply burdened in his heart.

CHINESE MINISTRY WORLDWIDE - by Thomas Wang

I have come with boundless appreciation and a deep sense of humility. I was born in China, Peking, 55 years ago. I am a living testimony for the missionary efforts of many nations, many people and many churches. Someone has cared enough to pray, some churches have cared enough to send, and some Christians have cared enough to come, to the ancient land, the Middle Kingdom. My grandmother, who helped in a missionary's home, became a Christian, then my parents, and then myself. I am a convert under the ministry of Dr. John Sung, the greatest evangelist God has given to China. But indirectly I am the fruit of the missionary endeavor in that ancient land. I therefore want to represent the Chinese people and the churches and to give you our deepest gratitude. If it hadn't been for the missionaries who came to us, I may still be an unbeliever. The missionary mandate is valid and the missionary work shall never be in vain, and therefore the missionary work must go on.

Over Forty Centuries Without God!

Chinese people, as a whole, have been without God for over 40 centuries. We have had Confucian teaching for almost 2,000 years, Buddhism from India about 1800 years, Taoism the indigenous religion for about 1700 years, plus a host of other folk religions. We've only had the privilege of the pure gospel of Jesus Christ for a little over 170 years. God has His perfect plans in everything. Paul wanted to bring the gospel to Asia first. He was directed by the Holy Spirit to bring the gospel to the west. And after it circled around the world, almost 2000 years later, it came back to the East. God chose the western people first to be the carriers of the gospel in the past centuries.

After years of growth and persecution, many Chinese Christians paid the price with their lives for their faith, especially in the recent 30 years. My pastor in Peking, Mr. Wang Ming-tao, has been in prison for 23 years, and was released in January. I had the privilege of visiting him in Shanghai in April. In spite of his long years of imprisonment, he was very strong in his faith. He had been brainwashed twice. I said to him, "Pastor Wang, are you willing for me to try to petition for you to come out of China for medical treatments?" After consulting his wife, he said, "Our responsibility is not finished. We will stay with our people. When you go out again, you tell the churches outside, never give up their missionary zeal, and never give up their commitment of evangelizing the world. Tell the churches outside, hold on to their faith. Never allow anything to dilute their faith. Tell the churches outside, hereafter the most important ministry is the ministry of prayer." And I promised him that anytime I got the right opportunity, I would tell the churches of the world of what he said to me.

Two Categories of Churches

The churches in China today are divided into two categories: the Government-recognized churches and the house churches. There are about 50 official churches open. In spite of the fact that the messages are restricted in the freedom of expression, people are so hungry they flock to the church. Every official church today in Mainland China is filled with people. Some have to have three services every Sunday morning. Every service is jammed with people. The first service begins at 8 o'clock and people line up at the door at 6 o'clock. I saw the situation. I couldn't help but say in my heart, "O Lord, when can the churches outside, the Christians outside, have this kind of attitude." While I was in Shanghai, several members and leaders of the house churches came to visit me. One of them said, "In our area alone, there are 300 house churches." And I said to him, "How many people in the house churches?" He said, "Anywhere between 10 and a thousand people." And I said, "How can a thousand people meet in a home." And he said, "We no longer meet in homes. In some of the communes in our area, over 90% of the population are Christians. And one of the labor brigades is made up of Christians only. Every year, their production is on the top. They are most productive and most law-abiding. Therefore many of the local authorities, when they make a speech to all the commune leaders, will say, 'I want you people to follow the example of the Jesus Commune.'"

I saw their hymnbooks were done by a mimeograph machine. They told me, "The local authorities lend us the mimeograph machine to print these hymnbooks. After we print them, we give each one a copy. They also give us the big halls to meet, and many of them come to the meetings." Of course, this is an isolated case. We know today that the true spiritual force in Mainland China are these house churches.

A very conservative estimation is that there are about 20,000 house churches in China. This is a genuine people movement. Under His grace, this movement will continue. We anticipate that China may be one of the most evangelized nations in the world. It's not just a wild dream. I say this with reasonable expectation. We anticipate there will be a house-by-house people movement, a commune-by-commune people movement, and a tribe-by-tribe people movement. And when this begins to spread and operate, no power in the world can stop it. Human power can stop the organized or visible church, but it can not stop people-to-people evangelization.

Four Types of Chinese People

The people of China fall into roughly four categories. There are about 800 million FARMERS - 80% of the total population. For them, life changes very little. They are very hard to reach by the urban workers, but there are witnesses among the communes, and they are growing. Secondly, there are the OLDER GENERATION, the people above 50 or 60. They remember how life was before 1949. Many were educated in the mission schools before the changeover of Government. Today they are being sought after by the Government for their training and their skills. These are the people who are most receptive to the Gospel, because they knew the life before and now long for it to come back. Then, of course, there are the URBAN YOUTH. They are the "angry young men." Why? Because they were the Red Guards in 1966 and '67. They were the young people who roamed all over the country and tried to tear up everything. But now, they all of a sudden woke up and found out they have been cheated. They found out that they are now 25 or 30 years old, and they only have a 5th grade education. They have nothing to look forward to in their life. They are very angry and very skeptical of the Government. They want to know what is happening in the outside world. They listen to every word you say to them. They are receptive to the gospel. Then of course there are the PARTY MEMBERS, the youth league members. They are the managers of the country. There are about 50 million of them. They are the hardest to reach among all.

How Can we Help?

What can the churches and the Christians on the outside do to help? First, it is not advisable nor is it possible for any organized contact or help from the outside. This will be frowned upon and prohibited by the authorities. The only contact that is possible, in a limited way, is personal contact. While we are trying to do anything, we must avoid any kind of competitiveness, any pursuit of sensationalism, or any desire for instant result. We must be patient, have the overall view, and have long-range planning. We will not permit hastiness to destroy the long-range outlook of evangelization of the Chinese people. We must work hard towards a more relaxed religious atmosphere in China. We must exert our goodwill. We need a worldwide renewed burden for China and for the Chinese people. They are still there, a quarter of the world's people. We cannot write them off. God so loved the world. Indeed God so loved the Chinese, He created so many of them. We must not forget this fact.

How do we do it? You do not have to wait until the door of China Mainland opens. There are many Chinese people at your doorstep. Begin with them. There are many Chinese churches in many lands. Try to encourage them. There are non-believing Chinese in many places. You can be a missionary to them right where you are.

Secondly, we do not see the feasibility for the churches of many lands to go into China and evangelize in the traditional way. Before that time comes, you can help and work through the existing Chinese churches and Christians in the overseas area and through them. You can be contributive to the churches and Christians in China. How? For instance, there are urgent needs, especially for the house churches, for moral support. Many times they ask this question, "Are the outside churches remembering us, praying for us? Are the outside churches still interested about people in China?" We can give them moral and prayerful support. Many of them are in need of Christian literature, including the Bible and the hymnbook. I personally see some Bibles being torn apart because sometimes 2, 3, 5 home churches share one copy of the Bible. One house church has the Gospel of Matthew. Another has Mark, another has John. And then they copy them and pass them around. After a year each one of them has a complete Bible.

Many of them need tools and teaching materials. There is an inborn danger of the house churches, because they have a lot of enthusiasm but there is such a lack of teaching. This is our greatest burden for the house churches. They need teaching materials - the basic doctrines, the basic teaching of the Word, how to study the Bible, how to do personal evangelism, what is a church, how to tell between the true faith and heresies. It is our fear that with the relaxation and gradual opening of doors, many of the cults, many of the heresies will also go into China, and spread their teaching among the people and the churches. We can also support many of their preachers. I personally have met several fulltime preachers in China, which means they have no job over there, they need support.

If you have a desire to witness to the Chinese people, you can go back there. You can apply and go in as a scholar, a scientist, an engineer, a professor, or an English teacher. You can have a short assignment for a year or two. You will have opportunities to get in touch with intellectuals. They are so eager to hear what you have to say.

A Comparison.

If I make a comparison between the first entry of the gospel into China Mainland and of today, I can mention several important differences. The early carriers of the gospel were not Chinese. The evangelization of the Chinese people today, at least for the time being, depends mainly on the Christians inside China herself. I see this people movement is moving fast. I see the role of the overseas Chinese, and the role of the overseas non-Chinese churches through the overseas Chinese. Their role is a supportive one. Two years ago all the house churches were still underground. They could pray, they could share, but none of them dare to sing. But today when you go there, they are not underground any more. They open their windows and sing very loudly. I said, "Can you do this?" And they said, "Oh, we don't care. If someone wants to come in, we welcome them in, and they listen to what we have to say." Two hundred years ago when the gospel came, the culture was resistant and they were hostile. Today, it's mixed. There is some hostility of course, but also there is a big wide open attitude. The state of mind was traditional, closed, anti-foreign before. Now there is discontent and the desire for a better life. There are limited openness to things from outside.

There were no churches before, but now there are over 50 official churches and about 20,000 house churches. The young people were in the background before. Now they are in the forefront. They want to express themselves. Freedom of propagation was restricted before with limited freedom, and now it varies. Some areas are very restricted, some areas have limited freedom. What about other religions? They were strong, and they were co-existing before. What about today? They were all suppressed. Only recently, limited freedom was allowed. What about ideologies? It was Confucianism before. What about today? Marxism, with Confucianism, revived to a small degree. What about language? Diversified before. Today, unified. Everyone understands Mandarin. Putting all of this together, we have reason to believe that in the years ahead, you may see emerging from that ancient country, one of the most evangelized countries in the world. God has used the miseries and the tears and the price of lives in the past 30 years to create a vacuum in the hearts of the Chinese today. And that vacuum has to be filled with God Himself.

THE FUTURE

Edinburgh '80 - a milestone of missionary effort all over the world. Where do we go from here? My heart is extremely heavy and so are many of yours. Where does this great convocation lead us? We have seen God's blessings among us and yet at the same time we see areas that cause grief in our hearts. There is room for improvement in the areas of seriousness, of cooperation, and of big-hearted understanding. If Edinburgh '80 cannot be a facilitator of further missionary exchange, I am afraid Edinburgh '80 will fail of its purpose. And yet at the same time, we have reason to believe this could be a great turning point to make us see that the missionary effort in the world is not completed yet. This could be the opportunity to take away our false satisfaction and to open our minds and our eyes to see the hidden peoples that are yet to be reached. This is merely the beginning. The finer hour is yet to come. May I, with all humility, offer a viewpoint here for the future of our movement under the guidance of the Holy Spirit? Among our discussions, a number of our co-workers have put emphasis on the word "theology." Therefore, I believe if any missionary thrust is going to go on with renewed vigor, that movement must be faithful to the Scriptures. The Bible alone is our ultimate authority. We must be very much aware of words like syncretism or universalism. The Student Volunteer Movement survived for 40 years, having a great spiritual impact the world over. There could be many reasons why it disappeared. One of them is a gradual dilution of theology and diffusion of goals. Any time we shift our emphasis from the pure gospel, that will be the beginning of the death of any missionary movement.

One World

Secondly, we must stop polarizing. I do not belong to the First world or the Third world. There is only one world. It's about time we work together. It's about time we show true mutual respect. It must be more than skin deep. Yet at the same time, we should also have a sense of appreciation to the nations and churches who have pioneered missions work in the past two or three centuries, who have given their lives and their money and their sons and their daughters, and who have given the best years of their lives to many lands. This is one thing I am constantly reminding the Chinese churches of, that we should never forget the love labor and the sacrifice from the churches of many countries who have come to the Chinese people. Many of the graves of the early missionaries are still seen today in China. And for such love labor and such grace we, as Chinese Christians, could not and should not forget. Therefore, I believe that, among the churches of the world, there should be true respect and appreciation. If this can be the case, I believe there shall be true cooperation in this one world. We should plan together - not to put up a plan and tell the other people to endorse it. We should have a crusader's lifestyle.

Merely a simple lifestyle is not enough. A simple lifestyle can also be a fruitless lifestyle. This lifestyle should be the hallmark of missionaries today. We should be willing to identify within this one-world community and then we should have a feeling of urgency because the Lord is returning soon. I appreciate the theme of our consultation this time, but I think this theme was made under the assumption that our Lord would not return before the year of 2,000. By His grace, we would like to see a church for every people as soon as possible.

Every People Should Have a Church.

Furthermore, my dear brothers and sisters, never be discouraged and never be sidetracked from the high calling of the Lord. If God gave you today this burden, do it. Go ahead, preach it. And spread it. Every people should have a church. That is a command. Ever since the early church, indeed ever since the Old Testament times, there has always been the conflict, the inner conflict, between the prophets and the establishment. By God's grace, can we today look forward to see the cooperation between the prophetic voice and the establishment, between the dreamers and the builders. Must we tear each other down? Must we hinder each other from advancing the kingdom of God? The dreamers and the builders must work hand in hand. And therefore the mandate and the dream and the expectation of Edinburgh '80 must go on. This job shall never be finished until the return of our Lord Jesus Christ. The Chinese churches for one will stand with you together to see the great commission accomplished.

9
THE STUDENT CONSULTATION
EDINBURGH EXPERIENCE
Brad Gill

Although 243 had made it their ambition to attend, one hundred and eighty student delegates finally arrived for the ten days of intense meetings. There was little time to tour one of the world's most beautiful cities, yet this concerned the delegates little. They had set themselves to discuss a more consuming subject.

THE DELEGATES

The delegation was made up of the following types of participants: student recruiters for mission agencies (10); seminary students (10); graduates and young professionals (20); students on Christian campuses (15); students on secular campuses (30); leaders and administrators of Christian colleges (32); staff of student organizations (22); members of mission or student organizations involved in student mobilization (25); mobilizers for mission interest in local churches (3).

Although the bulk of participants were from the USA, there was more than just a superficial international representation - 66 non-USA delegates from at least 26 different nations. Great Britain and Scandinavia led the way, followed by South Africa, Germany and Indonesia. In attendance as well were key staff members from Campus Crusade for Christ, Navigators, Inter-Varsity Christian Fellowship, University and Colleges Christian Fellowship (UCCF), International Fellowship of Evangelical Students (IFES), Belgium European Student Missions Association, The European Missionary Association (TEMA), the African Society for Frontier Missions, the International Consultation of Christian Medical Missions (Lausanne), the AMEN Movement in Peru (Asociacion Misionera Evangelica a las Naciones), Word of Life (Kenya), and the Congo Team.

While an advance team had arranged accommodations, the steering committee, which had performed its administrative coordination by correspondence and telephone between Africa, America and Scotland, finally met in Scotland just a few hours before the convocation was to assemble.

THE BRIEFING SESSIONS

After a warm welcome from the Christian Unions of the Edinburgh University campus, George Verwer, founder and director of Operation Mobilisation, an organization which for two decades had called forth thousands of young people into world evangelization, challenged the delegates with the spiritual issues to be confronted if this generation were to be able to penetrate the Hidden Peoples. (See MISSION CHALLENGE Chapter 10 - ED.)

The following evening was the "Meeting of the Nations." A number of individuals were asked to respond to the question "Why am I Here". They included a Christian leader from Korea, Dr. Simeon Kan, a student leader from the Transkei, Mr. Edwin Mahlutshana, and one of the steering committee, David Bliss. After reviewing the multi-media production "That Everyone May Hear" (from the recent Consultation on World Evangelization in Pattaya, Thailand), each of the delegates was asked to reflect on why they themselves had decided to attend the Edinburgh gathering. The information from these response papers would finalize the framework and particular concerns to be dealt with during the forum sessions.

It was appropriate and indeed a privilege to have Patrick Johnstone, author of "Operation World", address the delegates on the subject "Intercession for the Nations." Prayer would play a critical role in the following days. Spontaneous prayer cells met all week, and an all-night prayer meeting took place Thursday night. Again and again the delegates pushed through frustrating and difficult periods of communication with seasons of prayer. Everyone realized by the end of the week that Patrick Johnstone had truly given a "keynote"—without sustained prayer, the purposes, plans and participants could not have come to final resolution. (See MISSION IMPERITIVE - ED.)

He was followed by Dr. J. Robertson McQuilkin, president of Columbia Bible College. It had been this man's impassioned call for laborers at the Consultation on World Evangelization in June which alerted the steering committee to his vision. His years of missionary service had sprung from a student missions thrust on the campuses of America (Student Foreign Missions Fellowship) and had implanted within him the burning desire to see men and women sent where the church of Jesus Christ had yet to emerge. He was asked to deal with the overall challenge of these harvest fields, the objective of the missionary vocation and the necessity for more laborers in this era of frontier outreach. (See MISSIONARY INVITATION, Chapter 12 - ED.)

By the end of these addresses, and even before, the delegates were prepared to address the subject at hand: the "means" by which God would use them to assist in a new movement of frontier missionaries.

THE FORUM SESSIONS

The delegates participated in the WCFM morning and evening sessions. In the afternoons they met together to discuss topics of student frontier missions mobilization. A number of issues surfaced ranging from stimulating students to actual involvement with the hidden peoples. This led to a number of task forces which dealt in depth with such topics.

Frontier-minded personal disciplines
Biblical and theological foundations
Christian campus mobilization
Secular campus mobilization
Seminary mobilization
Training and preparation for the field
Church mobilization and student/church relations
Distribution of information and resources
Tentmaking ministry
Prayer and intercession
Exposure missions or short-terms
Exploring possible structures for a student
    frontier missions movement and relations to
    existing student organizations.
Relief and development
New pioneer-sending structures
Mission agency relations

These task forces met an average of four times, but a few, such as the one considering possible structures, spent hours overtime, missing meals and other meetings, in order to come to a consensus. This was done after much discussion and much prayer. The various task forces were to present their reports to the entire group on Friday afternoon, but were frustrated because of the vast numbers of items to cover in so little time. Consequently, four specific concerns emerged which needed additional time and consideration:

a. In relation to the WCFM, the student delegates expressed the necessity for clear guidelines in pinpointing frontier peoples.

b. Delegates needed to be exposed to the many student mission thrusts already existing across the world. Some of these organizations were actually represented at the ISCFM.

c. While students were able to dialogue with mission leaders over meals, the limitations of time and resources during the consultations hindered task forces from more indepth discussion.

d. The predominance of American participants created a problem of international parity in the discussion. A great deal of time was required for the resolution of issues caused by cultural misunderstandings.

One afternoon, therefore, was spent reviewing the issues and strategic definitions presented at the WCFM. Another portion of an afternoon session was given to key student mission leaders to share what was taking place through their organizations. The rest of the time, both in the afternoon as well as over meals and late into the night, delegates sorted through what they believed to be the critical issues of seeing a new movement of young people "serviced" and "mobilized" for action.

When reports were finally given on Friday afternoon, a grid of concerns were introduced for consideration. Moving toward resolution was difficult: too many items needed discussion. The potential for meeting anybody's objectives was seemingly reduced every minute. But this group, through determined, prayerful intercession, saw God do something special in the next forty-eight hours. Out of what seemed to be disheartening frustration and disharmony there emerged a solid unanimity, a unified resolve, that could only be credited to the Lord himself.

I would like to consolidate the reports and concerns of the task forces in a seven-point grid. Hopefully, this will express the functions that seemed critical for this movement.

1. There was a concern that **information** regarding the Hidden Peoples be distributed on a vast global scale. With a booming church and accompanying student initiative in all parts of the world, the sharing of information with systematic regularity was required. The consultation had provided this in microcosm; now it needed to expand further to include many others who were not able to attend this consultation.

A specific task force, "Distribution of Information and Resources," dealt with the principles for this network of communication. According to its report, any communication was understood as "a servant to the movement," reflecting the nature and emphasis of its membership. "Considerations must always be made," it continued, "for the international scope of the movement, granting freedom to develop communications in ways appropriate to the different cultures and languages."

2. There was a deep concern for the primacy of **intercession**. One task force made this its sole purpose. It was the members of this task force that initiated the all-night prayer vigil. This was their strategy: bands of praying intercessors were essential to going, sending, upholding and mobilizing. When this task force realized that exactly 1000 weeks remained from the end of the consultation, it suggested in its report that a global prayer chain stretching from country to

country, continent to continent, be established as part of the ISCFM network.

3. There was a concern that appropriate <u>instruction</u> be available for frontier missions perspective and preparation. One task force on "Training and Preparation for the Field" outlined what it believed to be the requirements for frontier missionaries as a tool in determining a comprehensive plan of instruction. This task force recommended that students be made aware of the regional opportunities as well as "short term" experiences which could equip them for service.

More basic was the realization that many Christian academic institutions did not include frontier missions, or even missions, in their curriculum. The "Seminary Task Force" stated in their call to seminary professors that "a special type of training is needed for frontier-church planting, cross-cultural evangelists. Few seminaries offer it. Few have any focus on the frontier missions task ... . Education is needed in church planting, cross-cultural communication, evangelism, church growth, missionary apologetics, and in the theology of missions. Practical training is needed through supervised field education."

Many of the task forces, especially "Relief and Development" and "Tentmaking," recognized that an all-out invasion of the present curriculum of churches and schools would be necessary if laborers of quality were to be sent to these frontier fields.

4. There was a concern that there be an <u>integration</u> of frontier missions perspective and biblical lifestyle. Lives needed to be changed. While the original 15 principles had met both enthusiastic response as well as strong reaction, every delegate realized that his lifestyle needed to be impacted by this mandate. There was a deep willingness for radical reformation of heart and mind, without which the movement would prove weak.

5. There was a concern for immediate <u>involvement</u> with the frontier mandate. Whether it be "sharing the vision" with other Christians, working with international students, or reaching Hidden Peoples right at home—practical involvement was critical to the movement. A series of task forces were designed to formulate strategies at the "home base," i.e. in the churches and on the campuses. Together it represented a broad front of concern, of participation and practical initiative.

6. There was a concern that individuals be <u>incorporated</u> into task-oriented fellowships with frontier missions vision. Almost all task forces were convinced that student initiative would provide the means for spreading awareness and eliciting lifetime commitment to the Hidden Peoples. But certain task forces recognized that unless students were in viable fellowship groups, accountable to others of like mind and heart, their ability to continue towards personal frontier missions objectives would be greatly hampered.

The task force on "Mission Agency Relations" dealt with this issue of incorporation at another level. It was the problem of "wineskins": whether or not the "new wine" of frontier-minded recruits would be capable of incorporating into the traditional long-standing mission agency structures. Joining a campus-level fellowship was one thing— joining a long term accountability structure was quite another. This concern was illustrated as well by the task force on "Tentmaking." Was this generation of career-minded, professional students able to be incorporated into the traditional mission structure?

7. There was a concern that a proper infrastructure be considered for the movement. Would it be possible for students committed to frontier missions to relate together across geographical and organizational lines? This issue was laden with difficulty from the beginning. Some problems stemmed from a degree of suspicion on the part of some delegates that a new organization was definitely going to be formed, whether or not any or all agreed. Many of the problems were due to the cross-cultural nature of the experience. One Scottish delegate suggested that "during the consultation discussions we used various terms such as 'movement,' 'structure,' 'organization,' but the problem was that we tended to have different ideas as to what we meant by these words." Overcoming the subtleties of terminology, with so little time to discuss matters, was one of the greatest difficulties during the experience. But a strong foundation of agreement was essential for any viable framework.

One task force was thus charged with the responsibility of "exploring possible structures for a student frontier missions movement." This task force combined almost immediately with the group focusing on "working with existing student organizations for frontier missions." The reason for the merger was logical: all the various students with different points of view (and there were many!) about existing structures and/or a new structure, would discuss them together and work them out. This task force understandably was the largest, and spent many long hours of heated debate and earnest prayer together.

They also stated that "generally there seems to be no student mobilization entity focused single-mindedly on the frontiers, the Hidden Peoples. There is no unifying voice or effort for this specific vision: A Church for Every People by the Year 2000." After discussing different alternatives, one idea "emerged which would combine grass roots student mobilization with a relatively unstructured communication and coordination network internationally." It was at this point that the Caleb Project was introduced as a "directed but unstructured movement designed to mobilize students within their existing movements, organizations, and churches, to penetrate peoples currently beyond the reach of the Gospel."

THE PLANNING SESSIONS

Friday night, delegates again gathered to take action on their deliberations. Certain guidelines had been drafted by a subcommittee of the task force on structure and then accepted by that entire task force. These guidelines, representing as they did the consensus of one entire task force, gave the necessary impetus to the next 48 hours.

On Saturday morning, the author was asked to address the WCFM delegates as to the ISCFM developments. While final resolutions had yet to be decided, three things were outlined for the WCFM body:

1. The ISCFM delegates felt that the best way to alert fellow students to the Hidden Peoples was through a "grass roots" initiative in universities and churches.

2. From a student point of view, the convergence of mission leaders (WCFM) and students (ISCFM) was an important catalytic relationship. Students had been able to interact over meals and in between sessions with key mission leaders concerning issues being discussed in both consultations. In addition, quite a few WCFM delegates, especially those focused on students and recruitment, found time to join task forces and attend ISCFM discussion sessions. A few even participated in the all-night prayer meeting. The students found this to be very helpful—a source of insight and encouragement.

3. The ISCFM hoped to find the best possible "means" for mobilizing the necessary recruits for those WCFM agencies ready to send volunteers to the Hidden Peoples of the world. This alone was the most significant contribution a younger generation could render to mission agencies.

All night long the students had been readying themselves for decisive action. It had been a long and arduous week; almost one third of the delegates had been sick Others had spent late nights in deliberations, but sustained prayer had again and again pushed back any sense of hopelessness and fatigue. Now, in the last two hours before delegates were to leave, five unanimous decisions were made.

THE WATCHWORD

Paul Graham from South Africa, who chaired the planning sessions of the last two days, suggested that decisions be made by starting with what could be agreed on and then moving to the areas of dispute. He then moved that the ISCFM delegation vote on adopting the consultation's theme, "A Church for Every People by the Year 2000," as the watchword of any continuing ISCFM efforts.

This watchword was measureable. It assumed that the job could be finished. With just 1000 weeks until the year 2000, delegates knew that they were calling on fellow students to help them penetrate peoples of the world that were still without the church of Jesus Christ. Some of these had never been approached; some had long seemed resistant. But this watchword demanded that people go ...

it demanded that they send... it demanded that they offer up believing prayer.

A thrill ran through the entire group when the vote was unanimously and resoundingly affirmative! After so much debate for so many days, the students realized that with this first unanmious decision they had at last become a viable entity. This was the turning point. All the prayer and discussion, as frustrating and difficult as it had been, now began to pay off. However, this mandate, so descriptive of this group's objectives, still needed a framework for individual commitment.

THE PLEDGE

With the watchword as the goal, the pledge would describe the individual's response to that goal. Without individual commitment, the watchword would not accomplish much. When they came to the consultation, each delegate had in hand a "Declaration of Purpose," included by the original steering committee as part of the ISCFM application process. At Edinburgh ten more such statements of personal commitment and dedication were suggested as a possible pledge that the entire group could adopt. In order that each could be studied thoroughly and fairly, Paul Graham, as chairman, suggested the formation of an international committee. After three hours of very hard work, the nine delegates suggested the following pledge, which with two small emendations was unanimously adopted by the consultation as a whole.

> By the grace of God and for His glory, I commit my entire life to obeying His commission of Matthew 28:18-20 wherever and however He leads me, giving priority to the peoples currently beyond the reach of the Gospel (Romans 15:20-21). I will also endeavor to impart this vision to others.

THE GUIDELINES

The next item put before the group for consideration was a list of 17 guidelines, submitted by a subcommittee of the task force on structure the previous day. Again, after discussion and a few amendments, the entire list was unanimously adopted. While no regard was given to style or format, the entire list of guidelines was adopted in principle in order to proceed to definitive action. They are listed below as submitted to the ISCFM body.

1. A willingness to relate to, work through, and reinforce the work of existing student organization, churches, mission agencies and movements.

2. Motivate and inform other Christians regarding hidden peoples.

3. Seek to link students with missionary agency initiatives towards hidden peoples.

Page 178

4. Demonstrate that in the power of the Holy Spirit students can and will go to even the most difficult places on earth.

5. Challenge others to in turn go to hidden peoples.

6. Stimulate international cooperation and communication of student initiatives towards helping penetrate hidden peoples.

7. Stimulate an international prayer network to reach hidden peoples.

8. Support local church initiatives to penetrate hidden peoples.

9. Formation of an international communications committee.

10. An express commitment to the frontiers through a common pledge, declaration or covenant.

11. God's word as base of authority.

12. Concerned with a holistic approach to frontier missions.

13. Committed to fulfilling the watchword, "A Church for Every People by the Year 2000."

14. Based on Biblical principles.

15. Freedom for local and national expression.

16. Culturally flexible.

17. Maintain a minimal structure to encourage student initiative and creativity.

THE TWO COMMISSIONS

In addition to these three actions, the delegates felt it was necessary to provide a catalytic means for continuing the relationships and efforts of the ISCFM. No name was to be given other than reference to the historical roots of the ISCFM, nor was it to have any major organizational hierarchy. This movement was to have a grass roots initiative that had no membership rolls, as compared to student organizations worldwide.

The delegates did express the necessity of forming two commissions which could facilitate a continuing network of relationship between all who had attended the consultation. Thus, an International Communication Commission was set up with the mandate of communication, identification of resources and the stimulation of prayer. Gordon and Sherri Aeschliman from the United States were asked to take this post.

Secondly, the delegates decided that definitive action needed to be taken by the ISCFM in communicating to those student organizations and mission agencies which were vitally interested in the developments of the ISCFM. While they decided not to follow the same procedure as the WCFM continuation efforts, they felt that there were three functions the ISCFM needed to perform:

Page 179

1. Because many key individuals and student organizations were unable to attend the ISCFM, an international network of "advocates" needed to be formed.

2. Although the delegates felt that no new student organization should be formed, nevertheless they expressed the need for some way to measure interest at the grass roots for additional regional or international gatherings of this sort.

3. The delegates also felt it necessary to provide continual interfacing with the mission agencies represented in the World Consultation on Frontier Missions, which would in the future be the agencies under whose auspices many of those students would serve as missionaries.

After considering the various ways by which these functions could be provided, I was appointed as their representative, with the responsibility of developing the necessary network to fulfill these continuation functions, and suggesting that an advocacy commission be established through the ISCFM delegates from the various regions of the world.

CONCLUSION

Upon review, one is impressed with the way in which God led this small delegation. Concerted prayer, keen insight, sheer-dogged energy, and a determination to hear even the smallest voice on any subject— all this added up to a profound grasp of the essential characteristics of any student effort for frontier missions. With the solid direction and advice of missions leadership, this strong beginning could expand, providing an ever increasing number of frontier-minded recruits who believe God for "A Church for Every People by the Year 2000."

10
MISSION CHALLENGE:
Counting
the Cost

GEORGE
VERWER

Jesus said: "Which of you, intending to build a tower, sitteth not down first, and counteth the cost, whether he hath sufficient to finish it? Lest perhaps, after he hath laid the foundation, and is not able to finish it, all that behold begin to mock him, saying, 'This man began to build and was not able to finish.' Or what king, going to make war against another king, sitteth not down first, and consulteth whether he be able with ten thousand to meet him that cometh against him with twenty thousand? Or else, while the other is yet a great way off, he sendeth an ambassage, and desireth conditions of peace. So likewise, whosoever he be of you that forsaketh not all that he hath, cannot be my disciple. Salt is good: but if the salt have lost its savor, wherewith shall it be seasoned? It is neither fit for the land, nor yet for the dunghill; but men cast it out. He that hath ears to hear, let him hear." Luke 14: 28-35.

KNOWING THE SITUATION

At the beginning of a consultation such as this, it is appropriate to count the cost. It is important when we are in a spiritual conflict to know what our situation really is. The Bible teaches about spiritual warfare.

The church situation today in Britain is very divided. One of the leaders of the great evangelistic thrust going on in this country has written an article indicating that we are not ready to evangelize. My heart pounds in agreement with a lot that he states. There are great tensions and divisions in the British church. I am convinced, however, that considering the claims of Christ, we cannot wait until all the church is united, until all gossip ceases and everybody's loving one

Page 181

another. This is because we have a commission and we have an
example in the book of Acts that evangelism goes forward even in the
midst of weakness. Though at this time the British church in some
ways may be weak, God is greater. God is greater and evangelism, not
just nationwide but world evangelism, must go forward. It must go
forward as we also emphasize revival, holiness, spiritual life, and
simultaneously declare war against all gossip, unbelief, sin, all that
disunites true believers.

There is no reason why we cannot simultaneously work toward
renewal and revival, and world evangelism. I can share honestly with
you that my first burden is not world evangelism, but the Glory of
God. One of the reasons that we of Operation Mobilization have been
able to put men in the Muslim world and keep them there five, ten, or
even fifteen years is because as we went to the Muslim world twenty
years ago, our first burden was not the conversion of Muslims, or the
establishing of the church in the Muslim world, but the Glory of God.
I would rather be in the middle of Turkey working in God's will with
just a little fruit, than be somewhere else where I might be seen
great fruit, but not really in that first place that God wanted me.
Many of God's people, I believe, have missed His perfect will. I am
not convinced that it is the will of God for all these people groups to
have no witness. We cannot take some extreme Calvinistic cop-out and
blame it all on God any more than William Carey could do that when
they told him so many years ago, "If God wants the heathen to be
reached, then He will take care of it, without the likes of you." It is
God's plan because it's revealed in His Word that these people hear
the Gospel; that they receive a witness. It's impossible for us to
predict how much fruit there will be. Our first burden is the Glory of
God, therefore we obey Him and we go forth to lay down our lives in
witness.

RENEWAL

My second greatest burden is for renewal among God's people.
When I say that, I'm not referring to what any one stream would call
renewal. I'm happy to see people renewed in any way the Living God
chooses to do it. The way it happens in California isn't the way it
happens in Sweden, and the way it happens in Sweden isn't necessarily
the way it happens in Germany. Just last week I was in Denmark,
Sweden, Norway, Northern Germany and one or two other countries
and in every nation I go to there is a unique work of God. God does
not destroy our humanity when He works in us, nor our nationality.
Only as we understand these cultures are we going to be able to see
more recruits coming from these cultures, and of course, then they
will have the job of understanding the cultures they go to. In speaking
about the Holy Spirit and the victorious life, Billy Graham said, "I
don't care how you get it, just get it." I long to see a combination of
emphases on holiness, on Godly living, commitment discipleship, the
simple lifestyle, spiritual revolution, and to see them combined with
outreach to every nation, to every people, in world evangelism, and

cross-cultural communication. Count the cost. We know the words of the Lord Jesus in Matthew 9, "The harvest is plenteous, the laborers are few."

This is a very serious and very needed consultation. I can say that objectively because I had nothing to do with the organization. I know the criticism that goes on in our day against consultations and congresses and for people that are widely read it sounds like a lot is taking place. But the average person may not be that widely read. Most of you were not invited to Thailand, or Lausanne, or wherever these great congresses are going on. But somehow you've managed even as feeble, weak students to squeak in the door of this consultation. Such a consultation is needed because the situation is desperate. All kinds of consultations are taking place right now, not one or two, but many, to try to solve the Iraq-Iran crisis. Endless money will be spent. They know that this crisis in the Middle East could bring on World War III. Beloved, as followers of Jesus Christ we are already in a warfare that makes the Iran-Iraq crisis look small, at least spiritually speaking. Therefore, to have a consultation of people concerned about half of the people of the world, the unreached people, to pray together, to work together, to plan to do anything we possibly can to increase the thrust, to increase our numbers, to increase our unity, is well worth it.

BUILDING TOGETHER

It's very easy to criticize. There is far too much criticism among evangelicals today, and far too many negative thinkers. In Philippians we're challenged to think on that which is good, that which is pure, that which is right. Anybody can tear down, but it takes an architect to build. May God make each one of you a spiritual architect this week, to build for God as Nehemiah sent forth by God, built despite opposition, mocking, lack of resources. We are called to build together.

There's a verse in Nehemiah that often challenges me when I may be doing something I don't like to do (and you'll never be a missionary if you don't like to do some things you have to do.) The verse speaks about having a mind to work. Would you pray with me that God will give a mind to work?

This is a working consultation, not some kind of evangelical missionary jamboree, where we're going to come up and exchange missionary business cards, and pat each other on the back. It's a time of serious prayer and study. It's a time of declaring war afresh against the enemy and taking stock of what it's going to cost.

COMMITMENT

We're committed to Christ, to His Word, to world evangelism. But do we really know what that word means? It seems to me that in many countries and cultures, especially in the affluent society, this word is losing its meaning. People talk about total commitment and then drive away in their brand new car to live in their hundred thousand dollar home, and no one can say anything lest you be accused of being embarrassing or something worse.

In a world where millions are starving, where tens of millions have no homes, where evangelists in India are praying that they might have a bicycle, (and some have been praying for ten years), we in the affluent society, I believe, have sinned against God, and therefore, have failed to understand Christ's demands upon our lives. Luke 14:33 is very clear: "Likewise, whosoever he be of you that forsaketh not all that he hath, he cannot be my disciple." If there is going to be a powerful missionary invasion in our day, there must be a return to the standard of Jesus Christ and of the New Testament. What an abomination that some of our countries are now propagating a doctrine that teaches all spiritual people will financially prosper. This has confused thousands. When people get into that doctrine, and it doesn't work, they go away feeling that they are unspiritual or that they are not men and women of faith.

A. W. Tozer said that the more keen Christian is easily led astray. The more keen, (enthusiastic, excited, boldly dedicated) Christian is more easily led astray. When I first started out preaching about world missions twenty-five years ago, the main message was of course world missions, total commitment, all that side of the challenge which is in the Word of God, and as I went on I saw the strategy of the Enemy. I had to start speaking about extremism, calling people to spiritual balance, and to compare Scripture. One of the greatest hindrances to world evangelism and to the vision that you and I have is extremism. My whole life is involved with students, and young people, and the amount of extremism just in Europe amongst students is just unbelievable. There are little house groups that don't believe in world missions. I've heard tapes, widely circulated, more or less explaining that world missions is a thing of the past. Satan is going to counterattack that which God attempts to do through this consultation, and to get us into one extreme or another.

UNLIMITED POSSIBILITIES

As we count the cost, seeing the fields that are white unto harvest, there are unlimited possibilities for short term evangelistic opportunities. Isn't it amazing that the Mormons have 20 to 30 thousand men on the field? They have over 100,000 converts in Britain alone. They want to have some 70 or 80 thousand men on the field by the turn of the century. The Church of Jesus Christ should have at least, at any one time, (apart from the standard missionary force) 100 thousand men on a one or two year program. I read something only yesterday countering the concept that we needed a great number of missionaries, and that there were so many of us that we would start to get in the way. I wonder if they have ever visited countries like Italy. When I went to Italy, the student work there consisted of two middle aged ladies trying to reach all the university students in Italy. It has not improved very much since. A few other groups have come in.

At the University of Calcutta, there was a Christian Union there years ago when I was in a Christian campaign in that city, and I think that there were 15 in that meeting. That university must be a 100 thousand strong.

The challenge of world evangelism is as great as ever. These huge numbers of missionaries that are being prayed for can be used if they are Spirit-controlled, and Spirit-guided committed men. I don't think that they will get in the way of each other, and hinder the national church if they know a few of the basic rules of the game, like submitting to the leadership in that country, working alongside people, not lording it over them but learning from them, and turning the leadership in any country over to the people in that country as quickly as possible. Let us count the costs and realize that we are in a spiritual warfare. Satan has a strategy and he will counterattack. He has many dead end streets into which he likes to get God's people.

COMMITTED TO EACH OTHER

We need to count the cost in terms of our commitment to one another. How easy it is in our day for each group and each individual and, to some degree, even churches to do their own thing. This has so overwhelmed me at times that I have wanted to leave my own fellowship, simply so that I could just be identified with the whole body. How we need one another, different fellowships, different organizations. We have different ideas and will never all agree on every point, but if we are going to evangelize the world, we are going to have to build up our relationship.

This is another one of the reasons that such consultations are to be valued. We get to know one another and to understand what others are doing. I attended and had a little mini-seminar at the World Congress on Evangelism in Lausanne, and found that a great experience. The greatest part of that experience for me was that it was a humbling experience. In OM, I'm the leader. People are very kind to me and I am esteemed. I walk into a place and they let me say a few words. But when you arrive at the World Congress on Evangelism and you're just one of a thousand, you're nobody, in one sense. All these different men of God, such as Dr. Schaeffer and John Stott, are there. You're just humbled.

When you get among a lot of God's people and you hear about their work and you put together all that God is doing around the world, I tell you that that is a good therapy. You realize that your little OM, with all its ships and whatever else you can put together, is just a drop in the ocean. What a great experience for our spiritual growth to be brought into a situation where we are just part of the body! You know that when you are in that situation, your joy will have to come from the Lord Himself. There is always the danger when we come to a conference, that we are trying to get bits of joy from one another or from saying something. The Word of God tells us not to be ministered unto but to minister, and I believe, with all my heart, that for many of us, this consultation will be a time in which we have to look to the Lord more than ever before. Some things that are said may blow us right off our feet, and we are going to have to look to the Lord, or we will be overwhelmed with a challenge. We may be overwhelmed with so many interesting people, and I'm convinced that God wants us to build our relationships.

In OM work we have been trying more and more in our nights and days of prayer to pray for other missions, fellowships, and groups. We bring in visiting speakers, look at their slides, find out what they are doing, and God has blessed us as we have done that. Many people in a particular country do not even know what other major works of God are doing in their own country, even in a peripheral way. I don't know whether they don't read Christian magazines or they don't like people. One fellow said, "Not that I am antisocial, I just don't like people." It is valuable to know what others are doing, because then we're knowing something about what God is doing. We should rejoice with those who rejoice. God help us if we only rejoice when OUR work has a victory. We rejoice when any member of the body of Christ is being used or being blessed, and we attempt as the Scriptures teach us to believe the best about other fellowships and about other groups.

BEING STRONG MINDED

When you get in missionary work, you are going to discover that you are involved with a wide range of strong-minded people. A lot of the missionaries in the world are such people. That's how they got out there in the first place. Very few of you are ever going to get to the mission field unless you dig your heels in a little bit. Auntie isn't going to want you to go, and maybe Mommy and Daddy aren't either. Probably your own pastor may not even want you to go, and your employer, because the big teaching in England now is: Go through a university, get a good job, make money, then when you are all settled down, if the Lord leads, go to the mission field.

I want to know how many have got to the mission fields through that kind of ridiculous philosophy! Once people are married and settled down, generally, they are stuck for life. Very few married couples with children in all of Europe are launching out to the mission field, apart from those who have alreay started to move before they got into that more interesting, complicated, frustrating phase of life. I believe the Enemy is very, very clever, and he has a massive propaganda machine, and that machine is opposed to world missions, to what this consultation stands for. We have got to have the wisdom and the discernment to know what is coming from the Enemy and what is coming from the Lord. A. W. Tozer said, "The greatest gift need in the Church today is the gift of discernment," and we desperately need this.

COMMUNICATING CROSS-CULTURALLY

We have got to count the costs, building relationships. Do you get on with people? Do you know how to listen to people, how to let love cover differences when someone says something that you don't like? If you don't, you are going to have difficulties, not only in missionary work, but with your life. I don't think that we can overemphasize the need to learn how to relate to people, to communicate cross-culturally.

Many of us have trouble communicating to our own culture. Here of course we must be very careful that we don't just get discouraged thinking about it. Someone wrote recently that we can't really communicate cross-culturally unless we have a gift of cross-cultural evangelism. I haven't met many people who claim to have this gift, and it's obvious that people who read such books are not planning on the mission field. For twenty five years I have seen simple humble people apply themselves in a foreign country, as a servant, as learner, walking Calvary's road, and I have seen them effectively communicate cross-culturally, encourage and work with nationals and vice-versa.

I am convinced everyone of us can communicate cross-culturally to some degree. Some of course will be more gifted, but everyone of us can communicate, and there are a lot of things that we have to learn. There are books that we can read like "Share Your Faith With a Muslim." One out of every six or seven people in the world is a Muslim. Less than two percent of the missionaries in the world are working among Muslims. Are we going to wait for those who feel that they have to have a special Muslim Cross-Cultural Gift? We have enough obstacles to get over to get people to the field, much less putting up new ones, and it is my sincere prayer that we will beware of this kind of thinking.

The idea that we need more and more studies so that we can do our job better and better is very much linked with intellectualism. It's a text-book theory. But be out on the field for 10, 20, or even 2 years and you will see that it is just not the truth. Think of the great movement of the assemblies under the leadership of Bakht Singh in India, a movement I'm personally familiar with. Ordinary men, many of them without much education, filled with the word of God, started churches, communicating cross-culturally. Muslims had come to Jesus Christ, and 300 assemblies exist today.

A DESTRUCTIVE ENEMY

Lately I've read of a number of Christian organizations that are going through tremendous times of difficulty and disunity. In the States, the whole Bill Gothard seminar program is going through the greatest spiritual test of its existence. Two years ago I spoke to the staff, trying to share with them that Satan would soon launch a vicious attack against their work. Now it has happened. I spent two or three hours on the phone with Bill, just after the crisis, sharing some of my burdens, about the spiritual warfare, about the strategies of Satan.

The warfare is real. As we've seen some of the greatest Christian personalities in America hit the divorce courts, even in the past year, our hearts have sunk, and we have been reminded that it is not a game, some kind of a religious carnival. It's an all out warfare, in which the Enemy is out to destroy people. I might have an incredibly difficult day, and very, very heavy activity of the Evil One upon my soul and my mind that day. Coincidence? When you enroll in the army of God and decide to reach out to the unreached and to be involved in God's great purpose of world evangelism you will be a marked man. About that time, if you don't know how to pray, to resist Satan, if you haven't got a disciplined life, and don't know how to share and fellowship in a way that is going to help you along, if you don't know how to wear the armor of God, and hold high the shield of faith, wherewith you can stop all the fiery darts of the devil, then you will be one more missionary casualty.

QUALITY, NOT QUANTITY

My greatest concern, (it may sound like a contradiction) is not firstly more missionaries. It is the quality of the missionary that we train or send out that is all-important. We have to count the cost of what it takes to gain quality of life - not perfection, not super spirituality, not the total supernatural disciplined man, a sort of bionic evangelical. Rather, quality of life is reality, brokenness, openness, and all that we can appropriate in Jesus Christ, for we are complete in Him. A. W. Tozer was a great missionary thinker, and very much involved in world missions. He said that the task of the Church is twofold: to spread Christianity throughout the world and to make sure that the Christianity she spreads is a pure New Testament kind. Christianity will always produce itself after its kind. A worldly-minded, unspiritual Church is sure to bring forth on her shores a Christianity much like her own. Not the naked Word only, but the character of the witness determines the quality of the convert. He goes on to say that the popular notion that the first obligation of the Church is to spread the Gospel to the outermost parts of the Earth is false. Her first obligation is to be spiritually worthy to spread it—to spread a degenerate brand of Christianity to pagan lands is not to fulfill the commandment of Jesus Christ.

Tozer's statement has meant a great deal to me. It would be a glorious thing if many of us here would renew our commitment first to the Lord Jesus Christ Himself wherever He leads us. The last thing we would want a consultation like this to produce is a lot of people with a guilt complex if somehow they don't quite make it to the Muslim world. God is wanting to deal with you and with me on the basis of love, grace, mercy. What happens is that people may go out to serve just long enough to get rid of the guilt trip and then they come home. I'm convinced that some of you who are afraid of missionary work have got these ideas of cockroach invasions and eating all kinds of weird food and suffering in extreme climates. If you would understand God's ways and move by faith, however, many of you would discover that you actually enjoy it when you get to those countries. The true missionary is not some kind of ascetic, who is perpetually pining for the California beaches and his MacDonald hamburgers. In any case, MacDonalds are getting there now faster then we are! I have seen on the mission field, in Spain, Belgium, Holland and then India, that in the midst of the battle there are many wonderful and enjoyable aspects of missionary life. It is one of the fullest, most challenging occupations anyone could ever get into. Of course we are all missionaries. But I'm talking here about when you move out of your own culture.

THE CALL

Let's count the cost, what it's going to take in terms of quality of life, and then let's have a plan over the next couple of years to build up our spiritual lives through the Word, prayer, fellowship, the Cross, feeding on some of the powerful Christian books, and the great ministry that we can get on cassette tapes. The Word of God says: "I commend you to His Word, the word of His grace which is able to build you up and give you an inheritance among them who are sanctified."

God may give you a crisis experience during this week which may be a turning point in your life. God is working in different people in different ways. Some people have very emotional missionary calls. They can tell you the moment and the hour. Johnny Jungle came back from New Guinea, and was showing slides in the church, and at that moment you were hit, "Lord, take me; I'll go." I've heard some of the most unbelievable stories of how people were called to the mission field. Praise the Lord! As long as he goes, and he perseveres and the Lord uses him, fine. But God works in different people in different ways.

Many of you are never going to get that kind of emotional call, so stop looking for it. If somehow you feel you must have it, let me know. I will send one of my co-workers and at midnight we will show some slides and we will play some music in your room, and the next morning you will be ready to go. I can assure you that you probably will not get very far! Some of the people who are doing the greatest work on the mission field are people with far less emotion, more phlegmatic people who maybe never had a special call, but just slowly it was revealed to them by the Lord guiding them, others instructing, or giving advice, that this was the way, and they walked in it. Sometimes messages on the will of God leave us all more confused than when we started because it's a narrow message, and gives a narrow way to following God's will. As well as working in different people in different ways, God is working in different groups in different ways. He is working through the Navigators, through Campus Crusade, through the Christian Unions, through others who maybe don't feel they should fellowship that much with these three groups.

RIGHT PRIORITIES

When we think of the size of the task, it is vitally important to count the cost about the quality of our life. Many of us have too many convictions. We have got to have discernment and wisdom to know what the PRIORITIES are! The good is the enemy of the best. Some of our nations' people are caught up endlessly in secondary issues. Brother, that's all right, if you feel that way, good. But let's unite on the major issues of God's Word.

Even important Biblical convictions, if they are not mixed with love, can turn to bitterness. If we're not careful, what we receive here eventually could turn to bitterness. I found this was possible, as I have been preaching the message about the Muslim world for 24 years - 600 and 900 times a year, in 30 or 40 nations. Considering the amount of people that have heard the challenge, the response has been small. In trying to reach out to these countries, it seems so often that most of the churches are not with us. It seems that often you are a lonely voice, crying out in the wilderness, and if you're not careful, you can become bitter, and God doesn't want bitter missionaries.

Probably most of us have heard of somebody returning from the field, who maybe had been suffering, and maybe was living on the barest essentials, and they saw the way people were living in the States or England. When they started to speak in the pulpit, you could sense there was bitterness, and harshness. It wasn't the sweetness of Jesus Christ. I feel no matter how many times we are walked on, our message is thrown to one side, no matter how few people respond to our challenge, we must remain always loving, kind, tender and compassionate. We have no axe to grind; we only have a Savior to serve.

We must be patient in spreading this unique vision that we have for all the people of the world. I may have a few strong points; I have too many weak ones. For example, I'd like to preach my convictions about television. I'd like to wipe every television out of O.M., except one or two we need for our video recorder. But I realize it is not that simple. With a wide range of people that we have, this is not a priority for me to go around preaching against television. I can make my mild statements now and then and let everybody make their own decisions. The young people are taking this message in. I find far greater interest on the part of youth to move out in evangelism than I do in the Church to send them out. That is not a statement against the Church because there are many good churches that want to send out missionaries or O.M. would not exist.

God has brought us to Edinburgh for a great purpose. Those of us especially in this student consultation are not the most famous, the strongest, or the most educated, but if Jesus Christ be for us, who can be against us? Let us stand together, uniting the great qualities of spiritual reality with this great vision of reaching all people with the gospel and believe by faith that it can come to pass. The decision of course is always ours. God will take us so far, lovingly pushing and drawing us, but the ultimate step to be a doer instead of just a hearer is always yours.

I hope you will take it.

11
MISSION
IMPERATIVE:
Intercession

*PATRICK
JOHNSTONE*

I want to speak to you about this urgent matter of praying
for the world. This is not the kind of thing that people usually get
enthusiastic about. I want to base what I say on II Kings 6:8-23.

"Once when the King of Syria was warring against Israel, he
took counsel... saying, At such and such a place shall be my
camp, but... Elisha, sent word to the King of Israel. Beware
that you do not pass this place for the Syrians are going down
there. And the King of Israel ... saved himself there more than
once or twice... .The King of Syria was greatly troubled...
and he called his servants and said to them,... show me who
of us is for the King of Israel? And one of his servants said,
None, my Lord, O King, but Elisha, the prophet who is in Israel
tells the King of Israel the words that you speak in your bed
chamber. And he said, Go and see where he is, that I may send
and seize him. And it was told him, Behold he is in Dothan. So
he ... came by night and surrounded the city, And when the
servants of the man of God rose early in the morning and went
out, behold an army with horses and chariots was round about
the city. And the servant said, Alas my master, what shall we
do. He said, Fear not, for those who are with us are more
than those who are with them. Then Elisha prayed and said, Oh
Lord, I pray thee, open his eyes that he may see. So the Lord
opened the eyes of the young man and he saw. And behold the
mountain was full of horses and chariots of fire round about
Elisha and when the Syrians came down against him, Elisha
prayed to the Lord, and said, Strike this people, I pray thee,
with blindness. So he struck them with blindness in accordance
with the prayer of Elisha, and Elisha said to them, This is not

the way, this is not the city, follow me, and I will bring you to the man whom you seek. And he led them to Samaria. As soon as they entered Samaria, Elisha said, Oh, Lord, open the eyes of these men that they may see. So the Lord opened the eyes, and they saw, and lo, they were in the midst of Samaria. And when the King of Israel saw them, he said to Elisha, My Father, shall I slay them, shall I slay them? He answered, You shall not slay them. Would you slay those whom you have taken captive with your sword and with your bow? Set bread and water before them that they may eat and drink and go to their master. So he prepared for them a great feast and when they had eaten and drunk, he sent them away, and they went to their master. And the Syrians came no more on raids into the land of Israel."

INTRODUCTION:

The Conditions for Jesus' Return - World Evangelization.

At this stage in the history of missions we are at a crossroads. Decisions must be made. We must move ahead in a new way, because we face crises in today's world that we cannot avoid. It's a very different world to that of the Colonial era. We don't want to go back to it. God has put us into the world for such a time as this, and therefore God has a plan for us to fulfill—that which He has commanded in His Word: to evangelize the nations and the peoples of this world. That job will not be finished until Jesus comes again in Glory. SOME PEOPLE ARE PRAYING FOR JESUS TO COME BACK, BUT THEY OUGHT TO BE PRAYING FOR THE WORLD TO BE EVANGELIZED. The Word of God is plain, that He cannot return until the world is evangelized. Therefore if we want to bring back our Lord Jesus, we must finish the job. But we stand at this crossroads.

The Dramatic Advances of the Gospel

If we look back, we see an immense amount of work that has been done. Over the last 200 years, there has been a dramatic advance of the Gospel in many areas. We have seen God working in mighty power in many countries. In the WESTERN WORLD there is a tendency to discouragement and despair about the state of the churches here. But what we are seeing elsewhere is not necessarily a reflection of that. We have seen the center of gravity of Biblical Christianity moving away from the western to the non-western world, and praise God for that. In most of these countries there were no believers at all 200 years ago, and so God has worked mightily.

Think of the great growth in LATIN AMERICA. Possibly there were only about 70,000 Protestants in 1900. Today there are 25 million. Think of AFRICA and the great turning to God and to the churches. I say both, because there are many nominal Christians in Africa, but also very many fine believers. I praise the Lord for what has been happening over the last 15 years. In many countries, persecution has come, and this has served to purify the Church and deepen its roots in Jesus. Today you will meet many fine, refined Christians in Africa. Some of you have probably already done so. Then again in Asia certain areas have seen great breakthroughs. It was a great thrill for me to be in the land of Korea just a few months ago and to see the astonishing situation in Seoul, the capital, and to hear that in that city of 8 million people, there are 3 million Christians today. There were none a hundred years ago. The place is swarming with people going to church, all carrying Bibles! The COMMUNIST WORLD too has seen great advances. Praise God for what is happening in China—there we have seen the Church growing in spite of all that the devil was throwing against it.

The Challenging Need for the Gospel

We must realize that although there have been great advances, our job is not yet finished. We have a belt of people right across the old world, stretching from the Atlantic across North Africa, the Middle East, up through the Asian Soviet Union, through Asia, where two-thirds of the world's population live. The Gospel has not really made a significant impact. And in this area lie most of the people that we are defining in this consultation as the Hidden Peoples, the people who are beyond the reach of normal witnessing Christian activity. In order for these people to be reached we've got to break through mighty barriers, enormous obstacles, to get the Gospel into resistant peoples that are not necessarily so willing to hear. But because our Lord Jesus is King and reigning at this moment, I believe that before He comes back again, we must see those breakthroughs. Otherwise Jesus is not Lord, and these other religions are more powerful. I do not believe this is true, and therefore, we must expect and wait for these breakthroughs in the world today.

But we face these challenges in the world. We see these very people we want to evangelize, dominated by resurgent religions and opposed to the Gospel we preach. We see what is happening in ISLAM today. How can we break open this tough nut? We've hardly made an impression on Islam. Of the 800 million Muslims in the world today, possibly there are only half a million who are now Christians, or who are the children or grandchildren of those who have been converted out of Islam. I could go on... these great blocs of people, the Hindus, the Buddhists, the Chinese and so on.

Prayer is the Secret.

We've got a job to do, but how are we going to tackle it? We see all these obstacles and the difficulties. It is only going to be as we mobilize people to pray. Now praying seems to many almost the last resort. And this is tragic. Unless we see that the only way we can move ahead is on our knees, we are not going to see those breakthroughs. It is not going to be with wonderful plans or clever ideas of men. We are going to speak about plans in these days, we are going to think of strategies, but unless those come from prayer, we are not going to see anything happen. I've seen too much in this

world as I've moved around of plans that have been given by God for
one area, and imported wholesale into another, and thinking this
method is the answer. Without the Holy Spirit behind it, it just falls
flat. And so we can have all these ideas of mobilizing students and
young people for evangelism, for world evangelization, and it's just
going to come to nothing, if it's not from God that the plans and
strategies come. That is why it is essential that we base all we do on
prayer and that is why I believe the conveners of this conference have
started off this our first main session on the prayer level.

Right through history, the great advances of the gospel have come
as a result of prayer. I can only give a few examples. In the Scripture
we find this is so. When Jesus gave the Great Commission to the early
church, He told them first to wait, and they spent ten days praying.
Then the Holy Spirit came, and they moved out. World evangelization
started with prayer. We find that again in Acts, chapter 4. When they
started to see persecution, they prayed and the Holy Spirit came down
in power again and shook the building where they were, and they
preached the word with boldness. We see a moving out and it came
through prayer meetings; earnest prayer before the Lord. The same
thing happened in Acts 13. When those leaders in the church in
Antioch prayed to God that they might be led, the Holy Spirit began
to speak to them about world evangelization and then came the great
missionary thrust of the early church to the gentiles. And so right
through history.

Any great forward movement of missions has started by prayer.
One example - the great example I believe - is that of the
Moravians. They were a little church that was chased out of what is
now Czechoslavakia, and took refuge in south Germany. This little
group was filled with dissension and problems but then God began to
work and they started to pray for world evangelization. And they
started a prayer chain which lasted for 100 years. That tiny little
church sent missionaries to North and South America, Africa, and to
Asia. They were there before any other Protestant missionaries and it
was largely through them that the Wesleyan (Methodist) revival came,
and then the modern missionary movement. It started in prayer.

We are facing this crisis today. We must start by praying. The
reason for "Operation World" was simply that we needed prayer
information. We were gathering Christians of different races with one
aim to pray for the world. We'd gather for a whole week, to pray for
different parts of the world,

I believe through those weeks of prayer, we saw breakthroughs in
many parts of the world. This then is my introduction, to show you
that prayer is absolutely basic to new advances for the Gospel.

Let us go over to the principles in the passage we read. We find
first of all PREVAILING PRAYER, that kind of praying that goes
through until we get an answer. Too often we say prayers and don't
expect an answer. We generalize our prayers sufficiently so that we

don't need an answer, and satisfy our consciences that we have done
our job. But prevailing prayer is getting what God wants us to pray
about and pressing through until we have the certainty in our hearts
of the answer even before we necessarily see it. That's the kind of
praying we need. And if we pray like that, it's going to have four
effects on our lives.

FOUR EFFECTS ON OUR LIVES

1. We Will Walk With God

The first is that prevailing prayer makes men and women of God.
Elisha is called the man of God, and that was enough of a definition.
Again and again through the life of Elisha you will find this. Other
people noticed his life style. That woman who gave him a place to
stay perceived that he was a man of God. There was something about
his life and his character that marked him as having something of God
Himself about him. We would say in New Testament terms he had a
Christ-likeness about him. But how do we get that Christ-likeness?
Today, we are in the age of instant Christianity - everything must be
at once. We must have it all in a rush. But it doesn't always come
like that. There are many who are seeking this kind of experience or
that kind of experience. Praise God for every experience. I am not
deriding them. But we think that we can have an instant holiness, and
it doesn't come that way. A man or woman of God is marked by the
character of God, because he or she spends time, earnest time, in the
presence of God.

So often we've gone out and we've spoiled the message we've
preached because we haven't lived it. But this man lived the message,
and everybody perceived that he was a man of God. Even the enemy
in Syria knew the man of God was there, and that it was his fault
that they were suffering defeat after defeat. And so we find this first
characteristic of those who prevail in prayer. They begin to share in
the character of the Lord Jesus Christ Himself. This comes with many
agonies. Probably many of you here can testify to this kind of
experience when you begin to feel so inadequate and wretched. God
humbles you and breaks you before the Cross and you begin to realize
that in yourself there dwells no good thing. You need God in a new
way—to break through in your life. This is often the turning point in
a person's Christian walk, and begins to make him effective, whatever
kind of experience we might call it. But the basic thing is that it
comes through agonizing before God, determining to go through with
the Lord in this matter. But too often we, in Christian work, begin to
get professional, and we dodge the issue of earnestness before God.
Let's not lose it. Because we're never going to see the Holy Spirit
working in the world without that earnestness, that kind of prayer
that Isaiah prayed when he said, "Oh, that Thou wouldst rend the
heavens." That's what we need. Let's remember it's not going to be
our clever, psychological methods or our advertising programs or our
slick leaflets, and so on, that is going to mobilize young people of

today to move out in missions—it's going to be prayer that will do it, and it must start in you and me. Then if we've got that stamp of God about us, we're just going to move other people with us. This one man, Elisha, changed history—one man alone. Later on, we see how the whole army of Syria came to capture one man, and they messed this up too because God was on the side of Elisha. You'll find that if one or two of that nature can be raised up by God, they are going to move multitudes with them.

2. We Will Know God's Will

But more than that, a man of God has a contact with the Lord so that he is able to find out how God feels about situations. In this narrative, Elisha had, as it were, a direct telephone line to Heaven as He knew exactly what the Lord was thinking and the Lord was telling him what other people were thinking. Elisha knew the will of God. Look at his authority as he moved around amongst the people. There's that calmness and authority about all he did. And so therefore, we find in Elisha, not only did he have that walk with God, but he was able to discern God's will. Isn't this one of our greatest problems in praying? We don't know quite how to pray. Most of our efforts in praying should be spent in finding out God's will. We don't change God's mind by praying. God changes us when we pray. So that we fit in with His plan and we know how to move ahead. If I know what God wants me to pray for, I can pray for it with earnestness and expect God to answer. But all too often, we have a presumptuous way of praying for things without really knowing if this is God's will. So often we have it by example in this matter of healing. We have the promises in God's Word that He can heal. But then we sometimes have awful situations in which we pray for somebody who is sick and that person dies, even though you have trusted, and there's definitely faith there, but God's plan was otherwise. We can't always tie them together. It's often a problem of not really discerning what God was planning to do as a result of this illness. Sometimes God receives greater glory by the way we die, as Jesus said to Peter after the resurrection. We don't find out God's will by only discussing it. And during this consultation, if plans come up, don't just talk about them, pray about them together. Put it through the grid of prayer, and then God will begin to put minds and hearts together with a common line. As you have that unanimity before God, and that witness of the Spirit in your heart, then perhaps you can move forward. The basis of all advances in Christian work is first of all, a person's walk with God. God is more interested in us and how we are before Him, than the work we do. Let's not make plans without really seeing our own hearts right with God, and having the stamp of divine nature upon us, having the mind of Christ. And so here we see, in Elisha, this was true.

3. We Will Wage Spiritual Warfare.

Prevailing prayer leads us into a spiritual warfare. This Is well illustrated in this story. That frightful King of Israel was certainly not a godly man, but he was still the leader of the people that God had chosen. Elisha sent a message to his king, and warned him about the plans of the enemy. As a result, the enemy became extremely frustrated. The King of Syria looked around for the spy, but then his generals had to tell him, "It's all the fault of that prophet!" And so the armies of Syria were diverted from the main plan they had and sent to surround that little town with one prophet in it. Isn't that amazing? And we see that if we walk with God and we begin to have effective praying the devil is frustrated, and he comes and attacks.

In Ephesians 6 we see the war in the heavenlies that goes on, and how we must be equipped to fight it. But all too often we, as Christians, are fighting a battle on a carnal horizontal level. We are striving with systems, with organizations, with personalities, and things on that level. We must deal with the vertical level. That is where the real enemy is - in the heavenlies. We have our organizations, but they're split, they're divided, they are backbiting, because we're fighting against the wrong enemy. We're fighting against flesh and blood, people, ideas, when really we're fighting against the devil. He wants to bring dissension when he sees that there are plans that might hurt his kingdom. We must realize who our real enemy is and fight him on the spiritual level. The level of the spirit is not in the level of organizations or plans. In Africa, if a lion is shot, he will often try to bite the bullet that has hit him and not go for the hunter who has shot him. There are too many Christians today who are trying to bite the bullet and not the hunter, Satan. When we walk with God, we begin to understand the nature of the spiritual war in which we are engaged. The wife of the leader of our mission often used to pray, "Lord I don't want to be in any work of God in which the devil is not interested." That prayer was answered very frequently! If we are going to be spiritually effective, the devil is going to pour out all his efforts to damage us, to stumble us, to hinder us from being effective.

One word of encouragement, if you are going through a really tough time. Maybe God has a great plan for you, and Satan is just attacking you. God wants you to press through and to trust Him in that, and you will come through to the place of victory. If the devil is frustrated by what is happening in your life or in your fellowship's life, and attacks, you can take comfort, the action is there and things are moving ahead. The devil will oppose everything that hinders his kingdom. We see this well illustrated by the way the Syrians came to capture Elisha. It was a pretty foolish thing to do, wasn't it? After all that Elisha had managed to get right, to think that they could still get him. But the devil is like that. He thinks he can achieve a lot. But as we walk with Jesus, the devil's got a hopeless task. Praise 's God, he's defeated. And so, we needn't fear him. We mustn't   n, underestimate him, but this principle is true on a worldwide scale. Let's apply it!

4. We Can Expect Spiritual Victories.

As we look at the world with all its upheavals, turmoils, and trouble, we mustn't look at it with despair and pessimism. We must see this as an answer to the prayers of God's people. In Revelation 8:1-5, we see a principle that the judgments of God are poured onto the world as a result of the prayers of God's people. "When the Lamb opened the 7th seal, ... another angel came and stood at the altar with a golden censer, and he was given much incense to mingle with the prayers of all the saints upon the golden altar before the throne. And the smoke of the incense rose and the prayers of the saints from the hand of the angel before God. And the angel took the censer and filled it with fire from the altar and threw it on the earth; and there were peals of thunder, and voices and flashes of lightning and an earthquake." So sometimes even the earthquakes and the shattering events of this world are sent from heaven by God because His people are praying.

I believe we are seeing this in all that has been happening over these last 18 months in Iran, and the rise of this fanatical Islam; some Christians have been killed, some missionaries are in prison , and others driven out of the country. Yet in Iran today, from all the reports I can gather, more people are earnestly seeking after God than ever in the history of the country. The same we find among Irani refugees in the west. Iranian people are coming to the Lord more easily now than ever before. And for that we can praise God. All these upheavals are stirring things up, that people might be opened up to the Gospel. Then we have the Gulf War that is raging at this moment. I believe this might be allowed of God. I cannot dictate to the Lord what is going to happen, but I can see how God could use this to break down people's confidence in their religion and make them open to something new. You see how God works in history.

Think of China. Think of the disappointment when open Christian work came to an end between 1951-1953 followed by the terrible persecution under the Red Guards, and the church went underground. We think of that as a great tragedy. But only now as the doors to China begin to open a little bit, we begin to hear a little of the acts of God in the intervening time. As far as I can reckon in most areas where there were Christians, they've either quadrupled or even increased up to twenty-fold, as many now as there were when Mao Tse-Tung captured the Mainland. So you see you can't stop God. He uses even the forces of evil and turns them for good for the sake of His Kingdom.

I was in Thailand a few months ago, and I heard about the refugees who were coming over the border. In 1970 Cambodia had possibly no more than 400 born-again Christians. But in one camp alone, on the borders just over in Thailand, over 20,000 have sought the Lord this year. It's dramatic. God has used the holacaust. It wasn't God who gave it, it was the devil himself and his anger to stop the work of God, but God turns the tables on the devil and gives a greater victory than the devil could have ever won. And that is our Lord, and it comes through prayer. Let's mobilize! Let's advance into the world in prevailing prayer, and we will yet see many more great victories. Let us go into this Consultation determined to be in a spirit of prayer throughout, and follow the pattern set by Elijah!

12
MISSION
INVITATION:
Harvest Time

J. ROBERTSON
McQUILKIN

> When our Lord saw the crowds, He had compassion for them,
> because they were harassed and helpless like sheep without a
> shepherd. Then He said to His disciples, "The harvest is great,
> but the laborers are few. Pray therefore the Lord of the
> harvest to send out laborers into His harvest" (Mt. 9:37).

I'd like to ask several questions about the harvest and harvesters
and seek answers to the situation in the world and in our own lives.

1. WHAT IS THE HARVEST?

A GROWING HARVEST

The population equivalent to North America, or to Russia, or to
Africa, was the entire world population at the time Christ said, "The
harvest is great." It was great then, but today it must be more than
15 times greater. We're not completely sure of this statistic but many
demographers tell us that if Jesus Christ were to come tonight, there
would be more people going out into a Christless eternity than those
from all the centuries preceding the 20th Century combined.

THE FOUR BILLION LOST

Figure 1 represents the four billion lost of the world. I speak of
the lost because of Christ's analogy here. Actually, He mixes His
metaphors. First it's the sheep and then it's the harvest. When He
speaks of the sheep, He says they are harassed and helpless, without a
shepherd. So the word "lost" is a good Biblical word. I have suggested
that there are 4 billion people who are lost.

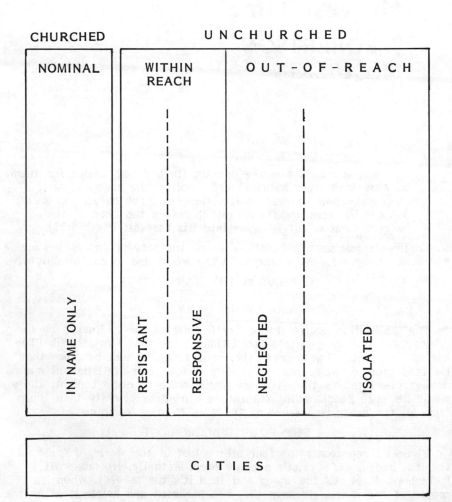

FIGURE 1

THE 4 BILLION LOST OF THE WORLD

MISSION INVITATION: HARVEST TIME - J. Robertson McQuilkin

THE LOST: Churched and Unchurched

The harvest is very great, as our Lord said. But let us separate these into the CHURCHED and the UNCHURCHED. I have called those "lost sheep" who belong to a church, "churched in name only". For example, a spiritually dark nation, like Italy, is churched, but a vast majority of them still need the Good News of life in Christ Jesus.

THE UNCHURCHED: Within-Reach and Out-of-Reach

We're concerned this week particularly with the unchurched, and not even with all the unchurched. We're going to divide the "lost sheep" even further—WITHIN-REACH PEOPLE, that is within reach of a church, or present missionary outreach, and the OUT-OF-REACH PEOPLES. Perhaps you call these the Hidden or the by-passed peoples. We are concentrating on this group that are presently out of reach of any organized church of Jesus Christ.

THE OUT-OF-REACH: Neglected and Isolated.

We can divide the out-of-reach peoples into those who are NEGLECTED and those who are ISOLATED. It may not be so much that the church has neglected certain peoples as that the church has been isolated from them for one reason or another, perhaps where it's illegal for foreigners to take the Gospel into that country. In the area of structural isolation, you would have considered China such until recently. As far as western missionaries are concerned, it still is structurally isolated with the door cracking just a bit. Libya is both structurally and ideologically isolated, and there are some that are just ideologically isolated.

There is another great proportion which is simply NEGLECTED. The door is open, but no one has gone in cross-culturally. In many of them, the harvest really is ripe such as tribes in Nigeria, where perhaps 25 tribes so far have been neglected, and not all of them Islamic. Certain areas of Indonesia would be "out-of-reach", but they are neglected. We simply have not gone there.

THE "WITHIN-REACH": Responsive and Resistant

There are churches throughout Japan, so it is a people "within-reach". It is also a RESPONSIVE people, although not nearly so responsive as Korea, for example. You can get 50% growth per decade if you work at it, and have the gift of evangelism. The problem is that the laborers are too few. Of 115 million people, less than 1% are Christian. And then there are the RESISTANT. Cross-cultural evangelists can get into Turkey, for example, but there is very little response.

THE CITIES: Ghettos and High Rises

A constant burden on my soul is the CITIES. They will include 80% of the world's population by the end of this century. The harvest

is great in those cities. There are people from every type, those who
are completely isolated, those who are out-of-reach but just simply
neglected, and those who are within reach of Christian neighbors.
There are believers but the laborers are too few. Even in a city that
is fairly homogenous like Mexico City there are different kinds of
peoples. In Seoul, Korea there has been a tremendous impact for the
Gospel for 25 years. In Sao Paulo, there is also this impact. But apart
from these, if there is another great metropolitan area where the key
has been found, I'm not aware of it.

INNER CITY GHETTOS often do not even appear in the
population statistics of the nation. They can ignore, for example, in
Jakarta, 3 or 4 million people because the government doesn't want to
recognize that those people are there. So you have the inner-city in
which virtually no one is willing to go, particularly Protestants who
are married and have families. Then you have the HIGH RISES. People
build barriers around themselves, barriers of protection. Who has
cracked the high rise? We've had some good probes in Hong Kong and
in Singapore, but where, really, have we cracked the high rises of
Paris, of Tokyo, of Osaka? In the cities of the world the harvest is
great, and is becoming greater by the day.

2. WHAT ABOUT THE HARVESTERS?

Jesus said that the harvesters, the laborers, are few. We need to
think about the kind of laborer that is needed to reap that kind of a
harvest.

Every Christian a Witness

I like to picture the local church with many functions—teaching
the Bible, discipling, fellowship—one body in Christ in which people
really care for one another, physically and emotionally and spiritually.
When the church reaches out, every Christian is called to be a
witness, to share the life of Christ in him, by his behavior and by his
talk.

Some Are Specially Gifted

In addition to this, God intends in every congregation for some
people to be specially gifted in bringing people to life in Jesus Christ,
(Figure 2). The specialists tell us that the most vital, vibrant
congregation can expect up to 10% of its membership to have a special
gift of evangelism. Now if we lay that responsibility on 100% of the
people, we're going to have a lot of people on guilt trips and we're
going to have a lot of people who would be so frustrated that they
will drop out of witnessing entirely. Everyone a witness, but certain
people anointed of God to consistently win others to Jesus Christ.

So here are your evangelists reaching out. In Figure 3, one
evangelist witnesses not only in his own community, but he goes to
another community, Samaria if you please, and establishes a church. It
takes somebody with particular gifts to go over there. Is he sent over

FIGURE 2

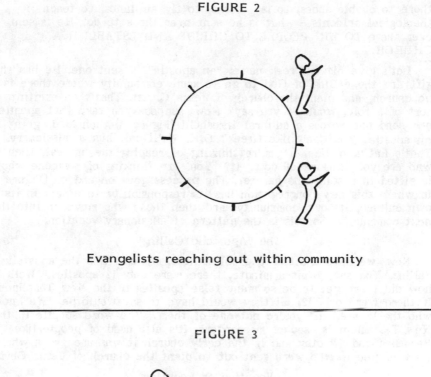

Evangelists reaching out within community

FIGURE 3

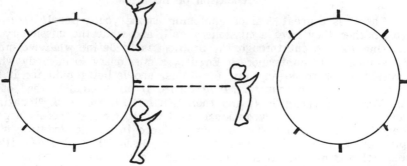

"Apostle", or missionary reaching out to another community

there to cobble shoes, to lay bricks, to fly airplanes, to teach
theological students - what is he sent over there to do? He is sent
over there TO WIN PEOPLE TO CHRIST AND ESTABLISH A
CHURCH.

Let's give him a Greek name: "an apostle", a sent one. He has the
gift and the calling of God to go to some community where there is
no church, and plant the church of Jesus Christ. That's an exciting
sort of a role, wouldn't you say? Now, suppose you take that apostle
and send him across a cultural threshold (Figure 4) then he is going as
an apostle. You don't like Greek? O.K. We'll call him a missionary.
That's Latin. Notice, if you're thinking of reaping the harvest, then
who are you thinking of doing it? You are thinking of someone who
is gifted in reaping the harvest. The process goes on and on (Figure 5)
in which this new congregation has its responsibility to others in its
own culture, its own community, and then those who move on into the
next community. So this is the pattern of missionary vocation.

The "Apostolic Calling"

Now we have a bit of a problem here. We call this the apostolic
calling. You say, "Wait a minute, there were only 12 apostles." Well,
how did there get to be so many false apostles in the New Testament?
If there were only 12, all they would have to say would be, "We know
who the 12 are, and you're not one of them." The word apostle in the
New Testament is used of messengers. It's also used of people like
Barnabas and Timothy and in the early church it was used of a whole
army of people who were sent out to plant the church of Jesus Christ.

Vocation or Location

There is a great deal of confusion among young people today as
to whether they have a missionary call, and what the missionary call
is. One way to cut through the problem is to define what we mean by
"missionary." In contemporary English, a missionary is anybody who
crosses water to do anything for Jesus, and is being paid for it by
people in his own country. We've turned it all around. Instead of
thinking first VOCATION, and then LOCATION, we think "location"
and wonder what our "vocational" call is. No wonder there's a great
deal of confusion. I would like you to zero in on the vocation of
pioneer or frontier church-starting evangelism. Why? Because it's
Biblical and because that's the only specialized person God has chosen
to get the task done. If there aren't people who are gifted and called
in that way, the task won't be done because that's what God chose to
use. Of all the gifts, He chose people with the ability to win others
to Christ and to establish the church of Jesus Christ. Now if you have
that ability or that vocation or God has stirred your heart to do that
sort of thing, what happens? Well, He may use you in the next town
over, or He may use you in the next state over, or He may use you in
some distant place. First "vocation" then "location."

FIGURE 4

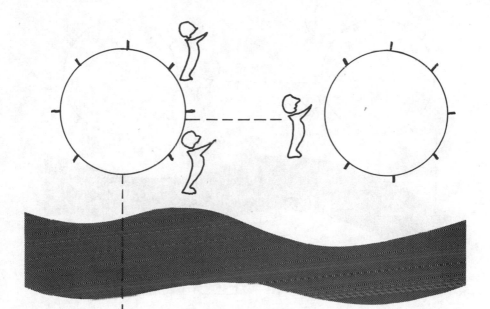
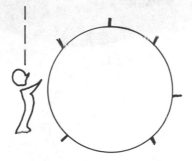

"Apostle", or missionary crossing cultural threshhold

FIGURE 5

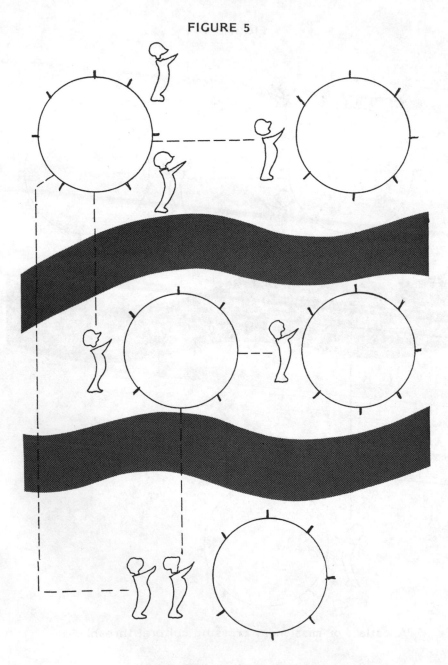

Continuing process of evangelizing
within communities and into new cultures

"First, Apostle...."

I agonized for a decade, trying to be a little Billy Graham, (I knew I couldn't be a big one) and finally in desperation I said, "Lord, we're going. I don't have the gift, but we're going." You say that's unbiblical. In First Corinthians 12:28 and 31, it says, "Covet earnestly the higher gifts—first, apostle, second, prophet, third, teacher." I discover, in the circles in which I move, that 95% covet to be a teacher, one of the higher gifts. But he says, "First apostle", and he says, "Desire it, covet it." When we got to Japan, we found that the American mass-produced, hard-sell approach was the very opposite of that which would appeal to the Japanese person. And we found that when we would settle down in a community and live among them and love them, then they would come, and they would come, and they would come, and we could establish a church. Then we would move into a new community, and love them to Jesus, and they would come. So don't conclude that you don't have this ability or this gift. Paul said, "Covet earnestly." That's old English. It means, "Go for it!" And maybe God will give it to you. If you're talking about frontier missions, if you're talking about Hidden Peoples, who are you looking for? You're looking for apostolic pioneer missionary evangelists.

3. HOW MANY HARVESTERS ARE THERE?

Let's look again at the "Lost of the World" Map (Figure 1). First I want to borrow a statistic from Patrick Johnstone. If we put on this map all the evangelicals in the world, we get the following: Evangelicals have sent out, maybe 40,000 to 50,000 missionaries. Where are those missionaries going? Three-fourths are going out to other evangelicals! That is, they are going to another culture, sure enough, but they are teaching theology, or they are preaching in a church, or they are doing some ministry for other Christians. THEY ARE NOT REACHING OUT IN TERMS OF EVANGELISTIC CHURCH PLANTING! Aren't all these evangelicals in America? No, they're not. In fact, a small minority of them are in America. They are all over the world. They are doing lots of good things, but they are doing them within the church. That means that we have perhaps 10,000 to 12,000 of these evangelicals who are going out to evangelize as a vocation.

I call the unchurched, out-of-reach peoples "the dark half." Why? Because there isn't even a flicker of a light. How many are going over there? Ralph Winter tells us that perhaps 3,000 to 4,000 (not just evangelical missionaries, but all kinds of missionaries) are going to this dark half of the world. Remember what Jesus said, the harvest is incredibly great, but "the laborers are few."

My prayer is that this conference will start something to break the logjam, to get the thing moving, to reach the dark half of the world. And what is it going to take? It's going to take people who are willing to get up and go.

4. WHAT ABOUT THE TENTMAKERS? CAN'T THEY DO IT?

Historically, any church that has really boomed in growth has done so with tentmakers. That is, the so-called lay people have been witnesses for Christ. But where in Christian missions are "tentmakers" comparable to the Muslim businessmen who sweep like a tidal wave toward Southern Africa? How many real tentmakers do you know? I've been around for a while, so I know one. His name is Roy Jensen. He was an executive with Airwick in Japan, and he moved to a certain area where there wasn't a church and planted a church. And then when he got that done, he moved to another place and planted another church. I've used him as an illustration for years. You know what that rascal did last year? He resigned Airwick and joined The Evangelical Alliance Mission. I said, "Roy, you've ruined my only illustration of an honest-to-goodness tentmaking apostle!" You see, there are a lot of lay people who witness for Christ, but we need TENTMAKING EVANGELIST CHURCH PLANTERS. We must develop new ways to develop tentmakers who will be used of God to start churches where fulltime missionaries can't.

5. WHAT KIND OF LABORER DO WE NEED?

You say, well they've got to be spiritual. I've lived and worked among missionaries all my life. I don't know any more spiritual people. You say, they've got to pray more. I don't know people who pray more. They've got to be more devoted. They are so devoted. You say, what's needed? People with a gift, for one thing. If they don't have it, we need to pray it down on the church. But we need a new breed of pioneers, a people with courage. They don't have to have such enormous gifts, such great gifts. But they must have courage, a courage that comes from faith, born of prayer. We need a whole new breed of young people who are not so concerned about their retirement benefits, the working hours and vacation time, but creative pioneers, dynamic men and women of courage. That's the kind of people we need, if we're going to get the job done. And I want to tell you, that kind are very, very few.

6. HOW LONG ARE WE GOING TO NEED THIS KIND OF LABORER?

The task will not be done until every person on earth has heard the good news in a way he can understand it, and until a local congregation has been established in every community. I don't think we can stop until then. God's the only one who knows what He meant when He gave the command through His Son. He's the only one who knows what it will look like when it's finished. But we can't quit until every person on earth has heard with understanding the good news and a church has been established in every community.

7. HOW ARE THEY GOING TO GET THERE?

Pray for Harvesters

Patrick Johnstone has pretty well preached it for us. I just remind you, Jesus said ... "PRAY THE LORD OF THE HARVEST TO SEND LABORERS." If God doesn't send them, they won't go. Even in this group of highly motivated people, if God doesn't get hold of you and thrust you out, the chances are you will never get there. This word, "send" is a very strong word. It's the word that is always used of casting out demons. Do you think they volunteered? He cast out the demons. It's the same word that's used in His cleansing the temple. Do you think all those people just rallied around and said, "I'm next, Lord let me go?" He thrust them out. We've got to pray that God, the Holy Spirit, will thrust out laborers into the field.

Recruit Harvesters

Pray the Lord of the harvest, but don't get caught up in an error. Some people say, that's all you can do. You can't recruit, that's God's business. I wonder what they think about evangelism. Regeneration is God's business, wouldn't you say? But how does He do it? Through you and me, through human instrumentality. How does He thrust them out? Through you and me, through human instrumentality. I think one of the most exciting things about the Student Volunteer Movement is that every one of those missionary volunteers took it as their responsibility to take others with them. They would take five or ten with them. When God set a fire burning in a man's soul, he took his buddy, and a whole group.

The Example of Barnabas

Barnabas didn't just wait around for Paul to volunteer. He spotted in Paul someone that could be used. He spotted Paul, and he kept his eye on Paul, and then at the right time, he recruited him. He didn't say, "Now Paul, if the Spirit moves you." He said, "Paul, we need you down here, will you come?" So they put him to work. Then the church got together and had a prayer meeting and thrust out Paul and Barnabas as the first great apostolic pioneer missionary church-planting evangelists.

So you have the responsibility, not only to go but to spot others, to enlist them, to put them to work, and then to give them some training. We need a new kind of training for this new breed. Do you know how many people are in training in all the seminaries, in all the Bible colleges of the United States? 100,000. Do you know how many of them will go to the mission field? Of the half who graduate, 3.7% will go to the mission field if past proportions continue. And that 3.7% includes all kinds of missionaries, not just evangelists.

8. WHAT'S GOING TO BE NEEDED?

We're going to have to recruit an army to get the task done. We've got to finance them. The Southern Baptists have a slogan, "Bold Mission Thrust." They are going to see that every person on earth hears the gospel by the end of the century. Does that sound familiar? Isn't that similar to our purpose this week?

"By the year 2000" has a fascination to it. Do you know why? Because, if we don't do it, it means that another millennium has passed, and we have not obeyed our Lord's commission. That's the thing that sometimes keeps me awake at night.

The Student Movement

You can't by-pass the local church, but the student movement has often been greatly used of God. In the 30's, a number of students became concerned that the Student Volunteer Movement had moved off almost totally into involvement in social action without evangelism, and so they founded a new organization called The Student Foreign Missions Fellowship. Have you ever heard of Urbana? Well, that's Student Foreign Missions Fellowship. Since World War II, about 40,000 have gone out from the United States. What did this student movement have to do with it? A recent sampling would indicate that 60% in evangelical missionary societies were either members of FMF or were influenced by it, by Inter-Varsity, by Urbana or by all three. One student movement veered off to one side, but God raised up another one that has been greatly used. So historically the student movements have been greatly used of God.

How are they going to be sent? God's going to send them, but He's going to use you and me. He's going to use the Church, and He may use a student movement to provide the laborers.

9. WHY HAVE WE DONE SO POORLY?

Why, if the harvest is so great, are the laborers so few? I think the secret is found right here in this same passage. When Christ saw the crowds, He had compassion on them because they were harassed and helpless like sheep without a shepherd. Do you know why we aren't getting the job done? It's because God's people don't care. They are not moved as Christ was. They shut their eyes to the harvest, to the need. And when someone pries them open to show them the need, they are moved with DISINTEREST. That's the problem—we don't have the compassion.

On the northern island of Hokkaido in Japan, four brothers were swimming in the Pacific when one of them let out a scream. "It's a shark, it's a shark." The three younger brothers clambered up on a shelf in the shallow water, and watched their 14-year-old brother in his race with death. That black dorsal fin sliced closer and closer. All of a sudden, the three of them let out a yell, and he knew what it meant. The fin disappeared, the shark dived to strike from beneath. So when they yelled, he flailed back in the water, and the shark struck and missed. As it was going past, he reached out and grabbed it around the belly. The 3 brothers on shore were safe enough. What do you think they did?

What would you do?

The average evangelical youth group would call a symposium, get an expert on sharks and analyze whether sharks are deadly or not. The women of the church would be spiritual and have a prayer meeting. The men would be practical. They would take a collection, and buy a harpoon for their sister to take and go after the shark! What do you think these three little guys did? They didn't look to see what the others were going to do, they didn't discuss it. Just like one, they hit that water, and one of them scooped a stone off the ocean floor, grabbed the shark and began to pound him on the nose. Another one grabbed him around the tail and began to beat him in the belly. That poor shark didn't know what hit him. He made a lunge, but got confused and went in the wrong direction.

The parents down the beach heard all the noise and came running. When they got there, there was a 9-foot shark on the beach, flipping out his last, and four proud shark killers circling it. The 7-year old looked up at his Daddy and said, "I was scared!"

Sure he was scared. And some of you will get very scared this week. It looks so enormous. He was scared, he didn't know that he was going to come back. He only knew he was going out. Why? Because his brother was in trouble, and he knew it. And he loved him. He cared, that's all. That's the motive. It's compassion.

You say, "McQuilkin, you sound like you get emotional about this." Maybe I do, but I'm in pretty good company. It says, "When Jesus saw the people... He was moved with compassion." Literally it says His stomach was tied in knots. What does your stomach get tied in knots over? When you fail an exam, when you lose a job, when plans don't go the way you want? That's when I get tied in knots. But when Jesus saw what we are seeing this week, His stomach was tied in knots, and He moved out to shepherd those lost sheep.

How do you feel about it?

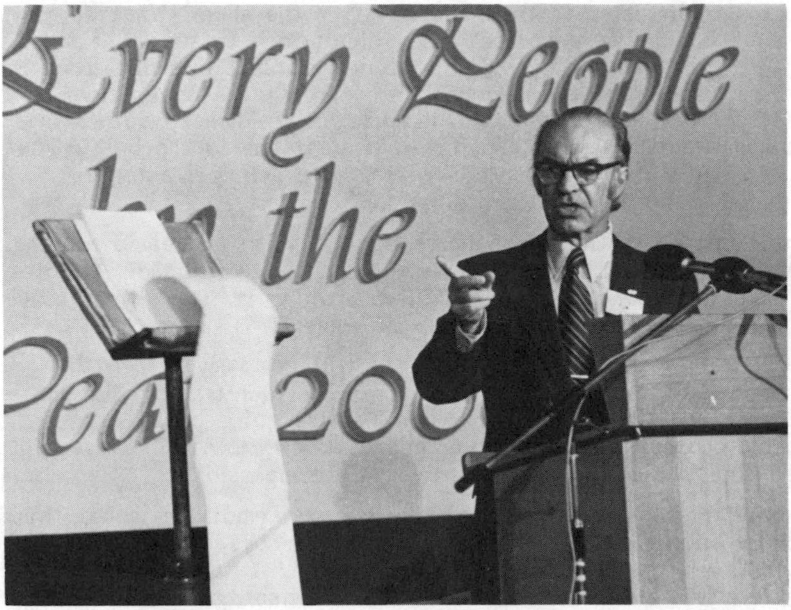
Every People
the
2000

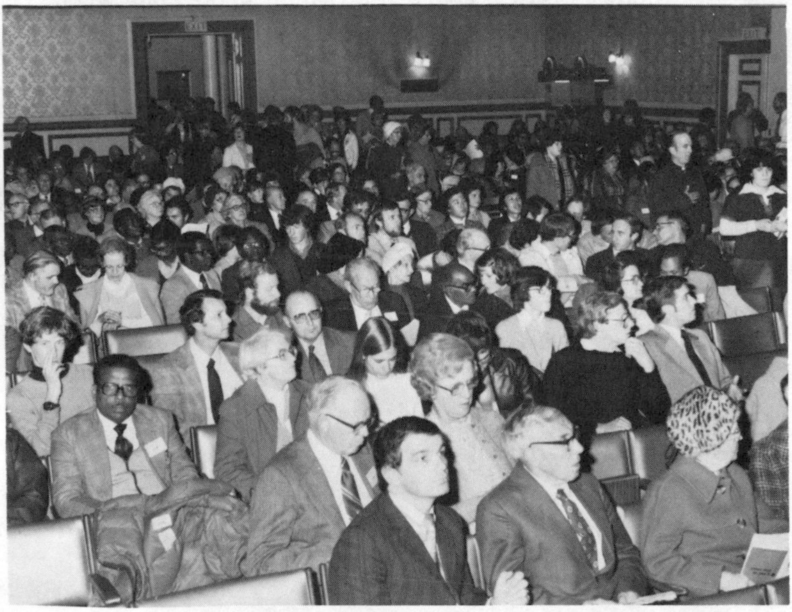

13
SINCE
EDINBURGH

The whole purpose of Edinburg '80 was to stimulate action by others toward reaching Hidden Peoples. The following examples are encouraging signs that the "Seeds of Promise" are beginning to sprout! (ED.)

ADVANCE IN EUROPE

During the conference, the combined Europe Study groups felt the need for specific attention to the Hidden People concept in Europe. Here is their report:

It was felt that adequate information should be made available at Mission '83 (sponsored by The European Missionary Association).

There was also a strong consensus that we should plan in such a way that others not present could take a full share of the responsibility, if they were prepared to do so.

The following tentative plans have been made:

-to gather information about European Hidden People
 for use in Mission '83;
-to organize a study-conference to prepare found
 information for use in Spring, 1982;
-to organize a general European meeting on Hidden Peoples
 in the period of October 15 - November 15, 1981.

In order to achieve this, an initiating committee has been chosen to act as steering committee for these activities. Its task will be:

-to initiate contact with missions and churches in
order to encourage and coordinate research and ministry
directed to Hidden People in Europe and the USSR;
-to maintain contact with other similar approaches
and the Centers for World Mission.

Report by Rev. Teo J. van der Weele

Over the last years the concern for "Hidden Peoples" has grown
considerably. The Lausanne Committee on World Evangelism (LCWE)
in Pattaya dealt primarily with the task of reaching the approximately
16,750 people groups, which have little, if any, witness for Christ
within their culture. There are 2.4 billion of these "Hidden Peoples."

Delegates attending the World Consultation on Frontiers Missions in
Edinburgh, came away with the commitment to establish: "A church for
every people by the year 2000." As Europeans, we are beginning to
recognize that there are still many "Hidden Peoples" within our own
borders, not only in the eastern part and beyond. Our heritage in
missions has been rich and we praise God for what has been, and is
being done by European missions, and churches, but there is still much
more to be done!

At Pattaya and Edinburgh and through interaction with the various
European Evangelical Alliances, many of us feel it is now time for
European Evangelicals to make a fresh study of the situations in
Europe. As the ad hoc European Hidden Peoples Study Group Steering
Committee we met in The Netherlands (7-8 January) to discuss the
issues involved and found we were confrontating by questions such as:

-What is our theology of mission and missions?

-How does this theology lead us regarding the "Hidden Peoples?"

-Where are the "Hidden Peoples" within Europe?

-What needs to be done to reach them?

-How do we prepare for and channel the rapidly growing numbers
of committed mission-minded young people?

We have found that others are wrestling with these questions as
well. We don't feel that a new organization is needed, but we do need
to come together as a consultation, study group or whatever, to do
research, inter- action and coordination. The present alliances and
committees provide sufficient structure and organization to give the
needed leadership to carry out the necessary tasks. However, we must
come together, as leaders and concerned believers, to understand the
present situation, discuss the possibilities and needs and establish some

responsibilities and priorities.

Our Steering Committee in consultation with various leaders of the European Alliances, LCWE and the World Evangelical Fellowship has arranged for a one-and-a-half day consultation on 6-7 May 1981 in West Germany.

This consultation will seek to establish a direction and plan for the vital work that needs to be done over the next years. This meeting will be very important to each of us. We are inviting only those people who understand and can represent the situation in their own countries.

STUDENTS ON THE MOVE

Ward Shope, General Secretary of the Theological Students for Frontier Missions, writes that his organization traces it's origin back to Edinburgh '80. Well, they don't have far to look back, but they have much to look forward to! They can justly associate with the title of this book - "SEEDS OF PROMISE". Following are excerpts from a statement signed by concerned seminary students (ED):

A CALL TO SEMINARY STUDENTS
CONCERNING FRONTIER MISSIONS

We, the seminary students assembled at the World Consultation on Frontier Missions in Edinburgh, do affirm that our Lord God created the world and all its peoples. We believe that He loves all nations... . In order to communicate this love throughout the generations, Christ has called His people as ambassodors and witnesses of this Good News to all unbelieving peoples (John 17, Acts 1:8)...

However, we have become aware of two situations which trouble us deeply: First, in her witness to Christ, the Church has yet to penetrate some 16,750 cultural-linguistic people groups that include about 2.5 billion people... . They remain the greatest challenge to the church and to those in our seminaries preparing for service. Yet, only about 9% of the world missionary force is actively carrying the Gospel to those people.

The second situation concerns our seminaries themselves. We do not believe that very many of our brothers and sisters are aware of or are considering the challenge... So little is said; so little is done; so much is needed.

In addition to urging students to sign the Edinburgh Pledge (see INTRODUCTION) they also provided a pledge for those not called to the foreign field (ED).

As a servant to a local church, whether in my country or abroad, I will seek to mobilize the congregation I serve to a deep compassion for the Hidden Peoples. I will encourage them to contribute to penetrating the Hidden Peoples with the Gospel through prayer, through finances, and through supplying Frontier missionary personnel. Furthermore, I will commit my life to be an example to others of what it means to be personally committed to Frontier Missions by praying, by giving of my resources, and by being informed.

In a meeting in Dallas, Texas in May 1981 the students put legs to their concerns. Ward Shope writes: "The purpose of the meeting was to give the movement which started in Edinburgh some basic foundational structures to ensure its progress. This was accomplished very successfully with the help of God. The meetings were long, and there were times of frustration and even hoplessness before we came to a resolution which seemed right to all." The new organizations stated purpose is "to mobilize graduate theological students to a lifetime commitment to the task of frontier missions for the glory of God. We are committed to the watchword, "A Church for Every People by the Year 2000."

THE BASIS FOR THE FUTURE — Samuel Wilson

On the final Saturday morning in Edinburgh, delegates to Edinburgh '80 voted to provide for the election of a permanent International Catalyst Committee through the ad hoc evaluating committee which had functioned during the consultation. The committee was to represent eight regions of the world, and was empowered to enlarge itself as it saw fit. Three pro tempore officers were elected until such time as the permanent committee could organize itself. Samuel Wilson was elected chairman, Leiton Chinn secretary and Larry Allmon treasurer. Under their leadership, the following international committee has been elected: Africa south of the Sahara, Panya Baba; Middle East and North Africa, Kundan Massey; Europe, Patrick Johnstone; East Asia, David Cho; South Asia, Chris D. Thomas; Latin America, Waldemiro Tymchak; North America, Samuel Wilson; Oceania, Petrus Octavianus.

The future should be assessed against the background of the motivation produced by Edinburgh '80. Visibility brings challenge. The awareness which was heightened in the hearts of those who attended carried over into a charge to Evaluating Committee members to nominate only those who would be willing to respond by becoming active for actually planting the Church through cross-cultural mission among Hidden peoples. Each Committee member has accepted responsibility for active promotion of efforts to reach those among whom no cluster of witnessing congregations currently exists. The vison which brought Edinburgh '80 into existence is bringing local and regional initiatives to fruition. Momentum is being built which will give substance to the dream of future consultations on a a growing scale.

Until now, it has been possible only to estimate the number of Hidden People groups. These estimates must yield to factual identification and planned penetration. Realistic evangelism with a view to planting a church discipled to the point of being able to carry on witness is the more meaningful and necessary goal.

Regional initiatives, like the ad hoc European Study Group, of which Teo Van der Weele is the leader, are providing the local stimulus to actual evangelism. Likewise, in West Africa Hidden groups have been identified and first efforts at penetration are being made. Regional consultations are alredy in the planning stage in several areas, such as Murree '81 in Pakistan.

In the long range, three participants at Edinburgh '80, Dr. Ralph Winter, the Rev. Teo Van der Welle and Dr. Samuel Wilson, are active in the planning process for a Consultation on the Nature and Mission of the Church in New Frontiers for Missions, to be sponsored by the World Evangelical Fellowship. This Consultation will take place in Wheaton, Illinois in the U.S.A. in June of 1983. It will undoubtedly serve as only the first step in a series of world events where information and experience can be shared, hopefully leading toward the serious pursuit of "a Church for Every People by the Year 2000."

APPENDIX I
MAJOR CONSULTATION PARTICIPANTS

ALLMON, Rev. Larry
General Director,
Gospel Recordings, Inc.   USA

Chairman, Convening Committee

BABA, Rev. Panya
Evangelical Missionary
Society of Nigeria

Ch. 4   Frontier Mission Personnel

CHINN, Leiton
International Students, Inc.
(Secunded to USCWM)

International Coordinator

COWAN, Dr. George
President, Wycliffe
Bible Translators

Ch. 5   Reaching Animists

GNANIAH, Rev. N. J.
Church Growth Assoc. of India

Ch. 7   Hidden People Among the
Hindus

GRIFFITHS, Dr. Michael
Principal, London Bible College

Ch. 3   Hinderances to the Gospel

HANNA, Dr. Mark
International Students Inc.

Ch. 1   Daily Bible Readings

JOHNSTONE, Mr. Patrick J. International Research Secretary,	Ch. 11 Mission Imperative: Intercession
McCURRY, Rev. Don Director, Zwemer Institute	Ch. 6 Hidden People Among Muslims
McQUILKIN, Dr. J. Robertson Principal, Colombia Bible College	Ch. 12 Mission Invitation: Harvest Tim
OCTAVIANIUS, Dr. Petrus Director, Indonesian Missionary Fellowship	Ch. 4 Frontier Missions Structures
RICHARDSON, Don Author, Regions Beyond Missionary Union	Ch. 5 Reaching Folk Religionists
RIGBY, Dr. David J. Principal, Lebanon Missionary Bible College	Chairman, Local Arrangements Committee
SPRAGGETT, Mr. Roy Scottish Mission Centre	Coordinator, Local Arrangements Committee
VERWER, Rev. George Director, Operation Mobilization	Ch. 10 Mission Challenge: Counting the Cost
WANG, Rev. Thomas General Secretary, Chinese Coordination Center of World Evangelism	Ch. 8 Hidden People Among the Chinese
WILSON, Ray (Black Buffalo) Founder, Black Buffalo Trails	Ch. 5 Reaching North American Indians
WILSON, Dr. Samuel Director, Missions Advanced Research and Communications Center (MARC)	Chairman, Continuation Committee
WINTER, Dr. Ralph W. General Director, United States Center for World Mission	Ch. 4 Frontier Mission Vision

APPENDIX II
DIRECTORY
OF MISSIONS

CONSULTATION ATTENDANCE

The following areas of the world were represented at the consultation: North America: 87, United Kingdom: 40, Europe: 35, Asia: 69, Africa: 24 and Latin America: 9. It is interesting to note that the so-called Third World countries (Africa, Asia, and Latin America) accounted for one third of the delegates. The 1910 conference had virtually none.

Total attendance, including the Student Consultation, was 451. This was less than that of the 1910 conference. However, in terms of agency representation, E-80, with 173 agencies, surpassed that of 1910 (160). It is also significant to note that one third of the agencies represented at E-80 were from non-western countries.

PROFILE OF AGENCIES REPRESENTED AT E-80

A brief profile of each of the agencies represented at Edinburgh is found on the following pages. Most of the headings are self-explanatory, but a few comments might help:

Groups: Here we wanted the number of people groups among whom the mission worked. This being a new concept and a new emphasis, it is not surprising that many agencies found it difficult to give a precise answer. In some cases this category was also not appropriate. For instance, Gospel Recordings provides recordings in over 4,000 languages and dialects, but cannot necessarily say that they are working in that many groups.

Missionaries: Within the scope of this publication we were not able to distinguish between home and field staff or nationals and expatriates. In addition, some organizations may not have been sure of what we wanted. Nevertheless this gives some comparative idea of the numbers involved and readers can write individual organizations for more information if necessary.

Tasks: Codes at the bottom of each page explain the different tasks represented by the numbers after this heading. No doubt there will be varying interpretations concerning each catagory. However, this should give some idea of the scope of each mission.

Names and Addresses: These are supplied along with telephone numbers for those wishing to communicate with the different organizations. Permission should first be obtained from the individual agencies before adding their names to any mailing list.

Accuracy of Information: This information was taken from E-80 application forms. A letter was subsequently sent to each agency requesting verification and we have sought to comply with all suggested changes. We cannot however guarantee the accuracy of any of the above statistics.

A.M.E.N., PERU
Apartado 5342, Lima 100, PERU

Telephone: 62 23 41   Founded: 1946
Rep(s) at E-80: Obed Alvarez, Edmundo Ravelo

Countries: 2 Groups: 3 Missionaries: 86 Tasks: 12

ACTION INTERNATIONAL MINISTRIES
P.O. Box 110, Greenhills, Metro Manila 3113, PHILIPPINES

Telephone: 70-92-47   Founded: 1974
Rep(s) at E-80: Doug Nichols

Countries: 1 Groups: 3 Missionaries: 20 Tasks: 1234567

ACTIVE CHRISTIAN TRAINING SCHEME (A.C.T.S.)
c/o Belfast Bible College
119 Marlborough Park South, Belfast BT9 6HW, IRELAND

Telephone: Belfast 664376   Founded: 1978
Rep(s) at E-80: William George Baxter

Countries: Groups: Missionaries: 4 Tasks: 7

AFRICA INLAND CHURCH
P.O. Box 45019, Nairobi, KENYA

Telephone: Nbi 333784   Founded: 1895
Rep(s) at E-80: Ezekial Birech, Joshua Chege,
Elijah Cherorot
Countries: 2 Groups: 9 Missionaries: 258 Tasks: 21

AFRICA INLAND MISSION
1440 Abbey Circle, Vinton, VA 24179 USA

Telephone: Founded:
Rep(s) at E-80: Charles Davis

Countries: Groups: Missionaries: Tasks:

AFRICA EVANGELICAL FELLOWSHIP, AUSTRALIA
10 Lyster Place, Melba, A.C.T. 2615, AUSTRALIA

Telephone: Founded:
Rep(s) at E-80: Sheila Draper

Countries: Groups: Missionaries: Tasks:

AFRICA INLAND MISSION INTERNATIONAL
Box 57909, Nairobi, KENYA

Telephone: Founded:
Rep(s) at E-80: Dr. Dick Anderson

Countries: Groups: Missionaries: Tasks:

ALL NATIONS FRONTIER MISSIONS
P.O. Box 446, Pasadena, CA 91102 USA

Telephone: (213) 794-7117   Founded: 1972
Rep(s) at E-80: Dr. Morris Watkins, Lois Watkins

Countries: 4 Groups: 10 Missionaries: 19 Tasks: 1234

(Codes: 1-Church Planting, 2-Evangelism, 3-Translation, 4-Literature, 5-Media, 6-Medicine, 7-Other)

AMBASSADORS FOR CHRIST, INC.
P.O. Box AFC, Paradise, PA 17652 USA

Telephone: (717) 687-8564   Founded: 1963
Rep(s) at E-80: Leona Frances Choy

Countries: 1   Groups: Missionaries: 15   Tasks: 247

ANGLICAN CHURCH OF UGANDA
c/o Enoch Drati, Fuller Theological Seminary
135 N. Oakland Ave., Pasadena, CA 91101 USA

Telephone: Founded:
Rep(s) at E-80: Enoch Lee Drati
Countries: Groups: Missionaries: Tasks:

ASIA EVANGELICAL MISSION
378 Kuo Hsing Rd., Kuo Hsing Nan Tou, Taiwan, R.O.C. 544

Telephone: Founded:
Rep(s) at E-80: John Hsieh, Charles Saunders

Countries: Groups: Missionaries: Tasks:

ASIA FOR CHRIST
18/3RT Prakashnager, P.O. Box 1700, Secunderabad, A.P.,
INDIA 500016

Telephone: Founded: 1975
Rep(s) at E-80: Dr. B.A. Prabhakar
Countries: 1   Groups: 5   Missionaries: 7   Tasks: 12

ASSOCIATION OF EVANGELICAL MISSIONS IN SWITZERLAND
Postfach 2107, 8028 Zurich, SWITZERLAND

Telephone: 01-251-75-40   Founded: 1965
Rep(s) at E-80: Traugott Staheli

Countries: Groups: Missionaries: 800 Tasks: 1234567

ASSOCIATION OF CHURCH MISSIONS COMMITTEES
1620 S. Myrtle Ave, Monrovia, CA 91016 USA

Telephone: (213) 357-5021   Founded: 1975
Rep(s) at E-80: Donald A. Hamilton

Countries: Groups: Missionaries: Tasks:

BLACK BUFFALO TRAILS
P.O. Box 2607, Hemet, CA 92343 USA

Telephone: (714) 925-8989   Founded:
Rep(s) at E-80: Ray and Priscilla Wilson

Countries: 3   Groups: 8   Missionaries: 12   Tasks: 234

BRETHREN IN CHRIST MISSIONS
Box 149, Elizabethtown,, PA 17022 USA

Telephone: 717-367-7045   Founded: 1871
Rep(s) at E-80: Curtis Book

Countries: 9   Groups: 14   Missionaries: 149   Tasks: 12567

(Codes: 1-Church Planting, 2-Evangelism, 3-Translation, 4-Literature, 5-Media, 6-Medicine, 7-Other)

CALVARY CHURCH MISSIONARY PRAYER BANDS
33 Siebel Avenue, Kirilla Pona, Colombo 5, SRI LANKA

Telephone: 073-3110   Founded: 1979
Rep(s) at E-80: Tissa Weerasingha

Countries: 1 Groups: 2 Missionaries: Tasks: 1

CAMPUS CRUSADE FOR CHRIST
Arrowhead Springs, San Bernadino, CA 92414 USA

Telephone: (714) 886-5224   Founded: 1951
Rep(s) at E-80: Paul Eshleman, Patty Burgin, Mary Graham,
Phil Hardin, Jeannie & Paul McKean; Doug Johnson, Karen
mohr, England reps; Daniel Porter, W. Germany rep; Warren
Willis, Guam rep.
Countries: 123 Groups: Missionaries: 11,400 Tasks: 256

CAMPUS CRUSADE FOR CHRIST, GUAM/MICRONESIA
Project Stop-Out, Box E, Agana,, GUAM 96910 USA

- See above

CANADIAN BAPTIST OVERSEAS MISSION BOARD, CANADA
217 St. George Street, Toronto, Ontario, CANADA M5R 2M2

Telephone: 416-922-5163   Founded: 1874
Rep(s) at E-80: Robert Berry

Countries: 8 Groups: 17 Missionaries: 100 Tasks: 1234567

CENTRO GUATEMALTECO DE TEOLOGIA   PRACTICA
Apartado Postal 102, Quezaltenango, GUATEMALA

Telephone: (061) 2108   Founded: 1962
Rep(s) at E-80: Ricardo Waldrop

Countries: 3 Groups: 4 Missionaries: 10 Tasks: 127

CHINESE WORLD MISSION CENTER
1605 E Elizabeth, Pasadena, CA 91104 USA

Telephone: (213) 684-0004   Founded: 1978
Rep(s) at E-80: Danny Yu

Countries: Groups: Missionaries: Tasks: 7

CHRISTIAN DYNAMICS
163/3RT Vijayanager Colony,
Hyderabad Andhra Pradesh, 500457, INDIA

Telephone: 36172   Founded: 1978
Rep(s) at E-80: P.D. Prasadarao
Countries: 1 Groups: 4 Missionaries: 2 Tasks: 2

CHRISTIAN MISSIONS IN MANY LANDS, JAPAN
Kaigan 2-3-22, Muroran 051, JAPAN

Telephone: Founded:
Rep(s) at E-80: Richard Goodall

Countries: Groups: Missionaries: Tasks:

(Codes: 1-Church Planting, 2-Evangelism, 3-Translation, 4-Literature, 5-Media, 6-Medicine, 7-Other)

CHRISTIAN MISSIONARY FELLOWSHIP
P.O. Box 26306, Indianapolis, IN46226 USA
Telephone: (317) 542-9256   Founded: 1949
Rep(s) at E-80: Dr. Harry Baird, James Smith, Joyce Smith

Countries: 4 Groups: 5 Missionaries: 40 Tasks: 21567

CHRISTIAN NATIONALS EVANGELISM COMMISSION
5, Watton Road, Knebworth, Herts SG3 6AH, UNITED KINGDOM
Telephone: 0438-811468   Founded: 1943
Rep(s) at E-80: David Winter

Countries: 37 Groups: Missionaries: 1000 Tasks: 12456

CHRISTIAN OUTREACH FELLOWSHIP
P.O. Box 3110, Kumasi Ashanti, GHANA
Telephone: 6186   Founded: 1974
Rep(s) at E-80: Ransford Senavoe

Countries: 1 Groups: 1 Missionaries: 1 Tasks: 2

CHRISTIAN AND MISSIONARY ALLIANCE CHURCHES
of the Philippines, P.O. Box 290, Zamboanga City,
7801 PHILIPPINES
Telephone: 55-27 or 35-16   Founded: 1947
Rep(s) at E-80: Benjamin P. De Jesus

Countries: 2 Groups: 9 Missionaries: 10 Tasks: 124

CHURCH GROWTH MISSIONARY MOVEMENT
36, Meiyappapuram 3rd Street, Madurai,
Tamilnadu, 625016, INDIA
Telephone: Founded: 1975
Rep(s) at E-80: B. Jeyaraj

Countries: 1 Groups: 3 Missionaries: 8 Tasks: 123

CHURCH GROWTH INSTITUTE FOR AFRICA
1st Floor Sandton City, 78509, Sandton 2146,
REPUBLIC OF SOUTH AFRICA
Telephone: 011-783-5400   Founded: 1980
Rep(s) at E-80: Johan Engelbrecht

Countries: 2 Groups: 4 Missionaries: 3 Tasks: 12

CHURCH MISSIONARY SOCIETY
157 Waterloo Road, London SE1 8UU, ENGLAND
Telephone: 01-928-8681   Founded: 1799
Rep(s) at E-80: H. W. Moore

Countries: 25 Groups: Missionaries: 310 Tasks: 234567

CHURCH OF PAKISTAN SIALKOT DIOCESE
Mission House 2, Mehmda Road, Gutrat, Punjab, PAKISTAN
Telephone: 3287   Founded: 1970
Rep(s) at E-80: George Fatehdin

Countries: 1 Groups: 1 Missionaries: 5 Tasks: 2

(Codes: 1-Church Planting, 2-Evangelism, 3-Translation, 4-Literature, 5-Media, 6-Medicine, 7-Other)

CHURCH OF THE NAZARENE WORLD MISSION DEPT.
1774 Sierra Bonita, Pasadena, CA 91104 USA

Telephone: Founded:
Rep(s) at E-80: Steve Hawthorne

Countries: Groups: Missionaries: Tasks:

CHURCH OF CHRIST IN NIGERIA
Rock Haven, Box 643, Jos, Plateau State, NIGERIA

Telephone: Founded: 1950
Rep(s) at E-80: Graham Weeks

Countries: 2   Groups: 5   Missionaries: 56   Tasks: 1346

CHURCH OF GOD WORLD MISSIONS
Keith at 25th, N.W., Cleveland, TN 37311 USA

Telephone: Founded:
Rep(s) at E-80: Bill Parson

Countries: Groups: Missionaries: Tasks:

CO-LABORERS DO BRAZIL
C.P. 290
87500 Unuarama PR, BRAZIL

Telephone: Founded: 1958
Rep(s) at E-80: Maurice Sand, Verna Sand

Countries: 1   Groups: 2   Missionaries: 8   Tasks: 27

DEN NORSKE SANTALMISJON
Postboks 6886,,   St. Olavs Plass, Oslo 1, NORWAY

Telephone: Oslo 209815   Founded: 1867
Rep(s) at E-80: John Victor Selle

Countries: 4   Groups: 9   Missionaries: 131   Tasks: 12456

DEN NORSKE TIBETMISJON (NORWEGIAN TIBETAN MISSION)
Brogaten 8, Oslo I, NORWAY

Telephone: 02-414911   Founded: 1938
Rep(s) at E-80: Asbjorn Voreland, Asbjorn Holm

Countries: 1   Groups: 4   Missionaries: 12   Tasks: 67

DIOCESE OF HYDERABAD, CHURCH OF PAKISTAN
Church House, Jacob Road, Hyderabad, Sind., PAKISTAN

Telephone: Founded: 1976
Rep(s) at E-80: Bashir Jiwan

Countries: 1   Groups: 4   Missionaries: 57   Tasks:

EAST-WEST CENTER FOR MISSIONS RESEARCH AND DEVELOPMENT
C.P.O. Box 2732, Seoul, KOREA

Telephone: 792-5542   Founded: 1973
Rep(s) at E-80: John Du Hyuk Yoon

Countries: 2   Groups: 3   Missionaries: 100   Tasks: 123

(Codes: 1-Church Planting, 2-Evangelism, 3-Translation, 4-Literature, 5-Media, 6-Medicine, 7-Other)

EVANGELICAL MISSIONARY SOCIETY OF EVANGELICAL
CHURCHES OF WEST AFRICA, P.O. Box 63, JOS Plateau State,
NIGERIA   Founded: 1949
Telephone:
Rep(s) at E-80: Panya Baba

Countries: 2   Groups: 4   Missionaries: 428   Tasks: 12

EVANGELICAL CHURCH OF INDIA
No. 1 Second Street
Ormes Road Kilpauk, Madras 600010, INDIA
Telephone: 663178   Founded: 1954
Rep(s) at E-80: M. Ezra Sargunam

Countries: 1   Groups: 5   Missionaries: 230   Tasks: 12

FOREIGN MISSIONS COMMITTEE OF THE K.P.C.
34 Am Nam Dong Seo Gu, (P.O. Box 190), Pusan, KOREA
Telephone: 26-3181   Founded: 1956
Rep(s) at E-80: Ho Jin Jun

Countries: 2   Groups: 3   Missionaries: 3   Tasks: 12

FEDERATION DE MISSIONS EVANGELIQUES FRANCOPHONES
c/o TEMA, 1032 Romanel, SWITZERLAND
Telephone: Founded:
Rep(s) at E-80: Eric Gay

Countries: Groups: Missionaries: Tasks:

EASTERN EUROPE FOR CHRIST
FREE CHURCH MANSE
Tomatin, Inverness-shire IV13 7XY, ENGLAND
Telephone: 08082-324   Founded:
Rep(s) at E-80: William Bell Scott

Countries: Groups: Missionaries: Tasks:

ELIM PENTECOSTAL CHURCH INTERNATIONAL MISSIONS
P.O. Box 38, Cheltenham, Glos., UNITED KINGDOM
Telephone: 519904   Founded: 1946
Rep(s) at E-80: David Ayling

Countries: 14   Groups: Missionaries: 42   Tasks: 123456

EPISCOPAL CHURCH MISSIONARY COMMUNITY
1567 E. Elizabeth Street, Pasadena, CA 91104 USA
Telephone: (213) 797-8323   Founded: 1974
Rep(s) at E-80: Louise Hannum

Countries: Groups: Missionaries: Tasks: 7

EVANGELICAL MISSIONARY ALLIANCE OF THE NETHERLANDS
Stationslaan 107, 3844 GC Harderwijk, NETHERLANDS
Telephone: Founded:
Rep(s) at E-80: Rev. T.J. v.d. Weele

Countries: Groups: Missionaries: 600   Tasks:

(Codes: 1-Church Planting, 2-Evangelism, 3-Translation, 4-Literature, 5-Media, 6-Medicine, 7-Other)

FELLOWSHIP OF EVANGELICAL FRIENDS
23, Isaac Street, P.O. 68, Nagercoil, Madras, INDIA

Telephone: 2771   Founded: 1960
Rep(s) at E-80: D.T. Rajah

Countries: 1 Groups: 2 Missionaries: 20 Tasks: 1246

FINNISH LUTHERAN MISSION, FINLAND
SF-12310 Ryttyla, FINLAND

Telephone: 914-67272   Founded: 1967
Rep(s) at E-80: Martti Myllarinen, Seppo Vaisanen

Countries: 12 Groups: 12 Missionaries: 74 Tasks: 1246

FOREIGN MISSIONARY SOCIETY OF THE
BRETHREN CHURCH, 3601 Linden Ave
Long Beach, CA 90807 USA

Telephone: (213) 595-6881   Founded: 1900
Rep(s) at E-80: Eric Smith
Countries: 8 Groups: 20 Missionaries: 114 Tasks: 214567

FOREIGN MISSION BOARD OF THE SOUTHERN BAPTIST CONVENTION
P. O. Box 6597, Richmond, VA 23230 USA

Telephone: (804) 353-0151   Founded: 1845
Rep(s) at E-80: Dr. Winston Crawley

Countries: 94 Groups: Missionaries: 3059 Tasks: 1234567

(Codes: 1-Church Planting, 2-Evangelism, 3-Translation,
4-Literature, 5-Media, 6-Medicine, 7-Other)

FRIENDS MISSIONARY PRAYER BANDS
SIPRI JHANSI, UTTAR PRADESH
284003, INDIA
Telephone: 1489   Founded: 1968
Rep(s) at E-80: Ebeneezer Sundar Raj

Countries: 1 Groups: 4 Missionaries: 80 Tasks: 13

FULL GOSPEL YOUNG MEN ASSOCIATION
Post Bag 609, Vellore, 632006, INDIA

Telephone: 22943 or 22828   Founded: 1972
Rep(s) at E-80: R. Stanley

Countries: 1 Groups: 5 Missionaries: 30 Tasks: 12456

GHANA INTERNATIONAL MISSION, GHANA
c/o Coordinating Committee of Christian Fellowship
P.O. Box 10042, Accra, GHANA

Telephone: Founded: 1970
Rep(s) at E-80: Dan Tei-Kwabla

Countries: 1 Groups: 1 Missionaries: Tasks: 2

GOSPEL RECORDINGS, EUROPE
Postfach 1264, Halver D5884, WEST GERMANY

Telephone: Founded:
Rep(s) at E-80: Marlene Muhr

Countries: Groups: Missionaries: Tasks: 235

GOSPEL ECHOING MISSIONARY SOCIETY
No. 7, 13th Cross Street, Chromepet, Madras 600044, INDIA

Telephone: 49349   Founded: 1971
Rep(s) at E-80: D. Dayanandhan

Countries: 1   Groups: 3   Missionaries: 42   Tasks: 1254

GOSPEL MISSION SOCIETY OF THE KUKI CHRISTIAN CHURCH
Dewlah Land, P.O. Imphal, Manipur 795001, INDIA

Telephone: IP. 1053   Founded: 1978
Rep(s) at E-80: M. Doungel, T. Lunkim

Countries: 2   Groups: 6   Missionaries: 14   Tasks: 12345

GOSPEL RECORDINGS, INCORPORATED
122 Glendale Blvd., Los Angeles, CA 90026 USA

Telephone: (213) 624-7461   Founded: 1939
Rep(s) at E-80: Larry D. Allmon, Colin Stott,
Allan Starling
Countries: Groups: Missionaries: Tasks: 235

HOME MISSION BOARD - Southern Baptist Convention
1350 Spring Street N.W., Atlanta,, GA 30367 USA

Telephone: (404) 873-4041   Founded: 1845
Rep(s) at E-80: M. Wendall Belew

Countries: 1   Groups: 77   Missionaries: 3033   Tasks: 127

HONG KONG-MACAU SOUTHERN BAPTIST MISSION
120 Wharf Rd. 1/F, North Point, HONG KONG

Telephone: Founded:
Rep(s) at E-80: Chu Wood-Ping

Countries: Groups: Missionaries: Tasks:

HONG KONG EVANGELICAL FELLOWSHIP
Box 96605TST, Kowloon, HONG KONG

Telephone: (3)691427   Founded: 1947
Rep(s) at E-80: Edwin Keh

Countries: 2   Groups: 4   Missionaries: 170   Tasks: 7

IN DE RUIMTE FELLOWSHIP NETHERLANDS
c/o T.J. v.d. Weele, Stationslaan 107, 3844 GC Harderwijk,
NETHERLANDS

Telephone: Founded:
Rep(s) at E-80: Herman Weele

Countries: Groups: Missionaries: Tasks:

INDIA CHURCH GROWTH MISSION
Pasumalai, Madurai 625004, INDIA

Telephone: Founded:
Rep(s) at E-80: N.J. Gnaniah

Countries: Groups: Missionaries: Tasks:

(Codes: 1-Church Planting, 2-Evangelism, 3-Translation, 4-Literature, 5-Media, 6-Medicine, 7-Other)

INDONESIAN MISSIONARY FELLOWSHIP
Jalan Trunojoyo 2, Box 4, Batu-Malang, East Java, INDONESIA

Telephone: Batu 99, 65,   Founded: 1961
Rep(s) at E-80: Dr. & Mrs. Petrus Octavianus, Jusuo Atusumi

Countries: 4   Groups: 8   Missionaries: 31   Tasks: 1234567

INSTITUTE FOR BIBLE TRANSLATION
Box 20100, Stockholm S-104 60, SWEDEN

Telephone: 08 94-54-14   Founded: 1973
Rep(s) at E-80: Simon Crisp

Countries: 3   Groups: 70   Missionaries: Tasks: 34

INSTITUTE OF CHINESE STUDIES
1605 E. Elizabeth Street, Pasadena, CA 91104 USA

Telephone: (213) 798-9151   Founded: 1977
Rep(s) at E-80: John Shindeldecker

Countries: Groups: Missionaries: Tasks: 7

INTER-VARSITY CHRISTIAN FELLOWSHIP
233 Langdon Street, Madison, WI 59703 USA

Telephone: 608-257-0263   Founded: 1941
Rep(s) at E-80: David Bryant

Countries: Groups: Missionaries: Tasks:

INTERNATIONAL STUDENTS INC.
P.O. Box C, Colorado Springs, CO 80901 USA

Telephone: (303) 475-9500   Founded: 1953
Rep(s) at E-80: Mark Hanna, Harvey Karlsen, Robbie Marvin

Countries: 3   Groups: Missionaries: 126   Tasks:

INTERNATIONAL MISSIONARY ADVANCE
1605 E. Elizabeth St., Pasadena, CA 91104 USA

Telephone: (213) 794-4102   Founded: 1975
Rep(s) at E-80: Ben Jennings, Mary Jennings, Won Yong Koh

Countries: 24   Groups: Missionaries: 2   Tasks: 7

INTERNATIONAL BIBLE PROJECTS
P.O. Box 21633, Nairobi, KENYA

Telephone: 337-500   Founded: 1979
Rep(s) at E-80: Daniel Kyanda, Frank Oyongu

Countries: Groups: Missionaries: 2   Tasks:

INTERNATIONAL CHURCH OF THE FOURSQUARE GOSPEL -
Department of Missions, 1100 Glendale Blvd.,
Los Angeles, CA 90026 USA

Telephone: (213) 484-1100   Founded: 1928
Rep(s) at E-80: John Holland, Doris Holland

Countries: 35   Groups: 33   Missionaries: 144   Tasks: 12

(Codes: 1-Church Planting, 2-Evangelism, 3-Translation, 4-Literature, 5-Media, 6-Medicine, 7-Other)

JAPAN FREE METHODIST OVERSEAS MISSIONS SUPPORTERS
3-7 1-Maruyama, Abeno, Osaka 545, JAPAN

Telephone: 06-652-3466   Founded: 1978
Rep(s) at E-80: Mamoru George Nakajima

Countries: 2   Groups: 2   Missionaries: 3   Tasks: 2

JUNTA DE MISSOES MUNDIAIS, BRAZIL
Caixa Postal 40022, Rio de Janerio, BRAZIL 20.270

Telephone: 254-0714   Founded: 1907
Rep(s) at E-80: Waldemiro Tymchak

Countries: 11   Groups: Missionaries: 370   Tasks: 12

KANYAKUMARI EVANGELISM FELLOWSHIP
Concordia Theol. Seminary, Nagercoil Tamilnadu, 629001,
INDIA

Telephone: 456   Founded: 1980
Rep(s) at E-80: J.C. Gamaliel

Countries: 1   Groups: 2   Missionaries: 0   Tasks:

KASHMIR EVANGELICAL FELLOWSHIP
Mission House, Udhampur J. and K., 182101, INDIA

Telephone: 318   Founded: 1973
Rep(s) at E-80: P.M. Thomas

Countries: 1   Groups: 20   Missionaries: 45   Tasks: 12347

KOINOINIA INFORMATION SERVICE OF THE W.E.C.
68 Summerleaze Road, Maidenhead, Berks SL68EP, ENGLAND

Telephone: 29623   Founded: 1974
Rep(s) at E-80: Leslie Brierley

Countries: Groups: Missionaries: 2   Tasks: 4

KOREA CHURCH INTERNATIONAL MISSIONARY SOCIETY
22-1 Ka, Pumin-Dong, Pusan, KOREA

Telephone: Founded:
Rep(s) at E-80: H. Paul Ko

Countries: Groups: Missionaries: Tasks:

KOREA COUNCIL OF CHRISTIAN MISSION ORGANIZATIONS
1370 Soongin-Dong, Chongno-ku,, Seoul, KOREA

Telephone: Seoul 555-9824   Founded: 1977
Rep(s) at E-80: Sung-Hyun Hong, Simeon C. Kang

Countries: Groups: Missionaries: Tasks:

KOREA HARBOR EVANGELISM
49-45 Nogosandong, Mapogu,. Seoul, KOREA

Telephone: Seiul 35-3746   Founded: 1974
Rep(s) at E-80: Paul Kiman Choi, Dong Hyuk Shin,
                Ki Suk Chung
Countries: 5   Groups: 70   Missionaries: 17   Tasks: 24

(Codes: 1-Church Planting, 2-Evangelism, 3-Translation, 4-Literature, 5-Media, 6-Medicine, 7-Other)

KOREA INTERNATIONAL MISSION
C.P.O. BOX 3476
Seoul, KOREA

Telephone: 792-5542   Founded: 1968
Rep(s) at E-80: Dr. David Cho

Countries: 2 Groups: 3 Missionaries: 26 Tasks:

KOREAN CHRISTIAN MISSION SOCIETY
136-46 Yun Ji-Dong Jong Roku, Seoul, KOREA

Telephone: Founded:
Rep(s) at E-80: Dr. Simeon Kang

Countries: Groups: Missionaries: Tasks:

KOREAN MISSION TO BANGLADESH
97-412 Banpo Apartment, Banpo-Dong, Kangnam Ku,
Seoul 151, KOREA
Telephone: 599-2636   Founded: 1974
Rep(s) at E-80: Jong Dai Kim

Countries: 1 Groups: 2 Missionaries: 5 Tasks: 1236

LEPKI
Bromo 2, F.O. Box 101, Malang, INDONESIA

Telephone: Founded:
Rep(s) at E-80: M. S. Anwart

Countries: Groups: Missionaries: Tasks:

LATIN AMERICAN EVANGELICAL CENTER FOR PASTORAL STUDIES
(CELEP), Casilla 1307, San Jose, 1.000, COSTA RICA

Telephone: 011-50622-5038   Founded: 1973
Rep(s) at E-80: William Cook

Countries: 5 Groups: 5 Missionaries: 20 Tasks: 12457

LOYALIST LUTHERAN ANGALIDOM MISSION
Lumbatamia Castle, P.O. Box 142, Maragoli, KENYA

Telephone: Founded: 1961
Rep(s) at E-80: Dr. Angali

Countries: 3 Groups: 5 Missionaries: 9 Tasks: 2134

LUTHERAN CHURCH - MISSOURI SYNOD BOARD FOR MISSIONS
500 N. Broadway, St. Louis, MO 63102 USA

Telephone: (314) 231-6969   Founded: 1847
Rep(s) at E-80: Dr. Edward A. Westcott, Jr.

Countries: 21 Groups: 34+ Missionaries: 149 Tasks: 123456

LUTHERANS FOR WORLD EVANGELISM
1605 E. Elizabeth Street, Pasadena, CA 91104 USA

Telephone: (213) 794-7117   Founded: 1979
Rep(s) at E-80: Rev. John Ottesen, Mrs. Mildred Hilley

Countries: Groups: Missionaries: Tasks: 7

(Codes: 1-Church Planting, 2-Evangelism, 3-Translation, 4-Literature, 5-Media, 6-Medicine, 7-Other)

MARTHANDAM DISTRICT EVANGELISTIC FELLOWSHIP
Mission House,, Marthandam Pin, Kanyakumari Dist., Madras,
S. INDIA 629165
Telephone: Founded: 1973
Rep(s) at E-80: C. Samuel

Countries: 1 Groups: 4 Missionaries: 90 Tasks: 21

MANIPUR PRESBYTERIAN MISSION
Presbyterian House
War Cemetary Road, Imphal, Manipur 795001, INDIA
Telephone: 924   Founded: 1964
Rep(s) at E-80: S. Lalkhuma

Countries: 1 Groups: 1 Missionaries: 30 Tasks: 124

MARANATHA FULL GOSPEL ASSOCIATION
91 Dr. Alagappa Ghettiar Rd., Madras 600084, INDIA
Telephone: 612128   Founded: 1963
Rep(s) at E-80: D. Henry Joseph

Countries: 1 Groups: 1 Missionaries: 3 Tasks: 124

MISSAO ANTIOQUIA
Caixa Postal 582, Sao Paulo, 01000 BRAZIL
Telephone: 632796   Founded: 1976
Rep(s) at E-80: Decio de Azevedo, Helcio Lange da Silva

Countries: 3 Groups: 3 Missionaries: 4 Tasks: 124

MISSION AVIATION FELLOWSHIP
Box 202, Redlands, CA 92373 USA
                                    Founded: 1945
Telephone: (714) 794-1151
Rep(s) at E-80: Ken Simmelink

Countries: 22 Groups: Missionaries: 250 Tasks: 7

MISSION EVANGELIQUE BRAILLE
Champ Bochereney, 1099 Les Cullayes, SWITZERLAND
                                    Founded:
Telephone:
Rep(s) at E-80: Charles Vuichoud

Countries: Groups: Missionaries: Tasks:

MISSION EN COTE D'IVOIRE
32, Chemin de Chatelaine, 1210 Geneve, SWITZERLAND
                                    Founded:
Telephone:
Rep(s) at E-80: Jules Varidel

Countries: Groups: Missionaries: Tasks:

MISSIONARY FELLOWSHIP OF SRI LANKA
"Sudharsana" Buona Vista, Unawatuna, SRI LANKA
                                    Founded: 1977
Telephone: 09-2659
Rep(s) at E-80: Lakshman Peiris

Countries: 1 Groups: 1 Missionaries: 2 Tasks: 2

(Codes: 1-Church Planting, 2-Evangelism, 3-Translation, 4-Literature, 5-Media, 6-Medicine, 7-Other)

MISSIONARY INFORMATION BUREAU BRAZIL
Caiya Postal 1498, 01.000 Sao Paulo, BRAZIL
Telephone: Founded:
Rep(s) at E-80: Paul Overholt

Countries: Groups: Missionaries: Tasks:

MISSIONARY APPRENTICE RESOURCE KORPS
P.O. Box 8040 Station ACU, Abilene, TX 79699 USA

Telephone: 915-677-1911   Founded: 1977
Rep(s) at E-80: Gaston Tarbet

Countries: 6 Groups: 5 Missionaries: 18 Tasks: 1247

MISSIONARY STRATEGY AGENCY
1054 N. Saint Andrews Place, Los Angeles, CA 90938 USA

Telephone: (213) 465-2267   Founded: 1964
Rep(s) at E-80: Dr. Masumi Toyotome

Countries: Groups: Missionaries: Tasks:

MISSIONS SOS, SWEDEN, WOHOLMS HERRGARD
54050 Moholm, SWEDEN
Telephone: Founded:
Rep(s) at E-80: Eric Stadell

Countries: Groups: Missionaries: Tasks:

(Codes: 1-Church Planting, 2-Evangelism, 3-Translation, 4-Literature, 5-Media, 6-Medicine, 7-Other)

NAVIGATORS, GERMANY
Hausdorffstrasse 130, 53 Bonn 1, WEST GERMANY
OR: ENGLAND office
22 Westbury Rd., New Malden, Surrey KT3 5BE, ENGLAND
Telephone: Founded:
Rep(s) at E-80: Paul Stanley, Joseph Bobb, Horst Gunzel
Countries: Groups: Missionaries: Tasks:

NATIONAL ENCOUNTER WITH CHRIST
25 W. 25th Ave., Eugene, OR 97405 USA

Telephone: (503) 687-1849   Founded: 1971
Rep(s) at E-80: Ruben Ortega, Carolyn Ortega
Countries: 45 Groups: Missionaries: 100   Tasks: 2

NEDERDUITSE GEREFORMEERDE KERK
P.O. Box 433, Pretoria 0001, SOUTH AFRICA

Telephone: 267-321 Pretoria   Founded: 1652
Rep(s) at E-80: Dr. Andrew Murray Hofmeyr

Countries: 16 Groups: 31 Missionaries: 222 Tasks: 123456

NEW LIFE ASHRAM
98/6 WHEELER ROAD
Cooke Town, Bangalore 560005, INDIA
Telephone: 51074   Founded:
Rep(s) at E-80: John Thannickel

Countries: 1 Groups: Missionaries: 21   Tasks: 72

NORTH AFRICA MISSION
12 Devonshire Square, Loughborough, Leicestershire,
ENGLAND LE11 3DW
Telephone: 0509-39525   Founded: 1881
Rep(s) at E-80: Ronald John Waine, D. Docherty

Countries: 6 Groups: 9 Missionaries: Tasks: 21435

NORTH AFRICA MISSION
"Les Pierides" Chemin Du
Coton Rouge, 13100 Aix-en-Provence, FRANCE

Telephone: 33-42-27-90-88   Founded: 1881
Rep(s) at E-80: A. J. Wiebe

Countries: 7 Groups: Missionaries: 100+ Tasks: 1245

NORTH EAST ASIA CHURCH MISSION COUNCIL
27.1 Ka Wonhyo-Ro,, Yong San-Ku, Seoul, KOREA

Telephone: Founded:
Rep(s) at E-80: Ho Choon Yu

Countries: Groups: Missionaries: Tasks:

NORWEGIAN LUTHERAN MISSION
Grensen 19, Oslo 1, NORWAY

Telephone: 332525   Founded: 1891
Rep(s) at E-80: Egil Grandhagen, Gudmund Vinskei

Countries: 10 Groups: 15 Missionaries: 486 Tasks: 1234567

NORWEGIAN MISSIONARY SOCIETY
Klubbgata 3, Box 226, N-4001 Stavanger, NORWAY

Telephone: 04-531065   Founded: 1842
Rep(s) at E-80: Odd Bondevik Gunnar Salomonsen

Countries: 11 Groups: 35 Missionaries: 430 Tasks: 1234567

O.C. MINISTRIES INCORPORATED
Box 66, Santa Clara, CA 95052 USA

Telephone: (408) 727-7111   Founded: 1951
Rep(s) at E-80: Bill Thomas

Countries: 11 Groups: Missionaries: 130 Tasks: 7

OMS INTERNATIONAL
1, Sandileigh Avenue, Manchester M209LN, ENGLAND

Telephone: 061-445-3513   Founded: 1901
Rep(s) at E-80: N. Dudgeon

Countries: 12 Groups: Missionaries: 463+ Tasks: 127

OMEGA WORLD MISSIONS
1605 E. Elizabeth Street, Pasadena, CA 91104 USA

Telephone: (213) 797-1937   Founded: 1980
Rep(s) at E-80: J. Gene Adkins

Countries: 2 Groups: 2 Missionaries: 9 Tasks: 34

(Codes: 1-Church Planting, 2-Evangelism, 3-Translation, 4-Literature, 5-Media, 6-Medicine, 7-Other)

OPEN DOORS WITH BROTHER ANDREW
P.O. Box 47, Ermelo 3850 AA, HOLLAND   Founded: 1955
Telephone: 03410-17844
Rep(s) at E-80: Johan B. Companjen

Countries: 3   Groups: Missionaries: 100   Tasks: 1234

OPERATION MOBILISATION
P.O. Box 14, Bromley, Kent BR1 3NJ, ENGLAND   Founded: 1960
Telephone: 01-464-9817
Rep(s) at E-80: Judith Davidson, Gary Dean, Gordon Magney

Countries: 25   Groups: 5   Missionaries: 1500   Tasks: 124

OPERATION MOBILISATION INDIA
Elim, 19 August Krant; Marg, Nanachowk, Bombay 400007,
INDIA   Founded:
Telephone:
Rep(s) at E-80: Miss Manjulah Shah

Countries: Groups: Missionaries: Tasks:

OUTREACH INTERNATIONAL
1718 Northcrest Drive, Arlington, TX 76012 USA   Founded: 1978
Telephone: (817) 460-0579
Rep(s) at E-80: Willard Walls

Countries: 4   Groups: 4   Missionaries: 4   Tasks: 23

OVERSEAS MISSIONARY FELLOWSHIP
2 Cluny Rd., Singapore 10, SINGAPORE   Founded: 1865
Telephone:
Rep(s) at E-80: Dan Bacon, US rep.; John A. Wallis, Eng.

Countries: 9   Groups: 38   Missionaries: 886   Tasks: 1234567

POCKET TESTAMENT LEAGUE
16 Holwood Road, Bromley, Kent BR1 3EB, UNITED KINGDOM   Founded: 1908
Telephone: 01-460-5317
Rep(s) at E-80: Geoffrey Simmons

Countries: Groups: Missionaries: Tasks: 24

PTL TELEVISION NETWORK
7224 Park Road, Charlotte, NC   28279 USA   Founded: 1974
Telephone: (704) 554-6080
Rep(s) at E-80: Vernon McLellan, Mrs Vernon McLellan

Countries: Groups: Missionaries: Tasks:

PENTECOSTAL HOLINESS CHURCH MISSIONS DEPARTMENT,
P.O. Box 12609, Oklahoma City, OK   73157 USA   Founded:
Telephone:
Rep(s) at E-80: Mark Kamleiter

Countries: Groups: Missionaries: Tasks:

(Codes: 1-Church Planting, 2-Evangelism, 3-Translation, 4-Literature, 5-Media, 6-Medicine, 7-Other)

REGIONS BEYOND MISSIONARY UNION
186 Kennington Park Road,, London SE11 4BT, ENGLAND

Telephone: 01 582 0193   Founded: 1873
Rep(s) at E-80: Geoff Larcombe

Countries: 5 Groups: 10 Missionaries: 72 Tasks: 213467

S.U.M. FELLOWSHIP
75 Granville Rd., Sidcup, Kent DA14 4BU, ENGLAND

Telephone: Founded:
Rep(s) at E-80: Alan White

Countries: Groups: Missionaries: Tasks:

SCOTTISH MISSIONS CENTRE
12, Sydenham Road, Glasgow G12 9NP, SCOTLAND

Telephone: 44-41-339-0173   Founded:
Rep(s) at E-80: Roy Spraggett

Countries: Groups: Missionaries: Tasks:

SCRIPTURE UNION
47 Marylebone Lane, London W1M 6AX, ENGLAND

Telephone: Founded:
Rep(s) at E-80: Dudley Reeves

Countries: Groups: Missionaries: Tasks:

PENTECOSTAL ASSEMBLIES OF CANADA
10 Overlea Blvd., Toronto, Ontario, CANADA M4H 1A5

Telephone: (416) 425-1010   Founded: 1919
Rep(s) at E-80: Bill Cornelius, Robert Taitinger

Countries: 18 Groups: Missionaries: 209 Tasks: 1245

PENTECOSTAL HOLINESS CHURCH WORLD MISSIONS DEPARTMENT
P.O. Box 12609, Oklahoma City, OK 73157 USA

Telephone: (405) 787-7110   Founded: 1911
Rep(s) at E-80: Ralph Arnold, Clifton Smith
    -see above also

Countries: 25 Groups: Missionaries: 102 Tasks: 21

PORTABLE RECORDINGS MINISTRIES INCORPORATED
681 Windcrest Dr., Holland, MI 49423 USA

Telephone: (616) 396-5291   Founded: 1967
Rep(s) at E-80: Ronald Beery, Alice Beery

Countries: 111 Groups: Missionaries: 17 Tasks:

PRESBYTERIAN COMMUNITY OF EAST KASAI
100 Colonel Kabangu no. 100, BP 1430 Mbujimayi,
East Kasai, REPUBLIC OF ZAIRE   Founded: 1966
Telephone:
Rep(s) at E-80: Ilunga Tshibangu

Countries: Groups: Missionaries: Tasks:

(Codes: 1-Church Planting, 2-Evangelism, 3-Translation, 4-Literature, 5-Media, 6-Medicine, 7-Other)

SINGAPORE CENTER, EVANGELISM AND MISSIONS
Ghim Moh, P.O. Box 1105, SINGAPORE 9127

Telephone: Founded: 1980
Rep(s) at E-80: Chris Thomas

Countries: 2 Groups: 3 Missionaries: Tasks: 217

SLAVIC GOSPEL ASSOCIATION
P.O. Box 1122, Wheaton, IL 60187 USA

Telephone: (312) 690-8900   Founded: 1934
Rep(s) at E-80: A. Reid Jepson

Countries: 21 Groups: 16 Missionaries: 230 Tasks: 123457

SOUTH AFRICAN ACTION FOR WORLD EVANGELIZATION
Posbus 709, 1620 Kemptonpark, REPUBLIC OF SOUTH AFRICA

Telephone: (011) 970-4320   Founded: 1976
Rep(s) at E-80: W. Murray Louw

Countries: Groups: Missionaries: Tasks:

SOUTH AFRICAN BAPTIST MISSIONARY SOCIETY
P.O. Box 1085, Roodepoort, 1725, REPUBLIC OF SOUTH AFRICA

Telephone: 766-1066   Founded: 1892
Rep(s) at E-80: HAV Beerens

Countries: 1 Groups: 7 Missionaries: 79 Tasks:

SUDAN INTERIOR MISSION
Cedar Grove, NJ 07C09 USA

Telephone: (201) 857-1100   Founded: 1892
Rep(s) at E-80: Gerald Swank, Malcolm Hunter, US reps;
Sam Burns, England rep.
Countries: 10 Groups: Missionaries: 1127 Tasks: 1234567

SWEDISH ALLIANCE MISSION
Box 615, 551 18 Jonkoping, SWEDEN

Telephone: 036-11-91-30   Founded: 1853
Rep(s) at E-80: Tore Gunnarsson

Countries: 9 Groups: 7 Missionaries: 75 Tasks: 2156

T.E.M.A.
1032 Romanel, SWITZERLAND

Telephone: 021 1 35 28 46   Founded: 1977
Rep(s) at E-80: Luc Verlinden

Countries: Groups: Missionaries: Tasks: 7

U.S. CENTER FOR WORLD MISSION
1605 E. Elizabeth Street, Pasadena, CA 91104 USA

Telephone: (213) 794-1111   Founded: 1977
Rep(s) at E-80: Len Bartlotti, Bob Coleman, James Buswell
Ernest Heimbach, Lee Roddy, Roberta Winter
Countries: Groups: Missionaries: Tasks: 7

(Codes: 1-Church Planting, 2-Evangelism, 3-Translation, 4-Literature, 5-Media, 6-Medicine, 7-Other)

UNITED PRESBYTERIAN CENTER FOR MISSION STUDIES
1605 E. Elizabeth Street, Pasadena, CA 91104 USA

Telephone: (213) 798-7527 Founded: 1972 Tasks:
Rep(s) at E-80: Franklin Satterberg

Countries: Groups: Missionaries: Tasks:

UNITED PRESBYTERIAN ORDER FOR WORLD EVANGELISM
1605 E. Elizabeth Street, Pasadena, CA 91104 USA

Telephone: (213) 791-1324 Founded: 1974
Rep(s) at E-80: Ralph D. Winter, Donald Roberts

Countries: Groups: Missionaries: Tasks:

VIENNA MISSIONS TRAINING CENTER (NAVIGATORS)
6 Old Landing Road, Durham, NC 03824 USA

Telephone: Founded:
Rep(s) at E-80: Bill Wolf

Countries: Groups: Missionaries: Tasks:

VOICE OF GOSPEL
Trichur, Kerala, 680005, INDIA

Telephone: 23532 Trichur Founded: 1975
Rep(s) at E-80: Daniel K.V.

Countries: 1 Groups: Missionaries: 3 Tasks: 1247

WORLD CONCERN
P.O. Box 33000, Seattle, WA 98133 USA

Telephone: (206) 546-7201 Founded: 1974
Rep(s) at E-80: Danny Martin

Countries: 4 Groups: 4 Missionaries: 55 Tasks: 67

WORLD LITERATURE CRUSADE
20232 Sunburst Street, Chatsworth, CA 91311 USA

Telephone: (213) 341-7870 Founded: 1946
Rep(s) at E-80: David Patterson

Countries: 46 Groups: Missionaries: 1982 Tasks: 24

WORLD MISSION CRUSADE
P.O. Box 18586, Los Angeles, CA 90018 USA

Telephone: (213) 463-8241 Founded: 1978
Rep(s) at E-80: Bong Eun Choi, Chung B. Kim

Countries: 4 Groups: 7 Missionaries: 20 Tasks: 1

WORLD OMEGA REVIVAL MISSION SOCIETY
K.P.O. Box 642, Seoul, KOREA

Telephone: 74-6775 Founded: 1974
Rep(s) at E-80: Hahm Sang Hoon, Heavy Stone Choi

Countries: 20 Groups: Missionaries: 50 Tasks: 12567

(Codes: 1-Church Planting, 2-Evangelism, 3-Translation, 4-Literature, 5-Media, 6-Medicine, 7-Other)

WORLD OMEGA MISSION OF AMERICA
P.O. Box 1216, Flushing, NY 11312 USA
Telephone: (914) 997-9306   Founded: 1978
Rep(s) at E-80: Joseph C. Toh, Heavy Stone Choi
Countries: 4   Groups: 4   Missionaries: 20   Tasks: 4

WORLD VISION INTERNATIONAL MARC
919 Huntington Blvd., Monrovia, CA 91016 USA
Telephone: 213-357-7979   Founded: 1966
Rep(s) at E-80: Samuel Wilson
Countries: Groups: Missionaries: Tasks: 7

WORLD-WIDE MISSIONS
P.O. Box G, Pasadena, CA 91109 USA
Telephone: (213) 449-4313   Founded: 1957
Rep(s) at E-80: Esther M. Howard
Countries: 36   Groups: 40   Missionaries: 61   Tasks: 12467

WORLD-WIDE MISSIONS, NORWAY
Larsok V.5, 4001 Stavanger, NORWAY
Telephone: Founded:
Rep(s) at E-80: Kari Bjorgaas
Countries: Groups: Missionaries: Tasks:

WORLDWIDE EVANGELIZATION CRUSADE
"Bulstrode" Gerrards Cross, Bucks SL9 8SZ, ENGLAND
Telephone: GC 84631   Founded: 1913
Rep(s) at E-80: Robert Mackey, Dr. David Burnett, Patrick Johnstone, Leslie Brierley, Roy Spraggett
Countries: 24   Groups: Missionaries: 850   Tasks: 1234567

WYCLIFFE BIBLE TRANSLATORS, AUSTRALIA
10 Lyster Place, Melba, A.C.T. 2615, AUSTRALIA

-see below

WYCLIFFE BIBLE TRANSLATORS, BRITISH OFFICE
Horsleys Green, High Wycombe, Bucks HP14 3UX, ENGLAND

-see below

WYCLIFFE BIBLE TRANSLATORS
19891 Beach Blvd., Huntington Beach, CA 92648 USA
Telephone: (714) 536-9346   Founded: 1934
Rep(s) at E-80: Dr. George Cowan, US rep; Lars Carlsson, Swedish rep; Richard E. Fry, English rep; Norman Draper, David Cummings, Australian rep; Earl Adams, Betty Adams, W. Germany reps.
Countries: 40   Groups: 650   Missionaries: 4200   Tasks: 3

(Codes: 1-Church Planting, 2-Evangelism, 3-Translation, 4-Literature, 5-Media, 6-Medicine, 7-Other)

WYCLIFFE BIBLE TRANSLATORS, West Germany
Postfach 603, 5909 Burbach 6, Holzhausen, WEST GERMANY

-see above

YOUNG LIFE
P.O. Box 520, Colorado Springs, CO 80903 USA

Telephone: (303) 473-4262   Founded: 1941
Rep(s) at E-80: George Sheffer, Jr., Martie Sheffer

Countries: 13   Groups: Missionaries: 714   Tasks: 2

YOUTH WITH A MISSION
P.O. BOX 1099 Sunland, CA 91042 USA
OR: Buccleuch Rd., Hawick TD9 0EH, SCOTLAND

Telephone: (213) 352-4661   Founded: 1960
Rep(s) at E-80: Tom Bauer, Lee Thompson, US reps.;
Brent Williams, Australian rep.; Lynn Green, Wade
Robertson, Michael Greene, Scotland reps
Countries: 100 Groups: Missionaries: 2500 Tasks: 27

YOUTH WITH A MISSION SLAVIC MINISTRIES, AUSTRIA
Postfach 13, A-2651 Reichenau/Rax, AUSTRIA

Telephone: 02666/835   Founded: 1973
Rep(s) at E-80: Elizabeth Kingston

Countries: Groups: Missionaries: 60   Tasks: 17

(Codes: 1-Church Planting, 2-Evangelism, 3-Translation,
4-Literature, 5-Media, 6-Medicine, 7-Other)

APPENDIX III

Minutes of the meeting of the Pasadena Committee on WCFM
Held--August 30, 1979

Attendees:

Leiton Chinn (ISI/WCFM)
Paul Fretz (GLINT; for
   Eugene Ponchot of Miss. Ch.)
Dale Golding (FEBC)
Ernie Heimbach (OMF)
Harvey Stranske (AIM)
Stan Roland (Agape/CCC)
Hugh Harris (Navs)
John Otteson (LWE)
Alvin Martin (for Art Glasser
   SWM/FTS)
Ben Jennings (IMA)
Bill Pencille (SAM)

Harvey Hoekstra (PRM)
Ralph Winter (UPOWE)
Sam Wilson (WVI/MARC)
Clarence Church (WBT)
Larry Allmon (GRI)
Don McCurry (SZI)
Carol Glasser (SZI)
Morris Watkins (ANFM)
Chuck Bennett (MAF)
Carol Yuke (CWMC)
Alan Gates (CBFMS/ICM)
Frank Satterberg (UPCMS)

After early discussion Ralph Winter expressed need at this meeting to determine and vote on the non-negotiables listed on the agenda in order to effectively move forward for the WCFM.

WCFM/PC 8/30/79:1

Voted to adopt the agenda with provision to interchange entries I with III.

WCFM/PC 8/30/79:2

Voted to appoint a Chairman and Coordinator for the following proceedings. Ben Jennings was nominated and elected as Chairman and Leiton Chinn as Coordinator.

WCFM/PC 8/30/79:3

Voted to adopt six qualitative goals with future refinement by a committee. They are as follows:

    1. Capitalize on the growing momentum, interest, and attention concerning hidden people groups.

    2. Allow mission executives to translate contemporary research and issues into immediate and projected strategies by 2000 AD and formally accept responsibility for specific hidden people groups.

    3. Participation of western and non-western missions as equals--as planners, partners, and participants in missions.

    4. Be a foundational consultation for subsequent consultations and determine subsequent meetings needed.

    5. Help meet the need for spiritual renewal and fellowship.

6. Provide opportunity for mutually informing each other of one another's involvement.

(It was suggested that quantitative goals be developed in a committee at a later time.)

WCFM/PC 8/30/79:4

Voted to include as a stated goal of the conference that there be as large a representation as practical of those agencies interested in hidden peoples.

(There was discussion and a suggestion that the credential committee should include in guidelines for attendees that the Lausanne, IFMA, and NAE statements (one or all) be found acceptable. Further discussion suggested that there be only two stipulations: 1. no universalism, nor 2. any equivocation in matters of biblical authority as participant acceptance guidelines.

WCFM/PC 8/30/79:5

Voted that the credentials committee should ascertain that participants are in substantial agreement with the Lausanne Covenant, IFMA, and NAE statements of faith.

(There was discussion to the effect that participants should include two levels: 1. active participants, and 2. observers. The committee agreed to include delegates sent by both church planting and supporting agencies (i.e.: MARC, Zwemer Institute) as participants.)

WCFM/PC 8/30/79:6

Voted that those formally participating consist of delegates from agencies with current involvement in or with formal organizational commitment to reaching hidden people groups.

WCFM/PC 8/30/79:7

Voted to allow in an observer category those organizations with interest in but not yet commitment to reaching hidden peoples.

(There was discussion which was concerned that the guidelines have a proportion of observer participants to active participants established. It was suggested that 1/3 of the group be observers.)

WCFM/PC 8/30/79:8

Voted that the principal category of active participants constitute at least 2/3rds of the total.

WCFM/PC 8/30/79:9

Voted that the credentials committee guidelines include the requirement that active participant agency representation include not less than 1 person representing the top leadership of the mission structure.

WCFM/PC 8/30/79:10

Voted to accept the five point statement suggested in August 1976 in Hong Kong

by the AMA as guidelines for agencies to be included at the conference:
"suggested that agencies to be invited would have to fulfill
at least the following minimum requirements: 1) that they
have a board of directors, 2) that their financial records be
available to the public, 3) that they supervise, not just support, missionaries, 4) that they have at least five missionaries
laboring in another culture (not necessarily foreign country),
or (if a smaller number) at least twelve years of supervised
field experience."

(There was an amendment to reduce the 12 years of field experience stipulation
to 5 years. The amendment was lost. There was another amendment to replace
the phrase "financial records" with financial reports. The amendment was lost.
There was another amendment that the AMA statement be a requirement for sending agencies only or be all inclusive.)

WCFM/PC 8/30/79:11

Voted that in the case of research or service agencies, at least 6 combined years
of supervised experience, following the stipulation concerning field experience
for sending agencies.

(There was discussion on the place of the conference: which was to remain open.
The time should remain in October 1980. The proportion of representation from
agencies was discussed.)

WCFM/PC 8/30/79:12

Voted that pending further refinement by a committee, representation should be
apportioned as follows:
        less than 100 missionaries = 1
            100-500   "   = 2
            500-1500   "   = 3
            1501-4000   "   = 4

(There was discussion on the structure of continuing administrative activities.
Sixteen persons volunteered to participate on a continuing committee, with some
subject to approval from their respective organizations to be charter members of
the "Pasadena" Committee. This committee would be open to others who would
wish to join.)

WCFM/PC 8/30/79:13

Voted to constitute those present and volunteering for service as the "Pasadena
Committee of the WCFM." Charter members include:
        Leiton Chinn (ISI/WCFM)   Alan Gates (CBFMS/ICS)
        Chuck Bennett (MAF)   Danny Yu (CWMC)
        Dale Golding (FEBC)   Ralph D. Winter (UPOWE)
        Ernie Heimbach (OMF)   Samuel Wilson (WVI/MARC)
        Stan Roland (Agape/CCC)   Larry Allmon (GRI)
        John Otteson (LWE)   Morris Watkins (ANFM)
        Frank Satterberg (UPCMS)   Ben Jennings (IMA)
        Harvey Hoekstra (PRM)   Harvey Stranske (AIM)

WCFM/PC 8/30/79:14

Voted to elect Larry Allmon of Gospel Recordings as Chairman, and convener of the next meeting of the Pasadena Committee scheduled for September 6th from 9-12:30 AM for final approval of the above statements.

WCFM/PC 8/30/79:15

Voted to constitute the Executive Committee of the Pasadena Committee as follows:
    Larry Allmon, Chairman (GRI)
    Chuck Bennett (MAF)
    Clarence Church (WBT), to be consulted
    Alan Gates (CBFMS/ICS)
    Dale Golding (FEBC)
    Ernie Heimbach (OMF)
    David Liao (OC)
    Don Richardson (RBMU)
    Harvey Stranske (AIM)

(Some of the Executive Committee members have accepted the positions pending approval from their organization.)

WCFM/PC 8/30/79:16

Voted that the Coordinator, Leiton Chinn, be an ex-officio member of the Executive Committee.

(The next meeting of the Executive Committee would be held at 10:00 AM, August 31st, in the Board Meeting Room of the Administration Building (WCIU).

The meeting was adjourned.

INDEX

General

INDEX

INDEX

Country

266
St 79

ABOUT THE AUTHOR/EDITOR

Allan Starling was born and raised in South Africa. He graduated from the Bible Institute of South Africa before joining Gospel recordings in their Cape Town office. He has served in various capacities with the organization, mainly in the U.S.A. and is currently coordinating their Research Division in Los Angeles, California, as well as acting as liaison with the U. S. Center for World Mission.

He recently developed the PEOPLESFILE, an extensive index of people-groups around the world and is currently enlarging and revising this as well as other publications designed to inform and inspire those seeking to reach Hidden Peoples.